Composing a Further Life

Composing a Further Life

 THE AGE OF ACTIVE WISDOM

Mary Catherine Bateson

KNOPF · NEW YORK · 2010

THIS IS A BORZOI BOOK
PUBLISHED BY ALFRED A. KNOPF

Copyright © 2010 by Mary Catherine Bateson

All rights reserved. Published in the United States by Alfred A. Knopf, a
division of Random House, Inc., New York, and in Canada by Random
House of Canada Limited, Toronto.
www.aaknopf.com

Knopf, Borzoi Books, and the colophon are registered trademarks of
Random House, Inc.

Library of Congress Cataloging-in-Publication Data
Bateson, Mary Catherine.
Composing a further life : the age of active wisdom /
Mary Catherine Bateson. — 1st ed.
p. cm.
Includes bibliographical references.
ISBN 978-0-307-26643-9
1. Women intellectuals—United States—Biography.
2. Women's studies—Biographical methods. I. Title.
HQ1233.B37 2010
920.72—dc22   2010001796

Manufactured in the United States of America
First Edition

LOOKING FORWARD . . .
> This book is dedicated to
> Anton Gregory Griffin, affectionate and curious always.

LOOKING BACKWARD . . .
> This book is also dedicated to
> friends with whom I have lost touch,
> especially during periods of working abroad
> or returning from abroad.
> Some I have been able to locate,
> others not, but I always welcome renewed connections.

Contents

Acknowledgments

THE SUBJECT MATTER of this book began to intrigue me in 2000–2001, when I was a fellow at the Radcliffe Institute for Advanced Study writing about lifelong learning. For three years after the fellowship, I taught a seminar on adult learning at the Harvard Graduate School of Education, building on the teaching and research I had done on life history narratives since I was appointed a Robinson Professor at George Mason University in 1997. In each of these positions, I benefited from colleagues and from students exploring their own life histories. Putting together an anthology of my own papers for publication in 2004 also stimulated my thinking about learning along the way.

My interviewing for this project began in 2006, and my greatest debt is to the men and women who sat down with me to discuss the decisions they were making or had made about later adulthood, patiently going back to early childhood as I asked about the origins of interests developed later, and trusting me to use and edit their words without masking their identities. Because I have also drawn on more fragmentary conversations with others who were not part of the larger project, I must leave their names, not used in the text, unlisted, but I express my gratitude to them. Early on, Lois Bateson helped me to hone my thinking and interviewing.

This project would not have been possible if I had not had the good fortune to share in discussions of aging and demographic change in other contexts. Knowing that I would need to connect with others working in the field of aging, in 2006 I accepted an appointment as visiting scholar at The Sloan Center on Aging & Work at Boston College, and in 2007 I received a research grant from the Sloan Foundation which, although it was originally intended for a single year, I spread over my working expenses for three years.

Other settings were important for my thinking and conversation. I was invited in 2002 to join a group of women exploring the personal meanings of growing older, and together we undertook the project called Granny Voter, described in Chapter III. For nearly a decade, I have been an intermittent member of a Harvard Medical School seminar on life histories and case histories conducted by Inge Hoffmann, where I presented some of my ideas. Starting in 2004, I served as a visiting lecturer and then a consultant for the Americans for Libraries Committee and their projects, Libraries for the Future and Lifelong Access Libraries. It was the library work that made me realize that demographic changes literally require a change of consciousness and led me to start a discussion group through the public library of the New Hampshire town where I live.

During this period, there has been a swelling tide of publication on aging. Because my primary focus is not on old age per se but on the period of active engagement that falls roughly between ages fifty-five and seventy, depending on circumstances, I have not extensively reviewed the geriatric literature. I obtained Sara Lawrence-Lightfoot's work *The Third Chapter: Passion, Risk, and Adventure in the 25 Years After 50* (New York: Farrar, Straus & Giroux, 2009), which focuses on approximately the same period, when this work was in the home stretch. My most important intellectual debt is to the work of Erik H. Erikson on the human life cycle, which has given me a theoretical base to build on. Permission to reproduce portions of his charts was given by Kai Erikson.

I owe a debt of gratitude to my agent, John Brockman; my editor at Knopf, Jane Garrett, and her assistant, Leslie Levine; and the copy editor who has worked on my last three books, Susan M. S. Brown. Portions of this work, not yet in final form, have been read and commented on by Melvin Bucholtz, Inge Hoffmann, and Father Joseph Brennan, S.J., and, as always, it has been read carefully in various stages of draft by my husband, J. Barkev Kassarjian, and my daughter, Sevanne Kassarjian.

Composing a Further Life

Prologue

WHEN I COULD WALK NO FURTHER, I simply collapsed. My previous image of the desert had been of a sandy waste, level or twisted into undulant dunes, but this was all rock and mountain with a few dry, thorny bushes. Two young men stayed with me while the rest of the group went ahead, and after an hour or so the three of us started up again, with one of them supporting me on either side. My feet could take turns moving forward as long as they did not have to carry my weight. That was 1956. I was sixteen, having joined an Israeli youth movement hike into the Sinai Desert, which was under Israeli occupation following the Suez campaign.

That feeling—of being supported on either side—came vividly back to me on a trip to Poland more than half a century later. I was sixty-eight, still busy professionally but working out new forms of engagement after retiring from teaching. I was in Poznán to attend and speak at a conference on conflicts between cultures, which would start the next day, but I had arrived on a holiday, the Feast of Corpus Christi. Corpus Christi is celebrated in spring, often with processions that move from one outdoor altar to another, suggesting a sort of pilgrimage as the consecrated Host is lifted up and prayers are said at every stopping place. Knowing that this would be the perfect day to get a sense of what it meant to the Polish people to have regained the right to public devotion—the feast is now an official holiday—after half a century of Communism, I had asked the conference organizers to arrange my pickup from the airport so that I could go to Mass and join a procession.

They had already been warned that, when it came time for me to speak at the conference, I would need to do so sitting down, so when we set out from the church in a great crowd of people, I found myself supported by a tall Polish nun who cares for congenitally disabled children on one side and one of the conference organizers on the other. I'm okay walking, but standing in one place gives me difficulty now, and there was as much standing to be done as walking. They had accompanied me expecting to help—it was part of their welcome and their thanks for my willingness to come to the conference. I learned a lot about the new Poland from being in that crowd, taking in its holiday mood, a relaxed but focused attention to the readings and homilies, a sustained blend of gaiety and reverence.

Back in 1956, hiking with the Israeli youth movement, I was learning a new way of thinking about what it means to be a part of a community, a new understanding of both dependence and independence. I have told the story before, but like many remembered events of youth, it turns out to have new meanings with the passage of the years. I had gone to Israel the previous summer for a two-week visit, accompanying my mother, who was acting as a consultant on the assimilation of immigrants from around the world, immigrants who combined a sense of unity as Jews with sharply different appearances and cultural backgrounds. I had quickly become fascinated by the idealism of the young Israelis I met and their sense of living simultaneously in the present and in ancient history. So, two days before we were supposed to return to New York, I had announced to my mother that I wanted to stay in Israel, learn Hebrew, enter an Israeli school, and complete my senior year of high school there. She had agreed, and friends had found a teacher of intensive Hebrew for me and a household in Jerusalem where I could stay, with a daughter my age and two younger children. I had promised my mother that, if war broke out, I would return to the United States, but when the Suez campaign began, I cabled to her my wish to stay and finish, and again she agreed. I had taken on the most challenging intellectual effort of my life and "declared my independence." I was competent by then in Hebrew, the school year had begun, and I had moved on and rented a room on my own.

Most of my classmates belonged to youth movements, so after the fighting was over, I joined a large group from several cities on a trip into Sinai during the Hanukkah vacation. The main portion of the trip was a three-day hike, away from the trucks, on which we would carry all our own food and water, the kind of challenge that was familiar to members of the youth movements and totally new for me. But it also had the flavor of a pilgrimage, a visit to the desert described in the biblical Book of Exodus, where the Jewish people wandered for forty years and were fed manna from the skies. By the time we went, it was clear that Israel would soon withdraw from its brief occupation of the Sinai Peninsula and return it to Egypt, so this seemed to my companions to be a single chance in a lifetime. We had celebrated Hanukkah by lighting kerosene-soaked rags in tin cans instead of candles, sitting in a wide circle and singing the traditional songs.

Before we set out, we had been warned that the trek would be grueling and that anyone who was not strong enough would have to be carried out. We confronted a first lap up a long, narrow path, just steep enough to require an occasional handhold and full of bits of loose stone. Three quarters of the way up, I realized how badly prepared I was, and it seemed irresponsible to go on and become a burden on the others, so I stepped out of the line, knowing that the trucks would still be at the bottom of the hill to pick me up when I returned. But no, I was not allowed to stay behind. Enthusiastic comrades took my backpack and sleeping bag and pulled me into the line without so much as a canteen to carry, assuring me that, unburdened, I would be fine, that they were happy to share the load. For two days I managed, but just barely, dozing on the rocky ground at every rest stop. It was in the afternoon of the third day, on our way to a kibbutz where we would spend the night, that I collapsed.

The next day, when the trek resumed and I was somewhat rested and still unburdened, someone asked if I would carry his camera and step out of the line from time to time to take a photograph of the group. I felt absurdly honored to be given a task I could do, the privilege of making a contribution, and found myself reflecting on the contrast between the ethos of mutual help that was fostered by the youth move-ment and my American emphasis on independence, on not being a burden on others. Half of me was euphoric and full of love for my com-rades. Half of me was ashamed and resentful that they had exposed my weakness, angry at my need for help.

Today, as I read the literature on aging, this story has a new meaning. Just as the theme of independence training is pervasive in American child-rearing advice, the literature on aging is full of discussions of independent living, the desire not to be dependent, the belief that one should take responsibility for oneself in order not to be a burden on others, stand on one's own two feet. All this came into focus as I walked in procession with my new Polish acquaintances, ready to help me stand, and I was glad of their help.

It seems to me that independence is simply an illusion. Certainly it is an advance when a toddler can walk across the room, deal with buttons and shoelaces, and brush his own teeth. Later on, he will be able to cross the street or the country alone, to manage money and time, and finally he will become an adult who can support a household. Perhaps the cus-tom, rare in human history, of isolating an infant in a crib in a separate room fosters the ability to cope later on, or perhaps it merely reflects the goals of the adults. Certainly it was a step forward when the thirteen colonies declared and defended their independence from Britain. But the United States depends on Britain today as an ally, and Britain depends on us. We depend on the Arab world as suppliers of oil, and they depend on us as consumers of oil and exporters of a vast range of goods. Countries depend on each other to maintain freedom of trade and hope that the integrity of local markets will be sufficient to protect global financial stability; far too little has been said about the way in which financial irresponsibility and turbulence in the United States harms people around the world.

Everywhere on the planet, the continuity of life depends on the rain forests and the bacteria in the soil and the plankton in the oceans, and we depend on the civility of other human beings and a vast network of exchanges to live our lives. Even where we "pay our own way," we are dependent on others for that possibility and for the availability of what we need. Even where we think of ourselves as taking rather than receiving—as when a man pulls a fish out of the water for his meal—we are dependent on the lives we take. In many places the fisherman wisely thanks the fish—for letting itself be caught—or the river—for offering the fish—or God—for providing the needs of his life; but this is easily forgotten—the more so when we depend on unknown fishermen and a chain of unknown handlers and shippers to get the fish we eat to the store.

With all these references to independence and to the need to avoid ever being dependent on others, we are caught in a false antithesis, for the choice is not between dependence and independence. The reality of all life is interdependence. We need to compose our lives in such a way that we both give and receive, learning to do both with grace, seeing both as parts of a single pattern rather than as antithetical alternatives. The modern disability movement and the legislation it led to in 1973 and 1990 were primarily concerned not with mandating support and benefits but with the possibility for interdependence;[1] the basic theme was the effort to increase the ability of people with disabilities to participate and to become contributing members of society. The larger society has the responsibility to offer not handouts but the context that makes participation possible.

Similarly, as parents, we can find ways to make our children aware that they are contributing members of the household and that the chores they are asked to do are tokens of trust and are received with thanks. From their birth on, we depend on our children for the joy and meaning they give to life, even though we are paying the bills. We could do the same with our parents and grandparents. As people grow older, some of the ways they have contributed in the past may no longer be possible, but the challenge to society is not only to provide help and care where these are needed but also to offer the opportunity to contribute and care for others.

What strikes me as I remember the story of that trip into Sinai is that the culture in which I had grown up had prepared me not only to avoid needing the help of others but to resent being helped. I do not think I am alone in that; I think it is a pervasive attitude in American society. Yet if I so dislike the idea of needing help, I may turn that negative attitude onto others in that position and dislike or despise those who need my help, offering it only reluctantly.

This notion of standing on one's own two feet and needing nothing from others resonates with American concepts of masculinity and with the mythology of pioneers, frontier scouts, and cowboys, but it is by no means limited to males. It is a style that works against mutuality and that risks encouraging taking rather than sharing, exploitation rather than cooperation. Yet most people's lives do provide opportunities to learn to value and practice interdependence and mutuality in some relationships, experiences that could be extended to other contexts. If we have had caring parents or caregivers, without which we would not have survived, we carry with us from infancy the experience of trusting others to nurture and care for us.

The cost of our emphasis on independence is high. It seems to me logically impossible, for instance, to build a sustainable environmental ethic on the myth of independence, just as it is hard to see the rejection of interdependence as compatible with any faith except the lonely cult of the self. We need to do more to give children the experience of both giving and receiving, teaching and learning, helping and being helped—and make sure to include some of each in our own lives from beginning to end. We need to practice accepting kindness as well as giving it and to avoid reacting to the offer of help as an insult.

At every stage, we are talking about learning. At later stages of the life cycle, we are learning to deal with the new circumstances of an aging body and a changing social setting, and drawing on a lifetime of experiences for helpful precedents. Not everyone has a story as dramatic as my Sinai trek, but everyone has had experiences of depending on and learning from others. Reflection on those experiences often reveals a degree of mutuality that offers a precedent for interdependence. Although children may not notice it, parents do learn from their children and teachers from their students, and often very young children find themselves cheering or consoling their parents.

Human life expectancy at birth in industrialized countries has increased by some thirty years since the beginning of the twentieth century. We are living in new territory, drawing the maps that will give it meaning. Older adults are healthy and active decades longer than they would have been in the past, reflecting on their lives in the effort to understand who they are in a newly emerging stage of life and discovering the wisdom they have to offer. Composing a further life involves thinking about the entire process of composing a life and the way in which early experience connects to later. It involves looking with new eyes at what has been lived so far and making choices that show the whole process in a new light and that offer a sense of completion and fulfillment. This book is a study of a small group of pioneers exploring that process.

We can look backward and be grateful for the river and the fisherman, and we can look forward to find ways to contribute that complete our stories.

CHAPTER I

Thinking About Longevity

IMAGINE A HOUSE that has been your home for a number of years, to which you unexpectedly have the resources to add a room. What will that room be? Will it serve a need that you were not aware of when you first moved in? You might, for instance, have decided that you now need a study or an exercise room. Or will it allow you to elaborate on something that has always been part of your life? Perhaps you have always cared about books and have bookshelves spread throughout your home, but now you want to gather those books together in a room you will call the library. You may not have had a room where a guest could stay but now want to offer hospitality to a married son or daughter with a new generation of children (will one room be enough?). You may want to take an avocation, like wood carving or work you have done for a cause you cared about, and develop it, so the new room will be a studio or an office. You may have become passionate about gourmet cooking and want a different kind of kitchen. Or you may simply want to use this opportunity to extend your traditional "living room" in some new and more inclusive way, with more space or wider windows or a hearth.

The first thing you will discover when you "add" a room to a house is that *add* is generally the wrong word, because the way you use all the rest of the house, the way you live and organize your time and even your relationships, will be affected by the change. Existing rooms will be used differently, sounds will echo in new ways, community and privacy will have new meanings. Gaps will open where familiar items have been shifted to the new space and new acquisitions will fill them. The new room is not simply tacked on to the east or west side of the house, it represents a new configuration of the entire building and the lives it shelters.

This is what longevity is like. In the United States, we have not "added" years to life (thirty in the twentieth century, twenty since World War II), tacked on at the end. We have changed the shape and meaning of a lifetime in ways we do not yet fully understand. Similarly, with increasing numbers of older citizens, we are changing as a population, becoming a rather different society, just as the Louisiana and Alaska purchases brought more than geographical space to the nation. Arguably, something even more profound has happened: we are evolving into a rather different species, inhabiting a new niche and challenged to adapt in new ways. Similar processes are occurring in other industrialized countries, but culture, legislation, and economy make them play out differently, so the examples in this book, drawn from the United States, need to be interpreted in the light of American conditions, particularly the continuing openness to immigration, the lack of mandatory retirement laws, and attitudes toward employment.

Here is the situation in which we find ourselves. Most Americans are aware that the retirement of the Baby Boom generation is creating a variety of new demands, so that "retirement" has changed its meaning. In fact, our assumptions about retirement already mask deep changes. Government retirement pensions were invented in Germany at the beginning of the twentieth century, at a time when sixty-five-year-olds were few and far between (life expectancy at birth was about forty-five), were mostly very limited in their ability to work, and would not be around for long. In other words, retirement was invented for people whose conditions were in some ways worse than those of eighty-five-year-olds in the United States today. Today's sixty-five-year-olds are starting new careers or continuing old ones, traveling around the world, and eloping with new loves.

What is less widely understood is that this is happening at a time when both individual life cycles and populations have taken on radically new structures. We have not added decades to life expectancy by simply extending old age; instead, we have opened up a new space partway through the life course, a second and different kind of adulthood that precedes old age, and as a result every stage of life is undergoing change.

Different societies look at age-groups differently. In some places status is governed by small differences of age, in others all children or all old people may be grouped together. However, virtually every society does make distinctions between children and adults and does recognize changes in the participation of older adults, creating at least three major stages of life, which may be subdivided further, stages that correspond for many individuals to generations: childhood (not yet adults), parenthood (adults), and grandparenthood (elders). With the survival of many grandparents to become great-grandparents and the improved health conditions of older adults, we have in effect created the first four-generation society in history.

Here I am not using the term *generation* to refer to twenty-year cohorts with catchy nicknames, although cohorts do indeed share characteristics determined by the changing contexts in which they have grown up and lived. I am referring to the presence of coexisting generations defined by their roles and activities, with individuals moving from one to the next as "the younger generation" becomes "the older generation" around the campfire or the table; children become parents, and parents become grandparents, often by about the age of forty, which was regarded as a fairly ripe old age through most of human history. Today's grandparents, including a considerable proportion of Baby Boomers, are different from grandparents in the past and much healthier and more numerous.

This is new. Every society has some members who are not yet

full participants—infants, children, and those approaching adulthood, whom we now call adolescents. And every society has adults who are simultaneously full participants in maintaining the society and in its perpetuation as they produce and rear children. And every society has at least a few older members who are past their reproductive and child-rearing years, often in declining health. This older generation typically withdraws from some kinds of participation, but the pattern always includes some continuing contribution, often of a sort that is not open to younger adults.

We know from cross-cultural studies that postreproductive adults—elders—have played a key role in human societies through time. Many of these elders have been grandparents and a few have been great-grandparents (a very scarce resource through most of history), but in terms of the ancient three-generation structure, they have played similar roles. This has been the human pattern: three generations or stages of life, diverse and changing through time, defined in relation to the others and to their forms of participation and only secondarily as age-groups.

Now, however, older adults, many of whom are grandparents but who have an unprecedented level of health and energy, time and resources, fit into society in new ways, often much like younger adults. And for the first time in history there are large numbers of *great*-grandparents, who look and act somewhat, but not precisely, the way grandparents used to. Biomedicine has once again created a profound change in the human condition. We have inserted a new developmental stage into the life cycle, a second stage of adulthood, not an extension tacked on to old age.

A decade ago some of us began calling this stage a second adulthood, but that phrase too easily evokes the second rate or secondhand—or even a second childhood of incompetence. I think we will need to think in terms of a first adult stage we can call Adulthood I, a very busy and productive time, which includes both our primary child-rearing years and the building of careers, and a new stage we can call Adulthood II.[1] Adulthood II may begin as early as age forty (for example, for athletes, whose first careers may last only twenty years) and extend past eighty (for example, for politicians, if they reach the Senate, and many self-employed people), for many years of participation and contribution. Both as individuals and as a society we are being taken by surprise by this change, yet so far most of the discussion focuses on its financial implications, not on its opportunities. How will the new room be used? How will the rest of life be different?

Those who are grandparents today are unlike the grandparents they remember. They adore their grandchildren, but they just aren't sitting still. They won't behave like stereotypical grandparents, with long memories and short walks, until they are great-grandparents. They are often colleagues to their own children, working side by side as adults. Historically, wisdom has been associated with elders. Today's grandparents combine the same length of experience with continuing mobility, so I think of Adulthood II as the stage of *active wisdom*, which precedes old age.[2]

We are going through a profound change in the status of the human species. The easiest way to assess that change is to consider the importance of an extended childhood in the process of becoming human, *Homo sapiens*. From very simple organisms up through mammals, learning very slowly became a key to survival; most organisms are hatched or born equipped with the specialized behaviors they need to survive in their environments, or can acquire them in a matter of days or weeks, without an extended period of dependency. Human development, by comparison, is exceptionally labor intensive, requiring the attention of multiple adults over long periods of time. Even in comparison to other mammals, human infants and children are helpless in a way that is conspicuous and seems terribly inefficient. But it is this helplessness that is the key not only to the flexibility that has allowed humans to adapt to every environment on the planet but also to the long adventure of exploration and invention that we call culture. Even more important, it is what prepares human beings to give and receive love and is the seedbed of conscience.

For humans, even the most rudimentary skills of survival must be transmitted from generation to generation early in the life course. Transmitting even a fraction of the larger culture requires a period of enculturation that now lasts twenty or more years and often continues to the end of life. It seems that the experiences of helplessness, dependence, and vulnerability are essential to becoming human. Human infants have no option of walking or flying away after a few weeks or months but willy-nilly are forced to stay with caregivers, normally creating the context for learning, along with an array of information and skills, how to love and how to trust.

When we look at aging from a Darwinian perspective, it is clear that the same apparent anomaly exists at the end of life. If the hen is the egg's way of making another egg, the hen that is no longer laying is useless except for the stewpot. In many species, the spider lays her eggs and dies—she has made her contribution to the future (and sometimes she kills her mate, his contribution also completed). Yet even as natural selection has reinforced a period of dependent learning for the survival of offspring in some species, natural selection apparently reinforces the possibility for elders in some species to live on while their young mature, sometimes to produce another brood, and sometimes beyond that capacity as well.

Studies of species that live in groups, where members of the pack or herd tend to be related—for instance, a herd of deer—have shown that the survival of a few postreproductive animals, in this case a few old does, increases the chance of survival of young born in the herd, because the old does remember where to find food or water in a year of drought or very deep snow, contributing to the *inclusive fitness* of the group.[3] Human society is conspicuous for the role played by adults other than parents in the rearing of the young—in fact, teaching is more distinctively human than learning, as is the institutionalization of teaching roles. Anthropologists have looked at human groups and demonstrated that the presence of grandparents—particularly maternal grandmothers—reduces infant and child mortality, which is to say, increases the likelihood that children will grow up to pass on their genes, presumably the same genes that kept their grandparents healthy and supportive. And here, too, love and trust must be part of the equation, particularly the trust between a new mother and her own mother, which allows her to accept help and advice more easily than from a mother-in-law.[4]

Most human groups value their elders, and a great many societies have evolved specialized and valued roles for the old, some of them depending on obvious assets, like length of experience, and others involving more subtle values. Among the San Bushmen of southern Africa, for instance, the hunt for game with poison-tipped arrows depends on moving rapidly across the veld, first to approach the quarry and then to follow for several days as the poison does its work. When men become too old to participate in the hunt, they become the makers of arrows—and tradition ascribes to the arrow maker the primary credit for the kill, so that in the distribution of meat to all the members of the community, the arrow maker is treated as the source. Looked at pragmatically, the making of the arrow is indeed a contribution, one that could be made by a younger man but has been reserved for the old, but less of a concrete contribution than the honor it is given, which makes it central to the solidarity of the band. Similarly, only when women are too old for childbearing are they permitted to become shamanic healers, a translation of the love and care they have given their children to the health of the wider community. In both cases, an appropriately limited effort is recognized as having a profound value.[5]

A similar alchemy occurs in a New Hampshire yoga class I have attended for over a decade, consisting mostly of women past middle age, and a few men.[6] Midway though the class, the participants pair off to give each other neck and shoulder massages. The younger members of the group have strong fingers and strong arms and give fairly energetic five-minute massages. But others, in their seventies and beyond, with arthritic fingers, can only manage the lightest touch, like butterflies alighting and taking off, and themselves need to be handled gently. Both kinds of touch are equally valued in the exchange. The older members of the group emerge as experts in a type of touch used in Swedish massage called light stroking, or *effleurage,* surely efficacious in its own way, for under this touch tension is released gently into the air. It is not easy to decide what counts as a valuable contribution, even through Darwinian spectacles.

In addition to our lengthy childhood and our postreproductive survival, a third evolutionary anomaly of human beings, which lends a distinctive character to human sexuality, seems to fit here as well. In most species across the animal kingdom, copulation occurs only when conception is possible and is triggered by the estrus cycle, most often by cues of scent—that is to say, it occurs only when the female is "in heat" and able to conceive. And of course in most species the reproductive pairing is relatively temporary and the presence of the male not necessary after fertilization.

Yet human beings seek sexual intercourse regardless of fertility— between ovulations, during pregnancy and lactation, after menopause, and into old age—so the decoupling of sex and reproduction was with us long before the invention of contraception and surely contributes to the maintenance of affection and joie de vivre over time. Nonreproductive sexuality has to be regarded as an evolutionary change, an emergent aspect of humanness, so the question is how nonreproductive sexuality has been selected for. One possible answer is that it helps keep couples together and available to care for their young, for each other, and even for their children's children. Sexual pleasure turns out to be an important ingredient in the human capacity for responsible caring.

Studies suggest that men at least live longer and healthier lives if they live with a partner.[7] Marriage is based on interdependence, and in every human society interdependence is increased by cultural elaborations on the biological division of labor. Yet interdependence is obscured in economic models where, when the family income is brought in by the husband, the wife is defined as "not working," which is to say as dependent, not contributing. Sometimes, too, sexual pleasure has been regarded as normal to males and not to females, which can lead to regarding sexual access and fertility as something the woman exchanges for economic support.

Since the end of the Victorian era, we have moved toward a model in which sex is regarded as mutual giving, and increasingly both partners contribute both earnings and unpaid labor, often specializing in different tasks, to their common life. Each of these models depends on the notion that partnerships last because partners come to depend on each other, to need each other, and, potentially, to look at each other with gratitude. All of this suggests that when economists talk about "dependency ratios," they are likely to be obscuring the real give-and-take—the reciprocity—on which human relationships depend. The language of economics biases our response by the selection between two closely related words that look like synonyms until you check the dictionary: *dependence,* it turns out, carries the connotation of reliance or trust, and *dependency* carries the connotation of subordination. The expectation that a man will be the sole support of his family puts a great and frightening burden upon him that may even drive him away and obscures the value of what a wife does as well as what she would be able to do in an emergency.

It is true that children can be a burden—especially when we define childhood as requiring vast amounts of unnecessary labor and equipment. But they are also a gift. It is true that the old can be a burden—especially when conventions and fashions cut them off from participation—but they, too, can make a contribution. The presence of Marian Robinson, Michelle Obama's mother, in the White House has carried a message about mutual support between generations almost as important as the fact that America put at least some of its history of racism behind it.

Part of the challenge, then, in growing older, is to discover the ways, arising from a lifetime of experience and in spite of reduced strength and stamina, in which it continues to be possible to contribute. The corresponding challenge to society is to recognize that contribution and to benefit from it instead of dismissing it. As we look for patterns of reciprocity at different stages of life, it may be important to consider every human activity and see the completed circuits of exchange rather than seeing benefits moving only in one direction. What does the physician gain from her patients besides fees? What does the teacher learn from his pupils? How does the comedian feed on laughter and the artist on recognition, and how does the politician rely on the trust and enthusiasm of supporters?

Through questions like these we can discover the reciprocities in the emerging shape of lives as we gradually become a four-generation society—a society in which great-grandparents are as common as grandparents were in the past and possibly more so. We may find that longevity contributes as much to our humanity as has the extension of childhood. In the meantime, however, the fear of becoming useless and dependent erodes the spirit as definitions are turned into fact, for the most toxic aspect of aging is the negative beliefs that seniors may come to have about themselves and about each other.

Aging today has become an improvisational art form calling for imagination and willingness to learn. Increased longevity will challenge us not only to revise expectations but also to discover unexpected possibilities, arranging life in new and satisfying patterns, and to explore how newly perceived possibilities relate to earlier life choices. In the process we will encounter gradual—or sometimes sudden—shifts of consciousness and identity that accompany awareness of the new situation.

When do you move from Adulthood I to Adulthood II? When you reflect that you have done much of what you hoped to do in life but it is not too late to do something more or different. The doorway to this new stage of life is not filing for Social Security but thinking differently and continuing to learn. Adulthood II is characterized by the wisdom culled from long lives and rich experience, the most acceptable and positive trait associated with longevity, but combines it with energy and commitment in the context of a new freedom from some kinds of day-to-day responsibility, a freedom that challenges expectations and may even be frightening. Together these produce the *active wisdom* that older adults have to offer, which gives them the potential for altering the shape of public and family life in America.

Adulthood II comes as a gift and offers new choices, but it may take time to assess the possibilities. Erik Erikson used the term *moratorium* for periods when young people put off commitment while they struggle for a sense of identity, sometimes lasting well beyond college. Many older adults take a somewhat similar interval for further study or travel or experimenting with some model of retirement that proves to be temporary, trying to find a meaningful activity they are ready to engage in during this new stage of life. I have sometimes used the metaphor of an *atrium* to describe Adulthood II, stretching my architectural metaphor, as if the new room added to the house were an atrium in the center, with doorways to all the other stages or rooms and open to the sky, but the metaphor seems most appropriate to the transition into Adulthood II, searching for the next step.[8] Adulthood II will eventually give way to old age and is marked by the consciousness of mortality, but for many it is a time of new beginnings or for the revival of earlier interests.

My hope is that this book will challenge individuals not only to thoughtful discernment and creativity in composing a further life but to greater engagement. We need the members of the grandparent generation—those in Adulthood II—to restore a dimension of long-term thinking to our decision making. For the great irony of our time is that, even as we are living longer, we are thinking shorter. We live in a society where working adults are experiencing ever-increasing stress and striving. Members of the parent generation are straining to meet next week's and next month's deadlines, quarterly reports, and a fast-recurring election cycle. Most women and many men are working two shifts. Under pressure, horizons are shortened.

We tend to assume that the old, because they have fewer years ahead of them, are less concerned with the future than younger adults, but in fact the group best equipped to advocate for the future are thoughtful older adults—those in Adulthood II—who have time and perspective for reflection combined with the willingness to consider new ideas and acquire new skills; who can speak up about issues that will affect future generations, particularly issues of the environment, and engage in bringing that future to pass. They are not ready to sit on the sidelines. Older adults are concerned about the future of their children, grandchildren, nieces and nephews, as well as students and the children of friends and neighbors, who will live in that future but cannot yet influence it. There is a potential for alliance between concerned young people and their grandparents, working together to protect the future. It is worth remembering that the environmental movement of today was once dismissed as consisting only of "little old ladies in tennis shoes."

Older adults have seen a lot of change and learned a lot about how to adapt through good times and bad, how to acquire new skills, and how to distinguish positive from negative change. Yet ironically the message that older adults receive from politicians and advertisers and even from each other is to be concerned primarily with their own comfort. Individuals coming up to retirement at this point in history are beginning to reimagine the shape of lives and escape from stereotypes. Ageism is pervasive, affecting young and old alike, slowing this process of discovery by shaping the way older adults look at others of the same age, making them hesitant to work together to influence the future.

Nevertheless, there are significant efforts to ensure that those who live longer can continue to contribute to society, including the work being pioneered by Marc Freedman in the areas of civic engagement and encore careers, and research supported by the Sloan Foundation on how workplaces and jobs need to be structured to optimize the contributions of older adults.[9] The movement of women into the workforce created gaps in child care and community life, which are partially being filled by retirees, and many industries are concerned about future shortages of skilled workers. There is already widespread interest in ways of reengaging retirees, either through flexible arrangements for paid work or as volunteers. The possibility of productive work lasting an additional decade will do more than supplement the workforce and can lead us to rethink the values and meaning of work. Freud famously said that what gives meaning to life is to love and to work—*lieben und arbeiten*—and these are the keys to understanding the restless searches of today's older adults.

Each of the liberation movements of the twentieth century has had to struggle against internalized prejudices and negative images of the self or of other members of the same group, which had to be overcome in order to embrace a different vision and believe that it could be achieved. In each such transition there have been risks—risks of excessive radicalization and acting out and risks of backlash. Yet beginning with the civil rights movement at mid-century and proceeding through the feminist movement, the disability rights movement, and the gay liberation movement, group after group that was excluded from full and equal participation has stepped forward, moving from a demand for equal rights into the fulfilled promise of new contributions.

Forty years ago, looking at their lives with the newly developed possibility of planning their childbearing, young women discovered the need to break out of inherited assumptions about who they were, what they could do, and what they should want in their lives. They had imagined their futures in terms of a set of culturally imposed stereotypes and had been trained to desire what society was ready to give them. Just as those women found they could not follow the model of their mothers, today's sixty-somethings remember their own grandparents as elderly without feeling elderly themselves. They are beginning to understand that they will not age in the same way and at the same pace, and above all that they must discover or invent new patterns for the years beyond traditional retirement, often as much as three decades, far too many years to spend on golf, television, and bridge, far too valuable to be expended on kinds of volunteerism that do not fully engage their skills or benefit from their perspectives.

Today, men and women approaching retirement (and the cohorts that will follow them), with newly achieved health and longevity, face the same challenge that new-wave feminism presented to women: to develop a new consciousness and to free their imaginations for the future. The same kind of process that occurred in liberation movements in the past is needed as older adults learn to discover and affirm who they are, the wisdom they have to offer, and how to make it effective in the world. I believe that, like the consciousness-raising of the sixties, this process of discovery must rest on learning, reflection, and conversation, leading to engaged action, and that consciousness will embrace responsibility as well as entitlement. To know what they will need and what they need to offer, both men and women must explore who they are.

This is the process I hope to simulate and stimulate with this book. One of the most insightful comments I received about an earlier book, *Composing a Life,* first published in 1989, was from a reader who said she had felt engaged in an unfolding conversation with six participants—herself and the five women portrayed in that book—although the actual words were drawn from separate interviews and then woven together.[10] We do not need formulas or rigid models to follow; we need to be drawn into a common process of search that will suggest new ways of being. We need distinctive individual voices rather than case studies. Particularly in an era of transition, the story is ill told with statistics. Both men and women have anxieties about losing their work because of age, and both need to articulate the meanings of love and work in their lives, what they would like to extend and what they would like to leave behind, so this book includes the voices of both men and women, sometimes individually and sometimes as couples.

Thus, the method of this book is an exploration of material from extended, open-ended interviews with thoughtful and articulate individuals—conversations with friends or with strangers who became friends—combined with my own commentary and introspection, and organized around emerging themes. A longer life span suggests a number of adaptations, all of which are occurring simultaneously. For some people, every stage is stretched: longer years of education, longer experimentation before marriage, late childbearing, and often deferred retirement. For others, life is started up again at midstream as if it could be repeated, a fairly common pattern for men with second families. For a third group, often women who have had a first career as homemakers, a new start on an autonomous career is involved. Some want to use an undeveloped talent, perhaps benefiting from emerging capacities to combine right- and left-brain functions by studying painting or dance or learning to play a musical instrument. Some want to build a legacy. Some go on to teach what they formerly practiced. Some want to focus their energies and passions on an area that received only a fraction of their attention in the past. For some there is a discovery of freedom. For others there is a chance for new or renewed dedication. And because we have not yet become fully aware of the possibilities, there will be for many an era of boredom and futility as the open doorways remain unexplored or are prematurely closed. These different approaches should not be contrasted so much as examined for common values and overlapping themes as we move into the new space opened up in our lives.

I like to think of men and women as artists of their own lives, working with what comes to hand through accident or talent to compose and re-compose a pattern in time that expresses who they are and what they believe in—making meaning even as they are studying and working and raising children, creating and re-creating themselves. Just as the use of a new room in a house depends on what is already there in the lives and relationships and possessions of the owners, the use of a new stage in the life cycle is related to what came before, ideally related in a way that is more than a sum of parts but rather an inclusive composition of grace and truth. It is often only in its final pages that a story reveals its meaning, so the choices made in later decades may reflect light back on earlier years.

If this is indeed a helpful way of looking at lives—if lives are composed somewhat like works of art, partly planned and partly improvised—then it is not enough to study what people do in retirement but essential also to study the relationship between what they do in retirement and what they did before—a relationship which, as in an artistic composition, may contrast or complete or reframe what came earlier, may be both profoundly surprising and surprisingly apt. Like the faces of wise and loving elders, lives so composed may be beautiful.

CHAPTER II

Small and Beautiful

THINKING ABOUT RETIREMENT involves thinking about work, why we do it, what its proper place is in life, and what that place could be.

Some people love their work, thinking of it in terms of a vocation or calling, and cannot imagine life without it. I remember my mother saying to me, when I was a child, that if she had to she would *pay* to be able to work—and there are women pursuing careers today whose earnings are totally absorbed by child care and other replacements for their services. For many people, their work is the most basic component of their identity, defining who they are. For such people, retirement may lead to rapid decline.

Some people hate their work, regarding it as something they are forced to do to support themselves and longing for the time when they can stop. Western attitudes toward work are haunted by the lines in the Book of Genesis in which God announces to Adam, "Cursed is the ground for thy sake, in sorrow shalt thou eat of it all the days of thy life: Thorns also and thistles shall it bring forth to thee; and thou shalt eat the herb of the field; In the sweat of thy face shalt thou eat bread, till thou return unto the ground" (3:17–19). This grim description of early agriculture in an arid climate continues to overshadow work of every kind to this day and may influence for the worse the way tasks and workplaces are designed.

Most of us have a love-hate relationship with our work that is hard to evaluate and keep in focus. Even those with the strongest sense of vocation may sometimes be heard to say, "My job won't let me do my work." Thus speaks the doctor who is concerned about insurance forms, the priest who must worry about budgets and the state of the church roof, the teacher who finds endless hours wasted on paperwork and committees. It is not easy to shed the job and continue the work, but this is one common aspiration for retirement.

At the bottom of the economic pyramid, men and women with little education often have very little choice in the work they do, working because they must at arduous and sometimes demeaning tasks, often at the lowest-paying unskilled jobs. It is ironic that the jobs that offer satisfaction and fulfillment also offer the highest pay. The labor movement has struggled to improve wages and working conditions but has not paid much attention to changes that might make work more satisfying—the emphasis is on shorter, rather than more meaningful, hours. This may be one reason for the movement's decline.

The use of skills seems to be a central component in the satisfaction people find in their work, especially the kind of skills that involve a measure of improvisation, addressing problems that call for specific and often creative solutions rather than repetition of standard solutions, even when these require high degrees of training. A carpenter modifying an existing building is always adjusting procedures to fit what is there, as a physician must allow for the variations in patients or a forester for the growth of particular trees. A farmer responds to the characteristics of different fields, and the captain of a ship to the shifting winds. But above all, work is the place where most of us encounter a variety of people, both as fellow employees and, if we are lucky, as those who will use the products of our labor in their lives, cooks selecting lettuces at a farmers' market, students in a classroom, home owners rejoicing in a remodeled basement.

I first met Hank and Jane Lawson when my husband and I were in Brooklin, Maine, visiting Richard Goldsby and his wife, Barbara Osborne, at the vacation house they rented for several summers next door to the Lawsons, who were also seasonal residents by then. The Goldsbys and the Lawsons had become friends over a series of summers, and while I was interviewing Dick for this book, he urged me to speak with them about how they were spending their retirement. So during an extended visit to the Goldsby household, I spent several hours interviewing the Lawsons and followed up with a visit to their winter retirement community in Arizona.

Hank and Jane are both natives of Maine. They have been married for over fifty years and have four children. Hank had good reason to look forward to retirement from his long-term job at the Brooklin Boat Yard, where he worked long hours, often handling heavy machinery. But of all the people I spoke to, he seemed the most ingenious in re-creating in retirement from his job what had been satisfying to him in a long life of hard work.

Hank's mother had died two days after giving birth to him, after which his father moved away from Maine, and he grew up in the homes of various relatives. He started doing neighborhood chores of various kinds when he was eight years old. He tried to join the Navy at sixteen, but they sent him back to finish high school, and he was finally sworn in at seventeen, the day after graduation. After the Navy, where he was trained in the maintenance and repair of big diesel engines, he worked at the local boatyard, then in commercial fishing, and then in construction in New Jersey, where his father was living. When he married Jane, however, they found they missed their hometown life in Maine, and Hank went back to the boatyard, where he stayed for forty-four years, fabricating metal parts when needed, and all this in huge, unheated sheds where boats were taken out of the water for repair or for storage during the Maine winters.

Hank is proud of his skills, but his greatest satisfaction came not from the work itself but from other aspects of his job. When I asked him about this, he told me, "What comes to mind is, not too long before my boss, Joel White, died, when he was already sick with cancer and his son had pretty much taken over, I said to him one day, it would have been about 1996, I said, 'I know you think that I think that the boats are great and all that, and you're absolutely right, but that really wasn't what I was interested in doing.' I said, 'I enjoyed doing the work, but more than anything, it was just a lot of fun dealing with the people that we were making the boat for or repairing the boat for.' I enjoyed that more than I did the actual work itself."

"Because you're a people person," Jane said.

"Yeah, and he never knew that," Hank continued. "He thought, Wow, Hank is pretty much into these boats. I didn't want to drop an anchor right in the middle of everything and destroy a friendship, because we certainly had a great, great friendship, but I didn't want him to go on thinking that I was the master boat person that he thought I would grow into. That wasn't the product for me at all. The product was the people. So I'm kind of happy that we had that little piece of conversation, because I know that I didn't mislead him into thinking something that wasn't going to happen."

"But you really enjoyed making those fittings for the boats. You were so proud of—"

"But you know why I was proud? It wasn't because of the fittings, it was because, when a person would come to pick up their boat, and they had all this work laid out for 'em, I would just, you know, I'd stand off to one side—I couldn't be in the center of attention, you know—just to see the surprised, happy look on their face; that meant more to me than the damn paycheck. I needed the paycheck to buy my bread; it's that simple. Joel didn't realize how much pleasure I was getting away from the product—the product for him being the work I was doing on the boats. And I was enjoying that, too, and proud of it, rightfully so. But that's where I say I really got a lot more pleasure out of it than he realized. So by telling him that, I removed the guilt feeling that I might have had."

Jane and Hank could have earned higher wages in New Jersey or far-
ther south, in a bigger boatyard, but that wasn't the life the two of them
wanted to have or where they wanted to raise their children. They
bought a dilapidated house in Maine that Hank worked on after hours
for over a year, waiting two years before they could afford a water heater
and rigorously avoiding going into debt. In all the years that Hank
worked at the boatyard, boating never became a significant part of the
life he and Jane shared, because Jane tended to get seasick. When the
time came to retire, "the plan was to go somewhere warm," Jane said,
"because he froze to death working at that boatyard all those years in
the winter. He was always so cold. He said, 'When I retire I'm not staying around here.' "

I commented that Hank had chosen the right industry, because people take such pleasure in their boats. He could have done other kinds of
skilled work someplace else that wouldn't have brought that look to
people's eyes and wouldn't have given him that connection between the
quality of what he was doing and the satisfaction he was getting out
of it.

"Well, you know, that is an issue that might even go back many years
to when the car industry was a big thing," he said. "Back then production was a good thing and all, but they wanted more than just production, they wanted some real good quality workmanship. Then as time
went on a lot of that disappeared. Production became such a big thing
that the quality kind of fell off, and so the guy that was doing this quality work, a little bit of him went down the drain. After that, if you went
to work for a car manufacturer, the job you were doing would be the
same thing over and over. I think in retrospect that, if we had it to do all
over again, we'd probably do it a little differently, because when you
take a person that's working and doing something, and take a piece of
that heart out—that's what you're doing, you know, if they can't do the
job that they want to do and be proud of—if they lose, for lack of a better word, it's pride, I guess, if you take that away, then I think you lose
an awful lot of the person himself because he's puttin' a lot of his feelings into what he does.

"One of the things that I always told the kids was, Don't let the dollar bill tell you what to do. If you're not happy doing what you're doing for a living, you're not gonna have a happy life. You're gonna be working a third of your life, and a third of it you're gonna be sleeping, and you doggone jolly well better be enjoying the third that you have off, because that's all you've got left. But if you can work and be happy working the third of your life that you're working, boy, you've got yourself about as complete a life as you'll ever get on this earth. And I rest my case."

Hank settled back in his chair with a grin, and I turned to Jane. "But did you feel that way about working in the bank?" I asked her.

"Yes, I did," she responded. "I didn't have to work. I wanted to work and I loved meeting all the people and it was somethin' to get up in the morning and get dressed up for, you know, because otherwise you'd lounge around and watch TV and drink coffee and read a book and just not feel very productive. I really enjoyed meeting all the people. It was hard to give it up. And when we moved out to Arizona, I still went back in the summers, and even after I retired from that, the next two years when I went back I volunteered, filing and answering the phone—just to be involved with the people."

"You volunteered at the *bank*? I never heard of anybody volunteering for a bank," I said incredulously.

"Well, at first I'd just go back to my old job in the spring, but the worst part every year was learning the new whatever they put in the computer—you know, they change things every year. And it finally got to the point where I said, It's taking too much out of me, I get too nerved up, but I said I'd love to come back and do some filing, answer the phone, stuff like that. So that's what I did for two years, about three days a week. They appreciated it. They gave me a bonus at Christmastime for volunteering, so everybody was happy."

Many people begin retirement with travel, producing a new version of the *Wanderjahr* that was once a tradition in Europe for young men of means, who often traveled abroad for a year or more before settling down to marriage and careers. The *Wanderjahr* offered what Erik Erikson called a *moratorium* for sorting out issues of identity before marriage and commitment to a particular adult role, and it often serves a similar function today in the form of a "gap year" between college and professional school.[1] Since few people arrive at retirement with an understanding that this transition will involve a rethinking of who they are, an interim pattern has emerged, in which travel offers a way of fulfilling deferred daydreams of adventure while the next stage takes shape.

The first step in the Lawsons' retirement was the purchase of a mobile home, the kind of recreational vehicle designed for actual travel. They set off across the country, and along the way they visited a couple who were former clients of the Brooklin Boat Yard and had been spending their winters in a trailer park retirement community near Tucson. It was the wife who told Hank about learning jewelry making there and who had shown the Lawsons a promotional video about the park, part of the Rincon Country West RV Resort.

"She knew that I made all the hardware at the boatyard, and she said, 'You know what, you could pick up that trade and I bet you'd love it,' " Hank recalled. "So with that in mind, that maybe I should try that, I went up to the workshop where they made jewelry. It's called the Silversmith-Lapidary Shop. I went in there, and this fellow met me at the door and he says, 'What are you looking for?' I said I didn't know, I was looking around, and I thought this might be interesting to get into. And he said, 'What do you know about it?' I said, 'I don't know anything about it.' He asked me if I had tools, and I said, 'No, I don't have any tools.' 'Well,' he says, 'you don't belong in here.' So I thought, Well, you're absolutely right, I don't, so I closed the door, and I left. Then I was telling this lady friend that it didn't work out, and I told her my experience. 'Oh,' she said, 'well, you must have run into the wrong person, because,' she said, 'they love to have new people come in and they love to help them. The people are always helping one another.' "

It was two years later when the Lawsons revisited Tucson and Hank went back to the Silversmith-Lapidary Shop. "This time I went in and I bumped into some lady from Texas in there and she was very friendly and she grabbed me by the arm and, boy, she wheeled me around inside and told me this and that and everything. She made me really feel welcome. What a difference a person can make! That was probably fifteen years ago. And now I do have my own tools."

Jane laughed. "And now when people come through the door, he's the one who takes somebody on and tells them . . ."

Hank went on to describe the complex of workshops in the resort, where groups of residents do their thing, woodwork or ceramics or sewing and needlepoint; his favored "shop" specializes in silversmithing and polishing semiprecious stones, although he does woodwork as well. When I went to visit the Lawsons in Tucson, he took me around the workshop, stopping to confer and advise on ongoing projects and showing me the different machines, and then on briefer visits to other workshops. Jane's sewing and embroidery workshop is across the hall. Each craft group has its own officers, and both Hank and Jane have been involved as officers and in teaching newcomers.

The crafts complex is only one of many facilities at the resort. "It costs almost four thousand dollars a year to rent the spot we're on. If you take advantage of all the facilities, from crafts to dancing to hot tubs," Jane said, "it's not that expensive, but if you're just going to come out there and not ever go to the Center, which there are people that do that, to me that doesn't make sense."

Hank added, "If you're a pessimist who doesn't want to get involved, I mean you're welcome· there and there are plenty of people to be friends with, but it's hard for us to understand anyone wanting to just set in their place and do nothing."

The next step allowed the Lawsons to move from their mobile home to what I learned to call a park model, the kind of large trailer that can be towed from place to place by a truck but is basically designed to keep long term in a single park attached to utilities, often with add-ons that make it semipermanent. "Someone told us about this couple who had upped and left everything just the way it was in their park model, and she wanted to sell it really cheap. They had moved into a community that provided a skilled nursing facility for the husband, she wasn't coming back, and the rent was due soon," Jane told me. "I said, 'Hank, let's just peek in the windows and look at it on the way home from coffee.' Well, it was all my colors, and I loved it. I just fell in love with it and said, 'Oh, I would love to have this.' He said, 'Well, we'll sell our mobile home and get that, if this is where you want to spend the rest of our winters.' So it was like we had to make a down payment right then and there. And I said, 'I can't do this without talking it over with the kids'— mainly our son, who's the business person, he is part owner of a building supply company. And I said, 'He's coming out in a few days, and I want to have him look at it and talk it over with him.' So we put five hundred dollars down and they gave us a week and our son thought it was a great idea.

"It was on the site fully furnished with sheets on the bed, towels hanging in the bathroom. Everything you would want except clothes. So we bought that for $28,000, and we came home and put our mobile home up for sale for $28,000 and sold it within a week because it was new."

Four years later, after selling a house in Maine, the Lawsons upgraded to a larger park model that was also already on site, where children or grandchildren could be put up in foldout beds for visits, strictly limited by park rules. In this sequence they reflected two of the common ways of looking at space during retirement—they scaled down but made sure their new space would allow family visits. There are photographs of children and grandchildren all through the park model, family and friends gathered there last year to celebrate an anniversary, and Jane and Hank are on the phone with one or another of their four children virtually daily. The latest park model is on a site with an open field behind it, with a view of the sunset, and they expanded it with a sort of enclosed patio called an Arizona room.

Because of Jane's seasickness, although they had owned a small boat and taught their four children about boating, the sea was not central to Jane and Hank's dreams of retirement. Still, there were subtle echoes of sailing wherever I looked. The park model in which they lived was much like the living quarters on a ship—compact and carefully planned spaces that required putting everything back in its place after use. Between their seasons in Arizona and Maine, Hank and Jane started going on annual cruises, but these were always river cruises, where seasickness was not a problem: first the Mississippi, then the Rhine, then a cruise in China. Hank said to me one day, "My friends ask me how I can bear to be away from the sea, but now, just look at those mountains." The Tucson Range, arid rock with little vegetation. But as we looked, cloud shadows moved across it, the light shifted, and I realized that the living rock, deep founded in the earth, is as dramatically alive as the sea, constantly shifting, something to be gazed at for hours, just as we can gaze, the way our ancestors did, at the flickering flames of a campfire.

By the time I met Hank, he had learned a wide variety of skills in working with precious metals and semiprecious stones. The first example of his work that I saw was a chain necklace, given to me by Dick and Barbara. Such chains are made link by double or single link from different thicknesses of silver wire, then twisted together like a cable with a variety of textures. The Goldsbys, who are both biology professors, joked that the chain they gave me represented the double helix of DNA.

Hank showed me a variety of other products he had developed, which he was reshaping into a small business. He got out half a dozen silver mussel shells, produced from a few shells brought from the Maine coast to his Tucson workshop, where he had experimented for over a year until he had a mold to produce a pendant that met his meticulous standards. On each one, he pointed out small flaws that had allowed him to refine his technique, so that together they provided a narrative of his patient learning. The completed pendants, he said, show slight variations, so he numbers them like lithographs. The mussel shells are now on sale locally in Maine, but by the time I visited Tucson, Hank was repeating the process with sand dollars, more challenging because their markings are so faint. He spoke of producing enough pendants so that small quantities could be released each year after his death as an ongoing inheritance.

After our conversations in Maine, I was reminded of a novel I had read many years before, *Trustee from the Toolroom,* by Nevil Shute.[2] In the novel a man who has been developing miniature models of engines and clocks and publishing the plans in a hobby magazine finds himself on a quest to the South Pacific. He has very little money, but he ends up being given free transport from place to place by pilots and captains who have followed his model designs with pleasure and who use the time together to refine their own skills. The ability to miniaturize opens an entire world, from macrocosm to microcosm and back. A precise focus on machinery opens a series of human relationships. I sent a copy of the book to Hank, who read it with great pleasure and asked, when I came to Tucson, "How did you get to know me so well?"

When people's lives go through major transitions, different strategies come into play. Some people choose discontinuity and look at retirement as a fresh start, sloughing off the skills and habits (and sometimes the relationships as well) of earlier years, going to a strange place or returning to school and learning a new profession. Some pick out a single element of their earlier lives to pursue without the distractions and stresses that characterize so many jobs. Others find ways of connecting the new and the old that allow them to transfer their skills and passions into forms that appear to be discontinuous but are actually based on subtle metaphorical translations—How is a mountain range like the sea? How is a park model trailer like a ship? How is the fashioning of delicate jewelry like the maintenance of great diesel engines? We call the people who articulate their recognition of such relationships poets. The sensibility that can make these transitions in daily activity is also, I suspect, making them in deeper ways, so that the conscientiousness of Hank's craftsmanship expresses itself as a kind of fidelity in relationships that has led to friendships with writers like E. B. White, a client of the boatyard, and scientists like Dick and Barbara, based on commonalities that are not obvious.

I approached the Lawsons partly because I wanted to understand the effect of moving on people as they grow older. Throughout human history, place has been a basic element of identity, as basic as family of origin, yet in contemporary America both have been partially set aside.

Almost all of the people who turn up in the chapters of this book have initiated their years of Adulthood II with changes in their housing, and I find myself struggling with phrases that combine a sense of grounding with different kinds of mobility. Definitions of home have as much to do with human connections as they do with real estate.

The Lawsons, having been attached to Maine all their lives, took one approach, scaling down and moving away from the winter cold and into a setting designed for retirees, in a mobile home that is not designed for mobility, but they wisely retained a base to return to in Maine in summer. Considering their choices, I have found myself enumerating the variations I encountered in my interviews and my own life.

My husband and I have owned our apartment in Cambridge (where we first met as students in 1957) since 1969. We moved there when I was pregnant with our daughter, and it was extensively renovated, but it was rented during years when we lived abroad. After our daughter married, we expanded into part of the second-floor apartment to create a guest room. When we returned from Iran, Cambridge was home, but then the center of gravity of our lives shifted to New Hampshire, where we built on the footprint of a dilapidated barn on the property we have owned since 1962 and originally used seasonally. In both cases, construction was triggered by the need to have space for extended visits by our daughter, her husband, and first one and then two grandchildren.

My father, Gregory Bateson, remarried when I was in graduate school and started another family—he had in the end three only children, one from each marriage, but his third wife, Lois Camack, had a son from a previous marriage, and my half brother joined the household for several years before Gregory and Lois had their daughter, Nora. After he married Lois, Gregory decided he was ready to deal with his roots, and they went to England and brought back the Bateson family possessions that had been in storage for decades—books, furniture, and artwork, surely a symbolic statement of settling down on Gregory's part. Yet Gregory and Lois continued to move around, spending time in the Virgin Islands and in Hawaii on research projects and taking a group of students on a round-the-world educational voyage.

When Gregory's health began to fail, they had settled in a big old house in Santa Cruz, but after he died, Lois moved to a small apartment near Zen Center in San Francisco and then gave that up to spend time at an ashram in India. When she came back from India, she decided to settle in North Carolina, where she had grown up and where her parents were living, initially so that she could look after them as they aged, but later she moved into a retirement community there—and out again, partly so that she could afford the flexibility of spending summers near her grandchildren. Twice she has set up housekeeping near them, only to have them pull up stakes and move elsewhere.

Ruth Massinga, a social worker and foundation executive who had twice moved far away from her family of origin in Louisiana, first to the East Coast and then to the Northwest, took a different tack, remodeling her Seattle apartment so she would have a more inviting guest room for her son and his family.

The Goldsbys, both tenured professors, had earlier followed career opportunities from place to place but eventually built in Maine and remodeled in Massachusetts, partly because selling their company suddenly gave them the financial flexibility to do so.

James Morton, dean of the Cathedral of St. John the Divine, and his wife, Pamela, lost their home of twenty-five years, the deanery in the cathedral close, which went with the job, when Jim retired, and now live in an apartment in the same New York neighborhood.

Jane Fonda owns a ranch near Santa Fe, which she seems to be developing as a long-term home base, but she still keeps a base in Atlanta. Last time I saw her, she was living in New York and performing on Broadway, beginning to look again toward Los Angeles.

Of the people described at length in this book, only Dan Jepson and Michael Crowe have not made significant changes, continuing to live in the house that Dan inherited in a suburb of San Francisco.

One of the emerging emphases as Americans reach old age is on making it possible for them to remain in their homes in spite of frailty or disability, but during Adulthood II, there is a lot of shifting and building as location is less determined by employment and people try to find the place that will make long-term sense for them. Some of this is simply the American pattern. We move constantly, shifting homes and replacing spouses. We are increasingly skillful at constructing new circles of acquaintances but often without real closeness.

In 2007, I started a discussion group on aging at the library in the small town of Hancock, New Hampshire, and many of those who joined it were newcomers, looking for ways to meet people. One of the themes the group pursued for weeks was the search for old friends with whom they had lost touch—we gave ourselves the homework assignment of reconnecting with at least one person and came back with stories of search and reunion. As many friendships are lost or attenuated through retirement moves as through death, but the loss, although just as real, is not specifically mourned. The human cost is also often unconsidered when retirees think about relocating, sometimes trading friendship for sunshine.

Moving is both liberating and debilitating. Undertaken too late, it is a very stressful process, one that sometimes seems to catapult people into frail old age, and undertaken too soon, it may preempt other possibilities. One of the topics that came up again and again in a group of women in their sixties that I belonged to was the problem of clearing out the accumulation of years of living, either for the sake of the next generation or to make a move to smaller quarters possible. Lightening up and giving stuff away is easier to do in the context of a move, with a deadline ahead by which time everything must be sorted and its future designated. But it isn't easy to determine what will be of value to the next generation or to know how to divide familiar treasures among multiple children. Sorting gets harder as time goes on—it requires a sort of ruthless decisiveness, while indecision results in endless dithering. Five moves, they say, equal a fire. But those who haven't moved may begin to need a fire.

Each of these strategies involves questions about relationships and how to manage the partially reconstructed relationships of previous decades. My husband once commented to me that in his Armenian tradition, the main way adults form new friendships is with in-laws when their children marry, but American children tend to marry peers met at residential colleges or in start-up jobs, far from home. Grandparents who move to be close to grandchildren, even when they get separate housing, are giving up their networks and support systems, rather like young brides in patriarchal societies, who cease to be full members of their own families while becoming probationary newcomers among their husbands' kin.

Hank and Jane are happy with their housing arrangements and the circle of friends they have developed. With proprietary hospitality, they took me to see the sights around Tucson: an old Spanish mission, Saguaro National Park, the edges of the Sonoran Desert. As I tried to see the desert and the mountains with their eyes, I found my imagination shifting. I have always felt uncomfortable with the metaphors that compare God to a rock or a mountain: mighty, yes, as close to eternal as we can get, perhaps, but static and lifeless. So I have instead conjured up the ocean or the atmosphere that moves around our planet, supporting life and never still. Now I see the mountains and the desert differently—kaleidoscopic with light and life.

CHAPTER III

Liberation Time

T HERE IS CHANGE ALL AROUND US, more rapid change from year to year than in any previous era. In some cases one can simply say of changed perceptions that they arise gradually from new experiences and cumulative learning, but in other cases one may feel a deeper change, a change of consciousness. The entire picture shifts, sometimes very rapidly. The world changes, becoming suddenly different. The idealism of one era may become the common sense or the nightmare of another, and common sense may be revealed as illusion.

Some of these shifts have been global. The twentieth century saw the breakdown of colonialism around the world, the liberation of many nations, and the affirmations expressed in the Universal Declaration of Human Rights. Some of these shifts were the results of technology creating new possibilities, others of new forms of expression or understanding.

There was a change of consciousness for great numbers of Americans in the sixties and seventies, who suddenly saw the world around them and their place in it differently. This kind of change is comparable to a religious conversion that has a "before" and "after" quality, punctuating experience and infusing it with new and different meaning. It's like falling in love or suddenly seeing one's life in relation to a newborn child, perhaps like learning that one has only a short time to live. The Copernican revolution must have felt this way to those who understood it, as human beings were forced to see their position in the universe in a new way, or Freud's demonstration of how much goes on in our minds that we are unaware of. For many people the dropping of atomic bombs on Hiroshima and Nagasaki, with the potential threat of nuclear annihilation, altered their understanding of the human condition forever. To describe a shift in consciousness affecting an entire society or civilization, some writers have borrowed from the history of science the metaphor of a *paradigm shift.*[1] In speaking of individuals, a more common term is *transformational learning.*

The American social revolutions of the twentieth century were based in experiences of this kind that offered to group after group a new sense of possibility, with the potential to grow into a new sense of responsibility. First, African Americans took a new look at the way their situation had evolved since the Civil War, and large numbers for the first time affirmed that it could be changed. They looked at each other and recognized not only beauty and strength but the possibility of assertion. With the glory years of the civil rights movement behind us, and continuing frustrations and economic woes in the black community, we sometimes forget that children defied their parents and students their teachers, taking their lives in their hands to affirm a new vision of themselves and of a possible future.

Then, with the beginning of new-wave feminism, women went through the same process, identifying the methodology as raising consciousness by group discussion, a term that Marx had used earlier to describe the shift in vision when exploited laborers recognize their exploitation. The disabilities movement and the gay rights movement required similar shifts in the way people looked at themselves as well as the way they looked at others.

It is already possible to discern two such shifts that have taken place in the United States and other industrialized countries in the first decade of the twenty-first century, but it is not yet clear how the newly unfolding consciousness will play out.

The first is environmental—the awareness that we have brought our planet to the threshold of profound climate change, mass extinction of species, and humanitarian disasters, and that these changes are being produced by ordinary behaviors we have come to take for granted. Whereas fifty years ago many women ceased to define their aspirations as a house in the suburbs, two children, and a dog, today men and women are examining the way their self-definitions are anchored in their driving habits, the symbolism of high-powered automobiles, and the consumption of material goods that we use to measure success. At a deeper level, the awareness of a common vulnerability and responsibility is still in the process of inspiring a spiritual awakening that goes back to the first photographs that allowed us to look at our planet as seen from the moon, new affirmations of the ancient intuition of unity.

The other shift upon us is the result of increased life expectancy. The assumptions that people bring to their own lives are connected to their general expectations about the shape of lives, yet the shape of lives has changed. For most of human history, average life expectancy at birth was less than forty years, and the "threescore years and ten" of the ninetieth psalm was an aspiration rarely met, certainly not to be counted on. Today, with life expectancies in industrialized nations reaching and passing the biblical horizon, another change is indicated in the sense of self, one that is just beginning to reach consciousness. Who am I? and What do I want in my life? are very different questions when life is neither sweet and fleeting nor "nasty, brutish, and short," in the words of Thomas Hobbes. Here, too, the meaning of success is in question as we try to understand the meaning of a "successful life." Scientific and technological change have stimulated new possibilities and new spiritual search.

Thomas Kuhn, who developed the concept of paradigm shifts in science, discussed the way in which anomalous data begin to undermine an accepted theory.[2] For me the first such datum came when an American colleague working as a teacher in Iran told me that she was retiring at sixty and returning to the United States to look after her mother. Her mother? I was still in my forties. It had never occurred to me that a woman of her age would still have a mother to look after and be planning her life around that obligation. Shortly after my father died in 1980, his widow, Lois, who is only a decade older than I am, decided to relocate temporarily in North Carolina, where she had grown up and her parents were growing old, to contribute to their care, a responsibility that lasted fifteen years, long enough for her to grow new roots.

Our assumptions about the shape of lives and how long they last are necessarily changing. Over the years, I have watched families who had rallied around a deathbed when doctors said it was a matter of weeks struggling to sort out their responsibilities as weeks extended into months or years. And I have listened to friends, who had made choices for retirement as if it would last no longer than a few seasons, revising those plans as their healthy span extended and golf or fishing or travel proved unsatisfying.

In 2002, Ellen Goodman, author and syndicated columnist for *The Boston Globe*, then sixty-one years old, invited me to a small, informal conference with a group of women that she and Patricia Schroeder, who served for twenty-four years in the House of Representatives from Colorado, were organizing, to discuss the approach of retirement age and how they—we—felt about it. We met that December in Celebration, Florida, over a weekend, a group of seven women, all of whom had had careers and all of whom, somewhat to my surprise, were currently married and had grown-up children. We were all in our sixties, each with a range of degrees, books, and titles to her credit. A novelist. A psychotherapist. A college president. An entrepreneur. Women who had been active in different ways in the liberation movements of the twentieth century, and who had struggled for the right to work outside the home, now looking at retirement. Women who had "had it all."

Most important from my point of view, everyone there had already once in her lifetime had to reject ready-made answers to the questions of purpose and identity and think them through as women in a new way. We recognized that we had been struggling with similar dilemmas and decided, even though we came from different parts of the country, to continue to meet semiannually and to invite two or three others to join the group. Because all of us were busy and engaged on a number of fronts, we agreed to concentrate on developing our common understanding rather than undertaking any new form of activism.

The two comments that I remember most vividly from that first gathering were Pat Schroeder's, that in the women's movement "We thought we had won a war but in fact we had only taken a beachhead for women's equality," and Ellen Goodman's, that all of our obituaries were already written, neatly on file in newspaper offices, so that in a real sense we had nothing to prove. But there we were, wondering about how to be productive, how to contribute to a positive future for our children and our grandchildren, how to continue to make our lives meaningful. This last is a new question for healthy people in their sixties to be asking, for through most of human history elders have been treasured and have had established roles that only they could fill, and much less time in which to fill them.

One of those who joined us six months later was Ruth Massinga, an African American woman who lives in Seattle, Washington, then approaching retirement as president and CEO of Casey Family Programs. This foundation, one of a cluster started by the Casey family, works to provide and improve foster care and to prevent the need for it. Ruth also chaired the board of the Marguerite Casey Foundation, an independent grant-making organization where she and Pat Schroeder had become friends, and cochaired the board of the Jim Casey Youth Opportunities Initiative.

Ruth has spent her career on different aspects of social welfare, concerned with children and with the elderly. Her career has included service as secretary of the Maryland Department of Human Resources and president of the American Public Welfare Association. She has a son, Irving, and two grandchildren, Ben and Madeline, who were six and four when we first met.

It was Ruth who got us discussing the importance of grandparents to the well-being of children, and the connections between longevity, health, and the availability of grandparents. Ruth grew up in Baton Rouge, Louisiana. Her own parents had in fact lived with her maternal grandparents in the kind of community in which relatives and neighbors all took a role in child rearing—the kind of community in which "it takes a village to raise a child." Ruth was the oldest, the first grandchild on either side, and described herself as spoiled and overprotected, spending summers in Lafayette, Louisiana, and returning to Baton Rouge for school during the winters.

"We lived in a very communal fashion. I can still see the faces of the neighbors who watched me and my friends on the way to the Catholic school, three or four blocks around the corner, and would report to my parents and my grandparents what I had or had not done appropriately. 'Ruth,' they'd say, 'Ruth, I see you taking off your sweater. Your granny's not going to like that, 'cause it's too cold.' That was the routine. Every house along the way was inhabited by somebody who was a part of the extended family in that fashion, which is very southern. It was tremendously impressive . . . and oppressive . . . from the point of view of the child. But you felt absolutely safe. You knew what the deviations were, and you knew what the consequences were."

I commented that, by the time most people had television, that kind of awareness had decreased. People began to sit indoors, and front porches all over the country were abandoned—no more "Good morning, Mr. George," no "Good afternoon, Miss Mamie" as you walked down the street. Neighborhoods became less safe, and again less safe when families began to get air-conditioning and close their windows in hot weather. I have sometimes fantasized that older people who have become shut-ins might be enrolled in a program to watch the streets through their windows.

"But even so," Ruth said, "when I was in college and driving, my father said to me, 'You should stop driving so fast.' And I said, 'What do you mean?' He said, 'Don't you know that the police tell me where you go and how fast you're going?' Okay, so that was 'fifty-nine, 'sixty, still a small town. Still small enough for most people to know what you were doing, and if they cared enough, it got reported back. It was, in that sense, a very closed society.

"I think that's part of why I couldn't wait to graduate college. I went to college where my parents had gone, and then I went straight to New York. Because I thought not only 'big city,' exciting, et cetera, but 'Ooh, wouldn't it be good to get away from all this?' "

Ruth majored in psychology and studied social work in graduate school. While she was away, urban renewal came to Baton Rouge, and her grandparents' home fell victim to development. "When they were in their early seventies and I was nineteen," she said, "their little neighborhood and their house all fell to eminent domain. They were retired by that time. My grandfather had had a heart condition for a very long time, but he was functioning pretty well. My grandmother, I guess she lived another year and died. So they died at seventy-four, seventy-five."

"Not a good age to leave their home and have everything get jumbled up," I said, remembering that often when older people are forced into a move too late for them to adapt to the new place, their lives seem to be cut short. "It did them in?"

"It did."

"So then, in New York, did you feel like a country mouse in the big city?"

"I didn't, you know. I didn't stop to think about it. I was so busy doing things. I went to work right away for the City Department of Welfare. I worked in what they called foster care for older people, for adults. It was not what I wanted to do, not what I saw myself doing. However, it was just fascinating that—you know, things all come back in circles in their own fashion, and here we are thinking about growing old. I spent a year and a half finding board and care homes for elderly New Yorkers who were either receiving public assistance or the city was putting money into providing board and care for them. Or they could have been private folks who just needed referrals."

"That's a model that doesn't exist any longer, does it?" I asked. "I've never heard anybody talk about foster care for seniors. It makes sense."

"It does, but maybe in smaller places. In New York, this was a small unit, but it clearly was responsive to some of the people, like older men who lived in single rooms, SROs they call them now, and were in dire straits, so we would try to make sure that they were safe and well cared for and got what they needed to survive. It was a great way to learn the city. I rode the subways all over town, got to see stuff that I had never thought I'd see. Got to do a little bit of counseling, although that wasn't really the point. The point was really to get these people in the right place and to maintain them in the right place." Ruth's move to New York, followed by her later moves, suggested to me the fairy tales in which a young hero—rarely a heroine—goes out into the world in search of adventure.

"I'll tell you," she went on, "one of the things that it did was to explode my sense of what the universe was. Here I was, having lived in a very segregated environment for twenty-one years. I knew who white people were, I knew who Jews were, but they weren't a part of my everyday experience in the same way as they were when I went to New York. So I got a sense of this, of different ethnic styles of caregiving, different expectations, and of how we—Americans—collectively felt about older people." Ruth was working out of an integrated office where they didn't specialize her with black seniors, so she simply went where she was needed, becoming aware of different patterns of kinship and family structure and of the cultural differences in how people deal with pain or misfortune or even whether they grieve out loud. "That was during the day," she said. "And during the evening there were jazz clubs and the theater and new friends, and all of that. So I became, in my own eyes, fairly sophisticated, fairly quickly."

Ruth took some courses at NYU and a class or two at Columbia, not so much social work as what she called "just soap and little bit of suds." Ultimately she moved to Massachusetts, to attend the Boston University School of Social Work. "A lot of my preoccupation was with how I was going to do," she said. "I had graduated magna cum laude. I was, you know, highly regarded as smart, but that was in the segregated South. So I was very concerned with whether I would meet my own and

the others' high standards when I went to graduate school. I was dab-
bling a little bit, seeing how people do it in an integrated setting. And
when I did go to graduate school, in 'sixty-three, I spent a fair amount
of time worrying about that with my faculty adviser. He said, 'Why
are you worrying about this? This isn't an issue.' I had to convince *myself* that it was not an issue, and did." That's Ruth: "I had to convince
myself . . . and did." Decision made, issue resolved.

"I came back to New York. I worked at a community service society,
which was doing direct service. I had a caseload that was largely in the
Bronx and largely but not exclusively minorities, because I was able to
relate to single black women with children who were struggling and
trying to figure out how to manage. I was not married nor had a kid
and wasn't thinking of it at the time, but I figured out how to be real
with them."

During that period, Ruth met Joseph Massinga, who had come to
the United States from Portuguese Mozambique. "He came to this
country as a refugee, learned English, got a bachelor's at Lincoln, came
to New York and went to Manhattan College (that's when I met him),
and then to Fordham and did a master's," Ruth said. "And then we married, and we went to Geneva and he started on a Ph.D. in international
politics." The historic tide of liberation in Africa that brought Joseph
Massinga as a student was the same tide that brought President Barack
Obama's father from Kenya to study in the United States. Each married
an American woman, and each returned in the end to Africa without
his American wife and child.

"Here I am, a southern girl," Ruth told me. "I go to the big city, I'm
doing my thing pretty good, being very cosmopolitan, and I meet this
rebel, romantic and vivacious, with a compelling narrative that all he
wants to do is go back home and help free his people. And that's what I
signed on to. Do I know Africa? Of course not. But it's . . . This was the
time of liberation, both at home and abroad. I had contributed relatively nothing. I had gone to the March on Washington and I taught in
a freedom school in Boston, but I hadn't ridden buses and I hadn't registered voters or done any of that hard stuff. But I was sure that I could,
so . . . 'I'll help you to free your country.'

"So we went marching off to Geneva, and we had— It was tough. Harder than he imagined." As a foreigner in Switzerland, Ruth had difficulty getting a job. She did some clerical work and also some research for the International Labor Organization on the growth of multinational corporations.

"I also became pregnant," she said. "We had married in September 'sixty-seven, and Irv was born in December 'sixty-eight. So it wasn't that long that I was available to the workforce. And Lord knows, I hadn't saved any money. Joseph had a little bit of a stipend, we weren't starving. I guess it was maybe a little better than hand-to-mouth but not a whole lot better. Well, it dragged on. In the meantime, little Mr. Massinga showed up, and my husband and parents colluded to say the baby could not be born in Switzerland. I think my mother was really concerned, I'm putting it straight out, she did not know what kind of mongrel child I was going to have. She liked Joseph all right, but she— 'Who are these people?' That was her whole thing. 'How could you do this? We do not know these people.' "

I commented that my impression was that at that time African Americans didn't feel much identification with anybody in Africa and thought Africans were probably savages. "That was exactly their fear," Ruth said. "Ooga booga. So it was all right that he was in this country becoming a learned person, but now what does he do? They were somewhat mollified that he seemed . . . the veneer seemed all right. When it came down to my being pregnant, she wanted to be sure that she saw and touched this baby herself and was able to imprint her view of the world on it. And they colluded with Joseph. So I came back to the States when I was seven months pregnant, and had Irv in Baton Rouge in the same hospital where I had my tonsils taken out. They checked him out, and he seemed like an okay enough infant. They thought, He's like us. I was insistent that I was going to be a good wife, and that meant going over to his father in Geneva when he was just two or three months old.

"Meanwhile, the negotiation about this dissertation that was supposed to be getting done was much more contentious than my husband thought it would be. So again, he and my parents decided, to my great rage, that I should come home. And I said, 'If you send me home, this is the beginning of the end of this relationship, because I have a voice, and I don't want to do this.' And he insisted. In his mind, this was the right thing to do; he persuaded my parents it was the right thing to do. Again: I'm thirty-one years old, and he and my parents are going to decide for me? No. I did it, but that really started to erode the bonds between us."

"At some level your parents must have known it would," I commented. "They must have thought they were getting you back."

"Well, I guess they did. Yeah. I think they may have thought—and I might have had fantasies, too—that maybe we were going to replay their story, that I was going to go to live with them. Joseph stayed a couple of years in Geneva, really working diligently on the damn dissertation. But it took a long time to negotiate what it was going to be, and then to do it. I don't even remember what it was about anymore. Then the war really broke out. He was already a member of FRELIMO [the liberation movement], and he decided, 'Well, hell, if I can't get this dissertation written, I will do something to help my country and go back to Africa and fight.' So that's when the story veered off course. The longer the dissertation dragged out, the more he was feeling like, 'Time's a-wasting, I've got this wife, I've got this baby, I've got this nation. Why am I doing this?' And not only did he have this wife, he had this angry wife, because by now I was saying, 'If that's what you want to do, that's what you want to do. If you think you're going to run me around and tell me what to do, well, to hell with you.'

"We never figured out— I recognize now that I really never reached out to try to help him through. What was so damaging to the relationship were those expectations we each had. During the courtship, I had never seen what I considered to be this authoritarian behavior exhibiting itself. But of course we were in New York. That's different from being thousands of miles away with no resources of my own."

So Ruth and Irv went back to Baton Rouge, where Ruth got a job, while Joseph went to war. "My mother and father were terrific caregivers, without a doubt, but I said to myself, 'Self, I just don't see this kind of arrangement continuing for very long.' And funny, I don't think my mother did either. I think, as dearly as she loved that little boy, it wasn't what she had in mind for herself. She did it, almost reflexively. She had retired, I came home, there was a baby, so what do you do? I think she recognized (and I told her on a regular basis), that I wasn't going to stay in Baton Rouge. So she was helping me and him prepare for the next adventure. I think she knew that." Ruth filed for divorce, which came through in 1973. In June 1975, Portugal granted independence to Mozambique.

"Irv and I went to California," Ruth continued. "That was the second time that I have gone far away. I moved to California thinking I was going to remarry—someone I had known in New York, older by almost fifteen years, who had eagerly pursued me when I came back to the States. That was another reason why it was easy to say good-bye to Joseph, because there was another player. I moved to the West Coast with him, but along came this same strand of authoritarian stuff that I had seen before, and I was not prepared to see it again. I said, 'What's with you guys? What message am I giving that suggests that you can tell me what to do and that I'm going to pay attention?' So that relationship ended. And meanwhile I started to build myself a career."

I asked whether she and Joseph had lost touch. "I went to Mozambique after Irv graduated college. He went to South Africa to teach for a year, and I went to Africa to visit him, to South Africa and Zimbabwe and Mozambique, just before the elections in South Africa. So I got there thirty years later. And Joseph was at Irv's wedding."

When I went to stay with Ruth in Seattle in 2006 to interview her for this book, she was busy with plans to remodel her apartment to make it more comfortable for guests, especially for her son, Irving, and her grandchildren.

By that time, our group had met some seven or eight times, and I had persuaded them to undertake a first venture into activism. I had kept insisting that we were a part, through our combination of life experience and continuing health, of something new in history, a change in the balance of generations living at the same time. It is no wonder that, one after another, the pioneers of new-wave feminism have written books about aging. And no wonder that we should feel newly challenged by the questions Who am I? and What do I want in my life?

Letty Cottin Pogrebin, one of the original editors of Ms. Magazine and a successful novelist, had reminded us of the pattern of women's consciousness-raising groups a generation before. In our conversations (as in the books coming out about aging), I had heard references to Jung's "wise woman archetype," the crone whose gnomic utterances and knowledge of healing often made her suspected of witchcraft. And like women and blacks in the sixties and gays in the seventies, we had to free ourselves from looking at ourselves and each other in terms of obsolete stereotypes, to question the emphasis on youthfulness that we had shared, and to embrace the strengths as well as the stresses of a new stage of life. The word wisdom came up often—but it was not until three years after we first met that I put two words together and realized that we were exploring the nature of active wisdom—an entire cohort with something new to offer to the world as years of experience combined with continuing health. It was the novelty of this situation that convinced me that a new consciousness should lead to a new social activism.

I have always been out of sync with the activisms of my generation, occasionally ahead but often far behind. Out of a sense of the dissonance between what I heard at home and the largely Republican background of most of my schoolmates, I had volunteered at the age of twelve for the first Adlai Stevenson campaign. I arrived at college with a fine disdain for the conformity and political lethargy of my contemporaries, a disdain that came from spending my senior year of high school in Israel, where the idealism of the early years of that nation's independence and agrarian socialism still burned brightly. Then, instead of catching fire with my peers during the civil rights movement, I had already gotten involved in the much smaller antinuclear movement in 1959, before it was swallowed up in the anti–Vietnam war movement. I really did not begin to understand what feminism was about until the eighties, when I encountered blatant misogyny, which I had somehow failed to notice. Wiser than I, the other women in the group insisted that they were already overloaded with political commitments and public activity, and that they wanted to use our conversations to grow in understanding of who we were and where we were going. We continued to meet at six-month intervals in different locations and added some more members. We began to refer to ourselves as Next Step Women.

In March 2004, we did agree on an activist project, looking ahead to the fall presidential election and motivated by our distaste for the assumptions of politicians that people over fifty are only concerned with their own entitlements. We had been discussing the shortening time perspective of American politics. "We live longer," I argued, "but we think shorter." Since everyone in the group except Pat Schroeder already had at least one grandchild (by the time the project was launched she had a sonogram of a grandchild on the way), we decided to start a grandparents' campaign based on the twenty-year implications of current issues that our grandchildren would have to deal with: the environment, the deficit, enmities incurred that might lead to future conflict, availability of opportunity, and the preservation of rights and liberties. The slogan would be "I am voting for my grandchild."

Statistics show that seniors vote in much larger percentages than other age-groups, partly because we have more time to think about elections and perhaps partly because our approach to politics was formed before more recent episodes of corruption and the resulting cynicism. We hoped that the emphasis on grandchildren would inspire grandparents to put pressure on politicians of both parties to think beyond the next election or the next quarterly earnings report. We argued that any involvement adults might have with young children, whether as family members or students or patients, represents an investment in the future beyond our own lifetimes. Ruth played a key role in making us aware of the increasing child-care role of older adults across the country, either fostering their own grandchildren or helping out while both parents work. And we were all aware that our own grown-up children were under financial and career pressure, over-worked with jobs and child care. One of the things we did as a group was to commission national poll questions aimed at grandparents, which showed that our suspicion that grandparenthood influences voting decisions is correct. As far as we could determine, the question had never before been asked.

The various newspaper columns and op-eds that grew out of the launching of the project, which we called Granny Voter, seem to have led to a greater awareness of the legitimacy and potential influence of the grandparent generation, but we had no program to take forward at the grass roots, and among that heavily committed and engaged group of women, there was no one ready to make Granny Voter her primary project and build it as an ongoing movement. We created a website with the story of Granny Voter, the poll results, photographs of the launching, and the texts of speeches by Geraldine Ferraro, Ruth Massinga, and myself, which is still on the Internet as of this writing at www.GrannyVoter.org. The concept is still waiting for some group to take up the challenge. As long as short-term thinking governs decision making in Washington, we are all at risk.

The Granny Voter story offers food for thought for older adults. On the one hand, it poses the question of how we concentrate our energies in continuity with what we have done in the past. My friends in the group are all committed and continuing to work for goals that were important in the early years of the women's movement, which they still share, including a woman's right to choose, which continues to be under threat. Their loyalties are shaped by the priorities of organizations they want to continue to support and the ongoing participation of these pioneers is valued by the groups they have worked with over the years. Women's groups seem to value those who have played a historic role more than men's groups do—perhaps among women there is less of an oedipal thrust for young leaders to step forward. New leaders might come forward more quickly if they were less respectful of the pioneers.

On the other hand, perhaps the struggle to preserve the right to choose whether or not to have a child and how to care for and educate that child should be in the hands of younger women dealing directly with the issues, while older adults might be rethinking the right to choose death with dignity. Do we stay with the same causes and organizations, or do we translate the fundamental commitments they represent into a new form? Or do we move from local to more global causes? How, when energy is limited, do we choose? It is possible that our efforts carry more conviction when they address others' problems rather than our own. I was proposing a new activism on the part of older adults that was not on behalf of older adults—though both are important—an activism on behalf of the future beyond our lifetimes, more similar to the Gray Panthers than to the AARP. The concern I feel about our capacity to think deeply about the future of our nation and our planet grows as I live longer. As you think further into the future, you see more and more interconnections, and your concerns extend more widely as well, like a swath of light extending through a partly opened door into darkness.

The choice of where we put our efforts is also connected to how much we are willing to learn as we get older, and whether we can once again grow into a new consciousness and new forms of commitment, acquiring new skills. I have never tried to build a political movement from the bottom up, though many of my friends have, so in writing a book about a process of change, I am practicing an old skill in a new context. But I was impressed by the significance of the experience other women brought to the effort, even as I noticed that what was effective twenty years before might no longer be effective, notably that demonstrations for peace and justice issues no longer get much coverage from the press.

Mother's Day and Father's Day fall in the spring. There is also a Grandparents' Day, in the fall, which doesn't get nearly as much play, though I expect it, too, stimulates the greeting card market. On September 12, Grandparents' Day, 2004, less than two months before the election, we launched Granny Voter on the Washington Ellipse. We had gathered our children and grandchildren from across the country and met in Pat O'Brien's Washington apartment the evening before, creating banners with the multicolored handprints of the grandchildren. Then on a beautiful sunny day, we gathered in a semicircle of white rocking chairs. My assignment was to introduce the event.

"Never in human history have there been so many experienced and healthy elders with so much energy and potential commitment," I told the crowd. "As lives not only extend but extend with higher quality, we are becoming something new in history—a new and dynamic force, 70 million strong in America and growing. What can elders do with this unique combination of energy and knowledge? Too many politicians have been blinded by stereotypes that apply mainly to the sick or those in their last years. They seem to assume that seniors are concerned only with Social Security, Medicare, and prescription drug benefits. Political advertising literally instructs seniors to concentrate on these special interests.

"Candidates in this year's election would be wise instead to watch the grandparents as we take up an active role we may play for many years: The Grannies are coming! Most of us are just getting started: the average age of becoming a first-time grandmother in the United States today is forty-seven. And more and more Baby Boomers are joining in. We took a rocking chair as our symbol, but this rocker is jet propelled. We chose the term *Granny Voter* because *granny* suggests someone easy to dismiss and we aim to reverse that meaning. Our special interest is the future.

"Older adults matter for human societies, passing on the stories that tell young people where they came from and offering visions of possible futures. They are leaders and healers and workers. They care for children when parents are unavailable and give their time to the community. Our ancestors planted trees and vines to bear fruit long after their deaths. We will find new ways to work for the future today.

"The world shifts and surprises from day to day. The Twin Towers are gone, and so is the Berlin Wall. Those who have lived with history have the habits of learning and adaptation, but we don't want to see the costs passed on to the next generation. We worry about the long-term cost of pollution or a destabilized climate that might last centuries. We mourn the disruption of institutions and international friendships based on decades of careful building. We can remind youth of the real burdens of war or injustice. We know that short-term thinking is dangerous.

"We vote—over 70 percent of those between fifty-five and seventy-four voted in the 2000 presidential election—and as we recognize that we represent something new, we are beginning to speak out. Beginning today, we will work to change the political agenda from short-term to long-term thinking. We will take on a new role as advocates and trustees for the future. Realizing that we are freer than ever before to stand up for what we believe in, we can become the needed visionaries of our society.

"For those who have grandchildren or other ties to young children, even if we don't see them as often as we would like, the future that calls forth our energy and commitment to defend it comes readily to mind: it is the world that the children of today will live in when we are gone. Every grandchild is an argument for a better future, a light shining into the unknown—may it shine on promises fulfilled."

Geraldine Ferraro, who was vice presidential candidate in 1984 and the first major-party woman candidate for national office, spoke next, zeroing in on promises made in the past and pointing out that many had not been fulfilled. "We Grannies—both women and men—no longer are worrying about the children we made those promises to," she said. "They are old enough to worry about themselves . . . But we do worry about their children, our grandchildren, and what the future holds for them. There is no doubt that what is lacking in government is long-term planning. That's because most elected officials think in two-, four-, or six-year terms, depending on when they're running for reelection. We want that to change. . . . And from my experience, I know that our government is capable of making long-term, sometimes costly decisions. In the early eighties, when I was in the Congress and a member of the Select Committee on Aging, our country was faced with the probability that the Social Security system would run out of money before the end of the century. At that time, Congressman Claude Pepper of Florida and the National Commission on Social Security worked on legislation that would preserve the system to the year 2040. The legislation passed, partly because it was the right thing to do, partly because no legislator wanted seniors angry at him or her on Election Day. That may be precisely why many public officials seem to ignore the long-term needs of children—because children can't vote. At least until now. This year we are changing that. On Election Day, we are giving our votes to our grandchildren, and we ask every grandparent in America to do the same thing."

Ruth spoke next, emphasizing the contribution of grandparents to child care. "Census data tells us that 4.5 million children are living in grandparent-headed households (that is 6.3 percent of all U.S. children), a 30 percent increase of such households between 1990 and 2000. Whether the biological parents are not available because of military obligations, death, incarceration, substance abuse, these children don't come to visit Grandma and Grandpa—they are home. And the grandparents, especially grandmas, are rereading [T. Berry] Brazelton, arranging for teachers' conferences, doctors' visits, playdates, and music lessons.

"Even more dramatic and prevalent is grandparent-provided child care. According to the national survey of families and households, close to one half of all grandparents—that would be 45 million of us—provide routine, day-to-day child care to our grandchildren during their parents' work hours. And while there are more grandmothers who are the full- or part-time preferred child-care provider, a third of grandfathers with young children living nearby provide child care as well. Fifty-four percent—more than half—of employed grandparents with young grandchildren (under five) living nearby provide child care. . . . So, grandparents are vital to our economy. They are needed to support their adult children's part-time and shift work arrangements. And, they are the reliable supporters to help parents enjoy leisure and social activities during nonwork time. . . . But you know, as one of my work colleagues, who is the frequent weekend babysitter for her two little granddaughters, says with delight, 'They are so much fun—I have such a good time.' . . .

"That is why, because of the tremendous investments grandparents are making and will continue to make day in and day out for their children and grandchildren, we are resolved to continue to press those who want our votes to discuss their plans for the nation in the future tense—twenty years into the future—in order for us to cast responsible votes for our grandchildren."

Already in 2004, Ruth was making plans to retire from Casey in 2005, and when I visited her in 2006, she was in the first stage of her retirement. "If I were to be totally honest with myself, it was probably three years ago when I started to turn over in my mind that 'I am going to leave,' " she told me. "It was because the routine of administration and management, as much as I'd loved it for thirty years, was just becoming a little too taxing. I didn't want to do that. I didn't want to hear about the problems and who didn't do what. But I did enjoy sorting through ideas, and one of the things that is attractive to me right now is that I get asked, not a lot, but you know . . . What do you think about such and such? So that I feel like I'm exercising my mind, I'm still in the game in that sense, run ideas rather than execution. Because execution is for somebody else at this point."

Ruth and I switched the conversation to a friend who was staying with a postretirement job that she appeared not to like that was not financially necessary. "So why does she keep doing it? If she really didn't want to do it, you and I both know she would stop," Ruth said.

I agreed, but I commented, "The question is whether she would stop without a model of what her next thing would be. I think maybe she's sort of looking around to find out? In a sense you're doing something kind of brave, because you've stepped out of one job without a clear sense of what you want to do next, and you've taken it easy to see how it develops. And maybe it will develop into something, maybe it won't. I think a lot of people are worried about the vacuum. A lot of people feel that way about marriages, too. They find the next person before they get out of a bad marriage."

Ruth chuckled. "Yeah. Well, I may be postponing the anxiety, if I have any, with this four-, five-month remodeling thing. But then there really is nothing other than taking it easy. You know what I mean? There is nothing lined up after that. It's been good not to feel obliged to have an opinion."

Ironically, one of Ruth's trademarks as an administrator was an emphasis on having clear goals, an emphasis developed early on as a caseworker when she was assigned to make a weekly visit to a single woman with six children who was more or less coping on welfare. All these years later, Ruth still remembered her name. "One of the things I learned from her was if you do not know where you are going, you do not know that you have done anything, and that was what the record showed. I was just a nice, friendly person who came to visit her every week, and she didn't know why the hell I was there. So finally I say, 'One of our goals is that you're going to use birth control effectively. You don't want to have another baby, right?' 'No, I don't want to have another baby.' Huh. Well, guess what, I go off on vacation and I come back and what's happened? She's pregnant, she happily announced. I look at the record and I see I'm not the first person who said that to her, and I'm not the first person who's gone on vacation and she's gotten pregnant. I'm saying, 'Mm-hm, this is my baby I guess.' I'm the one who had decided that she shouldn't have a baby, she had never said she was going to do that. So I learned a lot about having realistic goals, and I learned a lot about where my power ended and hers began. And I said to myself, 'Okay, don't set goals for other people that either they can't carry through or they don't want to carry through, or you can't make happen. If you can't make it happen, it's not a goal.' So she was a—I learned a lot from her. She helped make me humble.

"I raised hell at the agency because I was saying, 'We don't know what we're doing. Why are we disturbing this woman every month when we don't know why we're there? She's not— She's polite, she's never going to tell us to leave.' I would take the kids on shopping trips, so she was getting something out of this. But she didn't know why it was that we were supposedly helping her. She didn't think she had a problem, I don't think. She was happy. So yeah, that was an important thing for me to learn, and I've tried ever since to—whether I was working directly with the client or working with somebody else who's working with the client—to be sure: Do you know what you're trying to do? And can you really do it? There's no point in putting it out there as a goal if you can't make it happen. That doesn't mean you should be shortsighted in your goal. You should be ambitious, I think, but you should also figure out, how am I going to get there, and who's it going to take?

"That's what Casey does with young people. A lot of times with young people, we adults figure out that, you know, Charlie is bright and he's got a lot of potential, da, da, dah. But unless *he* decides that he's got that potential and he wants to work on it, it's all for nothing. A lot of what I did in management was to try to promote realism and ambition at the same time. They're not antithetical, but they need to be thought through carefully. It also means that the people you're working with, your staff, have got to be willing to push themselves to be clear."

Ruth has maintained her connection with a project for improving the Seattle schools that was financed by a wealthy businessman and originally focused on kindergarten through third grade. Only now, after over a decade, is it really beginning to be possible to evaluate the results as a model that can be applied elsewhere, but many useful projects are abandoned before the results can be evaluated. She also has a continuing concern with mentoring young people, wishing she had done more over the years to help them take the learning forward. "It's so a young woman or a young man comes out on the other side, saying, 'I know that I am good, I know that I can do these things, I'm a powerful player, and I have the skills and the talents to back it up.' I think that's the transformative work that has to be done. When I've done my very best work, that's what has happened, that a person comes out on the other side and says, 'I know I can do this, I'm confident.' Sometimes it takes more than one generation."

"I think it's also what we want to do for older people, who have a kind of a self-definition of deficit," I said.

"Well, you know, you're right, because it is precisely that issue in my head that I'm struggling with about getting older, confident as I am. You know that I had my knee fixed last year? I had a knee replacement. And I have this image in my head of a fallen horse, like that racehorse? I have this image in my head that if you lose control of your faculties, particularly your limbs, that's it. They have to put you down. Now that's a crazy image in certain ways, but in other ways it's not. It's all about being in control of myself as an older woman who lives alone, and it's all about how I am going to do what I have to do to be as strong as I can be and be confident that I can do what I need to do as an older person. It's the same kind of thing."

"Which can also involve learning to manage a disability as a positive learning experience," I commented. "You know, I told my daughter that I was getting hearing aids, and she said, 'That will be so exciting for you, something new to learn!' Learning is different at different ages. You have to have different strategies. So what we're doing, we're not compromising, we're learning and adapting. At least that's how I see it."

"Well, I think it is, but you know the hardest thing for me, I don't know about you at this juncture, is to come to consciousness about that as well as accepting. . . . There is a certain part of me that says, 'Oh, I'm fine, I know how to be me, I know how to be this middle-aged me. I'll be whatever I was, but I don't want to be an *old* me.' It has been a struggle because of all of the prejudices that I've internalized, that I project onto other people who may not have them. I have a self-image that I don't want to lose, and I'm afraid that I'm gonna lose that. I have to work hard to maintain the self-image I've got that I like.

"Remember when we talked in Next Step Women about coloring your hair? Well, I did that for a minute, and then I said, 'I don't want to do that.' So I've decided that the 'me' that I know can live with gray hair. But there are other things about the 'me' that I know that I don't want to give up, walking proudly, all that kind of stuff. The 'me' that I know, that didn't take good care of myself, has to make accommodations now, and I'm finally saying, 'Okay, so I've got to eat the right stuff, even if I don't like it. I've got to do the exercises they gave me for rehab, make sure that I regularly take care of myself.' When I left the job, I bought COBRA insurance, and I'm gonna figure out what to do about that damned [Medicare] Part B. I've still got to do all that. But every time I recognize those things that I have to do, I go through this internal conversation where I say, 'No, it's not something you're comfortable with but you have to do it.' "

"And you have to do it *well*."

"Mm-hm, it's true. It's true. One of the things, you know, that everybody says you must do as you get older and you're retired is think about volunteering, doing something that you love to do. Well, that's a terrific idea and it goes to exactly your point. What is it that I really love to do, that may not be what I have done for the last five years or ten years, but I may have done twenty years ago? Whatever that was, reconnecting to that confidence that I felt, so I can really offer that and feel good about it. I don't want to volunteer to do something that I feel half-assed about. I want to do something that other people will feel is meaningful and that I feel is meaningful. And some of that, yes, is a process of rediscovering and reconnecting.

"I say, well, I really do like to read aloud, which I did when I was seven and I do now with my grandchildren when I see them. Maybe I can find an hour or two to do that, in a library, or recording for the blind, and I know I do that fairly well, that would give me pleasure, and it would be helpful. And it's a simple thing, but figuring it out . . . I think probably over time the simple things or little private things are going to be the most fun. The natural things. But then sometimes I lurch into the fantasy that it's got to be a *big* project; if it's not a *big* project, it's not worth doing. And if you think about it, it really doesn't have to be a big project. It can just be something I put my mind to doing and I do it on a regular basis and somebody else gets something useful from it."

"This book I'm working on now," I told Ruth, "is something I know how to do, and actually the way I'm doing it is a lot like *Composing a Life,* so I'm doing something that I know I can do and I can do at my own pace. That's the ambivalence that I feel about Granny Voters. There's a really good idea there, but there are aspects of implementing it that I don't see myself doing, so I need to think of some context that will give me some infrastructure for it."

"You and I keep going around and around on that," Ruth said. "One of the things I've never done formally is to drive toward a steady result in a campaign style, which is my fantasy of what is necessary for Granny Voters. That's what I don't know how to do. I know how to organize folks, you know how to organize folks, but the question is how to find those people and infect them with the bug."

"As I listen to you, Ruth, I think we haven't been clear enough about the goals of Granny Voters. I mean we're clear enough about the conceptual goal of longer-term thinking but not about what we actually want to have happen to bring it about."

"Yeah. We know the end goals, but what are the activities that will get you there? We have to figure out how to make them come alive."

When the Next Step Women met in Washington in the fall of 2009, many things had changed. Ruth's son, Irv, now divorced and remarried, had completed a foreign service assignment in China and was about to leave for Indonesia. Ruth had been in Washington for the Obama inauguration and was planning to stay on after our meeting to spend time with her grandchildren, but they were less likely to visit in Seattle. We were all energized and excited by the possibilities of the new administration and the new urgency about climate change, but I had been unsuccessful in proposing a new push for senior activism around the election, and we met as a smaller group because of disagreements that had developed two years before. The future we were concerned about was coming closer at a rapid rate, and the question was still unanswered whether our species—or even this small group of friends—has the capacity to arrive at and act upon a consensus for the protection of the future.

CHAPTER IV

From Strength to Strength

IT WOULD BE INTERESTING to trace here the entire history of cultural versions of the life cycle, each one elaborating on biological potentials and cues with culturally constructed rituals and expectations. It is enough, however, to say that every human society takes note of the recurrent patterns of maturation and development and weaves them into a shared system of meaning, one that represents fulfillment for at least some members of the community. Not every culture has a ritual to mark puberty, but every culture does make a distinction between childhood and adulthood. Not every culture includes an institution comparable to retirement, but every culture offers a way of thinking about old age, usually with respect. In effect, a division of the life course into at least three stages is probably universal, but many societies think of life as having half a dozen or more distinct stages, and these are represented in art and poetry from the biblical Book of Ecclesiastes to colonial samplers, from Shakespeare to contemporary coffee mugs.

During the twentieth century, childhood became a subject of scientific study. Arnold Gesell traced the landmarks on a map of child development, always setting the bar a little low so that his readers could be like the denizens of Lake Woebegon, all of whose children are above average.[1] Sigmund Freud was the pioneer in describing the stages of development of sexuality in infancy and childhood and connecting early experiences with neurosis and mental illness at later stages.[2] Adolescence was defined and described as a distinct stage in development that is managed differently in different societies.[3] Since then, the idea of life stages following childhood has been elaborated by biologists and psychologists and popular writers, while in the same period average life expectancy has increased by over twenty years, although there continue to be differences between men and women, rich and poor.

Erik Erikson took two giant steps, first in looking at the stages of the life cycle not only in terms of vulnerabilities but also in terms of the basic strengths (which he called *virtues,* using the older meaning of the word) developed in meeting the challenges (*crises,* offering both peril and potential) that come to a head at particular stages of development. He extended this model into adulthood and connected it with the societal challenges of different historical periods.[4] Erikson's model, which underlies my own work, had eight stages, to which Joan Erikson added a ninth after his death.[5] One of his charts is inserted as Figure 1 on p. 70. Daniel Levinson proposed an alternative way of dividing adulthood.[6] Gail Sheehy drew on all of these thinkers to popularize the model of life stages in her book *Passages* and then further refined it to fit contemporary changes and generational cohorts in *New Passages.*[7]

The Eriksonian model is best known for its description of the identity crisis of early adulthood, yet the real landmarks are not crises but the development of basic strengths that evoke the words of the Psalmist, "They go from strength to strength, every one of them in Zion appeareth before God" (Ps. 84). The aspect of Erikson's work that seems to have been least integrated into general understanding is that the central developmental challenge of each stage reappears or is anticipated in every other stage. Thus, the crisis of identity in youth is anticipated in every step of individuation and autonomy from birth on, and must be revisited at every later stage. That which is first represented at birth by physical separation from the mother is played out as differentiation and later on in new forms of autonomy and a search for continuity, so that in old age we ask not "Who am I?" but "Am I still the person I have spent a lifetime becoming?" I would argue that healthy longevity has presented us with a second identity crisis. No one is the same at forty and at seventy, but the changes can compose a story that rings true. To put it in terms of my own preferred metaphor, we may ask in old age, "How can this time of my life complete or balance what came before? How do these years form an aesthetic unity?"

Erik and Joan Erikson were family friends and remained close to both of my parents after my parents divorced, but I did not read Erikson's work, with its mingling of psychoanalysis and anthropology, until my final year of college, in a course taught by the anthropologist Clyde Kluckhohn. Erikson came to Harvard in 1960 with the rare and honorific title of university professor, but I had not studied with him directly when I joined the teaching staff of his course on the human life cycle four years later.

I had rushed to complete my doctorate in linguistics and Middle Eastern studies within three years of graduating, partly because Sir Hamilton Gibb, also a university professor at Harvard, with whom I had been studying Arabic poetry and Islam, had announced his approaching retirement. When I completed my degree, in 1963, I was invited to stay on at Harvard as an instructor in Arabic (an appointment that continued until 1966, when my husband took a job in the Philippines, which effectively ended my career as a linguist specializing in the Middle East). The following fall, at the age of twenty-three, I put my hair up in a bun, bought a couple of stodgy tweed suits to make myself look older, and began teaching, overcoming my hesitations from time to time with the advice that the best way to really learn any subject is to teach it.

Most Americans of my generation will make the immediate association between the fall of 1963 and the assassination of President Kennedy on November 22. As I ascended the steps of Sever Hall on that Friday morning to teach my class, one of my students ran up and told me that the president had been shot in Dallas and was in the hospital, barely alive. Within minutes after I entered the classroom, we heard the bells of the campus chapel begin to toll and knew that he had died. I dismissed the class and wandered off the campus in a state of shock, ending up in a Catholic church nearby, alone in near darkness.

At that time the voting age was twenty-one, so I had voted for the first time in 1960, in the Kennedy-Nixon election. I had supported Kennedy but not with great passion, and I had not been much caught up in the romance of Camelot. I found myself puzzled in the days that followed the assassination by the degree of personal grief I encountered—often in people who had been critical of the president only the week before. I had a different reaction—an overwhelming sense of the way in which this event would affect the security and optimism of people all around the world. I saw it as triggering a deep global insecurity, calling into question the peace and order necessary for their lives and the lives of their children.

For reasons that are still not clear to me, that loss was personified for me in an imagined peasant farmer in India, working with a simple plow on an arid hillside, struggling to feed his family, a man who would know of America and the American president through the occasional transistor radio in the village but who understood intuitively that violence breeds violence and that the assassination of a powerful leader on the other side of the planet could darken the course of history. As I sat in that empty church, my imagination of a faraway farmer, who could have been on any continent, came for me to stand for a global erosion of hope.

That day I made a sort of promise that I would work to make some small increment of hope in the world. I had no idea what that might mean in practical terms, but I was fairly sure it would take me away from Arabic grammar and the fascinating puzzles of linguistics. Abandon my newly minted degree and study theology? People I trusted urged that that was a bad idea. So instead I decided that I would at least reshape my teaching and research in ways that allowed me to engage more closely with the lives of others. As a new Ph.D., I was confronting issues of identity and vocation that I had drifted past while following my interests in college and graduate school.

Over the following months, as I struggled to understand the basic shift of commitment that had taken place for me, one of the first steps I took was to go to Erikson and volunteer to be a teaching assistant in his course on the human life cycle, as several other faculty members had done before me, in order to immerse themselves in his profoundly humane thinking. Three years later, I began teaching anthropology in the Philippines. My focus had shifted from language to lives as they are lived in different societies.

The connection of hope to Erikson was obvious, for the first and most basic of the strengths (virtues) he described is hope, developed when the infant struggles to resolve the conflict between basic trust and basic mistrust. The final conflict in his scheme of the life cycle is between ego integrity and despair; Erikson referred to the strength of that stage as wisdom. You might say that I turned to Erikson for a tutorial on hope, and here I am, some fifty years later, right on schedule, trying to understand wisdom.

As with the other virtues that Erikson explored, it is important to avoid limiting concepts like hope or wisdom to any one stage of life. Erikson saw the earliest beginning (epigenesis) of hope in infancy. There must be moments in even the most felicitous infancy when, at some level, a crying child begins to despair that help will ever come; then gradually the repeated experience of relief builds up a protective barrier against despair that can last a lifetime and is a basis for resilience. For some, this becomes trust in a benevolent cosmos or the foundation of faith, but hope plays a role at every stage of the life cycle. Infants whose care is so inadequate that it does not support the beginnings of hope may not survive.

The word hope came to the fore for Americans during Barack Obama's campaign for the presidency in 2008, this time with an emphasis not on infancy or early childhood (infants can neither vote nor canvass) but on young adults. And this time the issue that sub-

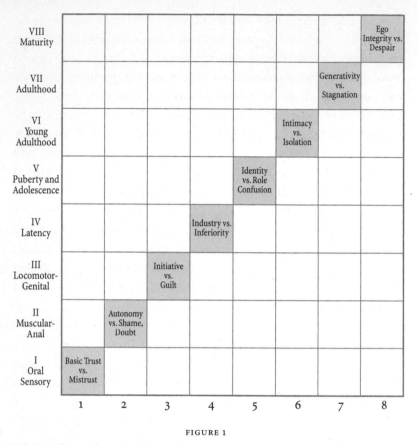

FIGURE 1

Erik H. Erikson: The Eight Ages of Man[8]

liminally represented the erosion of hope, even though it developed after the campaign began, was the financial crisis of that year. Still, every election challenges us to consider what it is that we hope for. Barack Obama reawakened an interest in politics in a whole generation of young people who had increasingly been coming to the conclusion that their lives would be harder and more limited than those of their parents and that the political process was something they could not affect and so was not worth paying attention to. No small part of this achievement was the way it echoed in renewed hope for all ages.

Hope and the need for a renewal of hope is an issue for older Americans as well.[9] When the economy slows, Americans who have retired must hope that the savings and benefits they have worked for and counted on will be there for them—indeed, we hope for better coverage and less red tape. Many of us hope to continue working and earning—unemployment is especially grim in late middle age—and even more of us hope to continue contributing to society. Meanwhile, we hope to live as healthily and autonomously as we can, and to die peacefully and with dignity. Many hope for an afterlife or for a reunion with loved ones beyond death, but this is not the business of politicians.

Whatever our faith or present life expectancy, however, there are hopes that go beyond this life. We would like to see our children and grandchildren prosper, the communities and institutions we have built develop and flourish. We would like future generations to be able to travel and to be greeted with friendship rather than enmity. We would like to see the natural world as we have known and loved it endure. Will the same birdsongs sound twenty years from now? Do we want the beaches fouled with oil sludge when we can no longer visit them? We would like our grandchildren—not only biological grandchildren but the children of neighbors and friends, future generations—to have the same rights and opportunities we have had, whether we are there to see it or not. And if our rights have ever been denied, we would like them affirmed and realized for the future. We hope to see the wounds of past injustices healed. We hope for peace and must resist sowing dragons' teeth from which future enemies will spring.

Hope makes a good political slogan because history suggests that, for the fulfillment of these specific hopes, we must look to the political process to ensure a framework within which citizens are given honest information and can make responsible choices. As a nation, we need to think of the long term, beyond the lives of the living. Hope, nurtured in infancy, provides the courage to think ahead for the sake of grandchildren and great-grandchildren fifty or a hundred years down the road, and hope is a necessary ingredient of any long-term commitment. The Granny Voter effort that my friends and I initiated was cautious about using the word itself, because our effort was nonpartisan, but in our push for longer-term thinking we were proposing action in the name of hope for the future.

Every cultural tradition includes a theory of how what has been treasured in the past is transmitted to the next generation, and this depends upon having an understanding of how human lives unfold, how the transitions are made from one stage to the next, often through rituals or ordeals, and how the torch is passed from generation to generation. How extraordinary it is to look at a newborn infant, helpless and totally dependent, and affirm that this child, growing and developing step by step, represents the future.

Today the human imagination roves further, connecting the past as it might have been with multiple possible futures. Next to these ideas of an orderly succession of stages there is also often a sense that any given life can be seen in terms of multiple layers of story, rather than following one single plot, and that the many roads not taken somehow continue to be available for wonder or regret. Even chronological narratives can have multiple versions as first one theme or interpretation is stressed and then another, each representing a way of seeing the past that offers a different approach to the future. In that sense, each significant choice made is a comment on what has come before, just as it is a partial determinant of what can come next.

When I began to think about this book, in 2006, I had become interested in the way people have thought about the future in terms of future generations and the need to take responsibility for the future far beyond their own lifetimes. I had decided that I would want to include among those I interviewed a partnered gay man who had, at some stage before coming to terms with his sexual orientation, been in a traditional marriage, had children and, eventually, grandchildren. This, in turn, meant finding someone whose life had spanned the years of gay liberation and who had survived the epidemic of HIV/AIDS and was willing to talk about it. None of my gay friends fit this multilayered description, but one kindly made an introduction, and I flew to California in May 2008 to meet Dan Jepson and his partner, Michael

Crowe, and stayed as a guest in their home. I had originally meant to focus on Dan, but I ended by interviewing them both. Dan and Michael have been together for over a decade and have celebrated their union twice during the brief periods when this was possible in California. It was Michael who got me thinking about the way our ideas about the past can shape the future.

Michael is a slim, elegant man with a neat mustache and a wide, engaging grin, who has worked for the National Park Service dealing with cultural and historic sites. He grew up in Cincinnati and has been involved with architectural history and preservation for most of his life. In 1985, at the height of the AIDS epidemic in the gay community, when many of his friends began to despair, he learned that he was HIV positive and made a number of decisions. As he told me, "I thought, I'm not gonna be that way. This is not gonna rule my life. It was shortly after that that I started working for the park service. I set out to think positively, and once you start to do that, you find circles of people that are like-minded." Michael began seeing a hypnotherapist and learned how to meditate, struggling toward a form of spirituality very different from the Catholicism he grew up with.

"I'd first become acquainted with the idea of reincarnation when I was preparing to go to India in the Peace Corps," he told me. "It was so different from being raised Catholic, you know, because I'd pretty much given up on that. I got intrigued with the idea and took a class in psychic meditation when I was still living in Cincinnati, which involves meditating and working on understanding your current life as possibly influenced by past lives that you had. . . . I'd been reading a book on reincarnation, *Many Lives, Many Masters,* by Dr. Brian Weiss,[10] who wrote about spirit guides as well. He was a hypnotherapist. . . . In a couple of sessions that he was having with his patients, they started talking about these lives, and he couldn't figure out what was going on. And he realized that they were talking to him about previous lives that they had had.

"So after a trip to Australia, when strange things seemed to be happening, I had this real urge to do something to understand all of this experience. . . . It turned out that I had had a previous life in Australia. I'd been transported in childhood from Ireland as an orphan, for stealing bread. And I could tell the hypnotherapist exactly what had happened to me. . . . And that's how I ended up finding Dan, who offered to help me get in touch with my spirit guides. . . . The Catholic equivalent would be guardian angels. At one point I found out that Dan had saved me from a disreputable life as a prostitute in medieval Italy. There are many people that you meet and think, Oh, I've known you for a hundred years—you know the kind of thing? You probably have, from previous lives. And I found this way of thinking to be extremely satisfying."

My comment was "You don't have to deal with everything this time around." But this seems to me now to be an oversimplification—a reason why the exploration of possible past lives might reduce stress in this life but only part of the story of why the concept rings true for so many people. It is interesting that surveys taken over the years say roughly one in five Americans believes in reincarnation.[11] I suspect that many common experiences—for instance, déjà vu—contribute to this belief, but it also seems to connect with the way memories are retained and unrealized possibilities remain with us. Perhaps vivid childhood nightmares of being a slave or a refugee, along with cherished ambitions of being an astronaut or a concert pianist, blend in with the past we carry with us, joining the different versions of ourselves at different life stages. Philosophers have speculated from time to time that worlds are multiplied by each decision, continuing simultaneously along divergent paths.

Michael seemed to be telling me that for him self-knowledge involved coming to terms with multiple narratives that he knew had not taken place in this life but that felt somehow relevant to the life he had lived, while for me the effort to understand others and the ways in which they compose their lives involves being willing to enter into their worlds with curiosity and respect. Through empathy and imagination we all live multiple lives.

Three months after this session with Michael Crowe, Jane Fonda came to stay with me while we interviewed each other for our respective books, and it occurred to me that another way people experience multiple lives is in theater, so I asked her how the very diverse parts she had played lived on for her. "In my life, nothing gets left behind," she said. This led into a discussion of acting and the Method derived from the work of Stanislavsky, in which she was trained. All past experience is a resource for the Method actor, a basic repertoire that allows her to connect with people in profoundly different situations, thinking herself into their lives. Fear, anger, and loneliness as well as love and laughter are there in reserve. If a part requires grief, the actor searches back through earlier experiences—a pet that died when he was four years old or the recent death of a friend—and speaks his lines out of that remembered emotion until the two fuse and he is no longer making stock gestures to represent grief or delight but out of the recalled experience letting his voice and his body—perhaps flooded with adrenaline or filled with contentment—express the feelings.

At times we all call up past emotions to deal with a present situation, remembering what it feels like to be brave when in danger or conjuring optimism. If I can remember what it feels like to be a "winner," perhaps others will hear it in my voice, perhaps my own responses will change and I can be one. If I can evoke the young woman I once was, my step becomes lighter. So, for instance, we see salesmen feeling their way into the conviction that they are about to make a big sale, a conviction that may sweep the customer along. If I find I am tensing up before beginning to address a roomful of strangers, I imagine myself greeting someone I love who has been absent and then try to extend that feeling to everyone in the room.

This process offers a curious mirror image of the effect of rituals and recurrent symbols. Every wedding evokes my own wedding, every funeral evokes the deaths of people I have loved, and the tears that come to my eyes sometimes when I am reading or watching a movie do not belong to any single time or place. Many people as they grow older—I am one of them—find that their emotions are closer to the surface, and this can be either liberating or embarrassing, depending on whether they have learned in the course of life that they should keep a stiff upper lip or have gained the opposite conviction, that responding with feeling to those around them is good.

I had sought out Michael and Dan in the expectation that they would help me understand the strength we call hope and the different ways in which people confront an unknown future. It seemed to me that Michael was describing a way of drawing strength for the present from the past, that foreign country of an infinite number of possible futures. Michael's explorations under hypnosis and during meditation also recall the various processes that have been developed to assist people as they grow older in reviewing and often in recording their lives, reflecting on them from different angles.

The belief that at death one's whole life passes before one in an instant is common, reported by a goodly number (but by no means all) of those who have had near-death experiences, and it supports the belief that one may have the opportunity to repent or affirm faith in a meaningful way in those moments. The past is active in the present, both as it occurred and as it might have occurred, whether as a source of strength or as a focus of regret. So, too, are the choices made, the roads not taken, which live on in the imagination. In a poem that I wrote for my husband on our fifth anniversary, using the metaphor of a juggler tossing possible alternative lives into the air, I grieved for alternatives foreclosed: "Those are bright spheres that fall away."

When Erikson speaks of *ego integrity*, however, he refers to "the acceptance of one's one and only life cycle as something that had to be and that, by necessity, permitted of no substitutions." But then he continues, "It thus means a new, a different love of one's parents . . . the style of integrity developed by his own culture or civilization thus becomes 'the patrimony of his soul,' the seal of his moral paternity of himself. . . . In such final consolidation, death loses its sting."[12] In these statements Erikson seems to relativize experience. Instead of referring to love or hope or integrity in ways that can be read as absolutes, he refers to a "new love," as well as the possibility of alternative versions of integrity.

As I listened to Michael, I reflected that only a small percentage of Americans who believe in past or future incarnations were affirming that belief as elaborated in the historic traditions of Hinduism and Buddhism, yet clearly there were ethical issues involved in Michael's meditations. Many years ago I heard a Tibetan Buddhist monk, Nechung Rinpoche, preach on the "recognition of the mother": since all souls have experienced an infinite number of incarnations, he said, it is possible to look at any sentient being and affirm that at some point in infinite time—in whatever unknown living form, human, bird, fish, insect—this being was my mother, and to feel compassion. At the same time that he was connecting all sentient beings, however, he was noticing the differences and remarking that Americans may not feel quite the same way about their mothers and should perhaps practice the meditation of the "recognition of the best friend."[13]

The corollary, it seemed to me, is to argue that in some other form at some other point in time, this being was my child—and to accept responsibility for the care and nurture of all life. More recently, a Japanese historian of Buddhism, Yoichi Kawada, explained to me the concept of the bodhisattva, the enlightened person who has arrived at the stage of release from the cycle of reincarnation but who, out of compassion, chooses to return to serve the enlightenment of others. There are other ways of thinking of alternative lives than "It might have been."

The strengths (virtues) that Erikson recognizes as emerging from the resolution of crises at the different stages of the life cycle are as follows. *hope* during infancy; *will* during early childhood; *purpose* during play age; *competence* during school age; *fidelity* in adolescence; *love* in young adulthood; *care* in middle adulthood; and *wisdom* in old age. (See Figure 2 on p. 79.)

Each of these strengths is prefigured at earlier stages, and each is reshaped to address the challenges of later stages. I once saw a bumper sticker that read, "It's never too late to have a happy childhood." In Eriksonian terms, this might mean "It's never too late to learn to hope; to acquire will, purpose, skills, and self-discipline; to make commitments and learn to sustain them, and to care for others; to see one's life in perspective." Each of these strengths builds on the previous ones and is flawed by struggles left unresolved.

It takes one kind of confidence to step out unsupported in early childhood, but that confidence metamorphoses repeatedly, becoming the precursor of the courage to face illness and death. Consider the cluster of terms that Erikson uses. He refers to the crisis of old age as the crisis of *ego integrity* versus *despair,* yet ordinarily we regard despair as the opposite of hope, the strength developed in infancy. Erikson refers to the virtue of old age as *wisdom,* yet at a certain point wisdom may become synonymous with trust, which arises in childhood, or even humility, by which a lifetime of learning tells us how little we know. He turns to Webster's to point out the complementarity in these terms; trust is defined as "the assured reliance on another's integrity." We can go trustful into that good night.

Whether we call them strengths or virtues, each in its turn is needed in meeting the ongoing demands of development and engaging with others, and each in its turn becomes an essential component at the next stage. All become a part of who we are as adults and how we respond to the transitions of aging. In our day, however, extended life expectancy and health often offer the opportunity to make new choices in exploring and developing ways of being in later life that were not possible earlier on. We now have a second era of adulthood, Adulthood II, after children have matured and careers leveled out. During Adulthood II, before the decline of health and mobility in old age, the crises associated with all three stages after puberty recur: the crisis of identity, the crisis of intimacy, and the crisis of generativity.

Generativity is the central challenge of adulthood, referring directly to reproduction and child care but also to the full range of contributions an individual makes to the community by work and creativity, to the need to nurture what we plant and what we initiate, and to continue caring for what is passed on to us, yet generativity builds on identity and intimacy. As a society, we often identify ourselves by our careers and jobs, and many people, men especially, fall apart when there is no longer an office to go to and a paycheck to bring home. Others, retiring from a career that has defined them, make choices that involve embracing a new identity, searching for ways to remain *somebody,* resisting being reclassified as nobody.

STAGE: PSYCHOSOCIAL CRISES	BASIC STRENGTH (CORE PATHOLOGY)
1. INFANCY: Basic Trust vs. Basic Mistrust	Hope (Withdrawal)
2. EARLY CHILDHOOD: Autonomy vs. Shame, Doubt	Will (Compulsion)
3. PLAY AGE: Initiative vs. Guilt	Purpose (Inhibition)
4. SCHOOL AGE: Industry vs. Inferiority	Competence (Inertia)
5. ADOLESCENCE: Identity vs. Role Confusion	Fidelity (Repudiation)
possible moratorium	
6. YOUNG ADULTHOOD: Intimacy vs. Isolation	Love (Exclusivity)
7. ADULTHOOD I: Generativity vs. Stagnation	Care (Rejectivity)
possible moratorium/atrium	
*ADULTHOOD II: Engagement vs. Withdrawal (reprise of 5, 6, 7)	**Active** Wisdom (**Indifference**)
8. OLD AGE: Integrity vs. Despair (reprise of 4, 3, 2, 1)	**Receptive** Wisdom (Disdain) **Humility**

FIGURE 2

An outline of the life stages, showing the relationship between the eight Eriksonian stages and the modifications suggested in this volume, which are in boldface. Note that Erikson's numbering has been preserved, so the inserted stage, Adulthood II, is indicated with an asterisk instead of a number.

Here are some of the ways in which Adulthood II replicates earlier stages in relation to identity. The physiological changes of adolescence that seem to trigger an intensified search for a sense of identity are mirrored by the physiological changes of aging. It was confusing in adolescence to be flooded with hormones, and it is confusing again as they dwindle; confusing in adolescence to discover zits on one's face and confusing again to deal with wrinkles; confusing to become an object of sexual desire and confusing again to be invisible. Physiological changes are accompanied by social changes as one suddenly encounters a new set of attitudes and expectations and must grow into new roles. There was a time when our parents said to us, "Act your age." Now, shockingly, our children may begin to say it. There was a time when I found it uncomfortable to be endlessly described as "the daughter of Margaret Mead," but now, with a daughter who is an actor and has adopted a stage name, I enjoy being "the mother of Sevanne Martin."

In Adulthood II, the new crisis of identity may be simultaneous with a new crisis of intimacy, as adult children move away and couples who have spent a long period as parents find themselves alone together and must adjust to each other's changes and changing roles. To lose the other is devastating, but much of what brought them together has changed, and something new needs to be built.

Given all of this, it is not surprising that there has been a great increase in late-life divorces by couples who would in the past have said, It's too late for me to imagine something new. At the same time, my husband and I seem surrounded by marriages. Not the marriages of our daughter's friends or the children of our contemporaries—those peaked out several years ago, although there are more to come, most of them after two or three years of living together. No, the marriages we are seeing today are marriages of people in their sixties and seventies, often after decades with the same partner but often, too, with someone new. Sometimes there are strong legal arguments for the decision, as estate planning becomes an issue, but what begins as a practicality often becomes an emotional turning point, and the word *forever* still retains its ancient force, both terrifying and reassuring, in the face of the need to make a new commitment or reaffirm an old one. After all, most of us have lived lives based on commitments made without any way of knowing where they would lead. The uncertainty is an essential element in commitment, the acceptance of consequences an essential element in fidelity.

This issue first struck me a decade ago, when I heard of a decisive refusal of marriage. Friends of ours who had been together for forty years or more and raised a large family split up after a period of increasing unhappiness, and the wife moved abroad for several years. I suspect that she belonged to that generation of women who had never lived on their own, going from college directly into marriage. In any case, it was for her an important liberation to leave the spacious house she had grown up in, in which she and her husband had raised their children. She filed for divorce. Some years later, after she had developed cancer and a first surgery had been followed by a recurrence that was clearly going to be fatal, she moved back again, staking out space for a small apartment in rooms abandoned by grown-up children. As her health declined and she continued living under the same roof with her ex-husband, friends and family urged a remarriage, if only to reduce inheritance taxes, but she steadfastly refused. Having escaped from an unhappy relationship, she was unwilling to reaffirm it on paper for reasons of convenience. Rejecting a failed marriage, she still clung to a concept of marriage she was unwilling to cheapen.

More recently, I know a couple who, although clearly in love, seemed committed to an intermittent relationship, living between different countries, who got married ostensibly to solve a visa problem—then set out to build a totally new life together, as if the legal formality had itself given birth to a new and deeper emotional commitment.

Dan and Michael celebrated their marriage for a second time in the spring after I visited them, during the brief period when same-sex marriage was legal in California. Much of the debate about legalizing same-sex marriage has concerned legalities and entitlements, but in many cases the real issue is the desire to affirm abiding love and to confirm the acceptance of responsibility and the willingness to commit to the well-being of another. Even at the legal level, the most wrenching effect of denying the right to marriage to same-sex couples is when a long-term partner is refused the duty and the privilege of being at the side of a dying lover because he or she is not "next of kin."

Within the last month, two long-term couples of our acquaintance have married. Few if any of their friends would think of them nowadays as having been "living in sin"—a huge change in mores in the course of my lifetime. Both couples are past the age when having children is a possibility. In one case illness is a factor. But what strikes me is that in these cases, although the commitment has been clear for a long time and the actual marriage is a reaffirmation of love, not so different from married couples who reaffirm their vows on a fiftieth anniversary, the decision to formalize the marriage acknowledges new circumstances that require the commitment to take a new form. As in the marriages of couples in their twenties, the vows of couples over sixty are made in the awareness of an uncertain future.

Human ideas about marriage vary greatly, but marriage in some form or other is a human universal, connected with varying ideas about paternity. We are just beginning to realize the impact that changes in life expectancy will have on the institution of marriage. Visit a colonial-era graveyard, looking at the intervals between birth and death, and then notice how sometimes a man would outlive several wives, often dead in childbirth, each tombstone marked as "beloved wife of ———", and then be outlived by the last, whose stone reads "relict of ———". Even with an exploding number of divorces, the average duration of a marriage in America at the end of the twentieth century was longer than in the colonial period.[14] Marriage did not evolve with life expectancies at birth of over seventy years, so continuing love in Adulthood II is still to be explored, with changing meanings of *forever* and a willingness to learn and relearn the identity of the other. Forty years ago—a great many changes ago—I wrote these lines, the meaning of which is still emerging:

> *We never promised we would stay the same,*
> *But only we would shape our change*
> *From this now single clay.*

Marriage has often been supported by the economic and political interests of families and clans, and often expressed in contractual form, both of which gave it more stability than a definition in terms of romance. Most cultures have some provision for the dissolution of marriage, although often, as in Orthodox Judaism and Islam, the initiative is limited to the man. Marriage was a late addition to the sacramental

system as it developed in Christianity, filling out the symbolically satisfying number seven. It is sometimes said that divorce is so common in
the United States that Americans have become serial polygamists.
There is another joke that divorce has had to be developed as a cultural
replacement for death, because so few marriages are sustainable for
fifty years or more, particularly since, as other family ties and supports
have weakened, the dependence of individuals on their spouses has
increased.

When my husband and I lived in the Philippines and Iran, I became
aware of the additional stresses on expatriate households removed
from familiar and familial support systems, but these challenges are
part of a larger pattern discernible in America of isolated, vulnerable,
and potentially brittle nuclear family units. Nowhere is the decay of the
extended family and the increased dependence on the nuclear family
more obvious than in the transitions of aging. Ironically, many couples
make decisions about where to live after retirement, moving to places
where the weather is warmer and their human ties are thinner, that put
them into the same situation as couples assigned to foreign military
bases or diplomatic posts.

Establishing new relationships is more challenging. Men and
women in their fifties and older who have lost a partner to death or
divorce face the same problems in looking for new relationships that
we all face in thinking about growing older, which is to say that we are
burdened by assumptions we grew up with. The very word *dating* carries connotations of artificiality and manipulation that we are happy to
have left behind as men and women have worked side by side and
learned to deal with each other as individuals rather than as "dates" or
possible "lays." Those who have had long-term marriages have grown
beyond the conventions under which we met our spouses, but the
process has been long and complex, and many women are still constrained by marriages contracted half a century ago to conceal their
intelligence, limit their ambitions, and accept second-class status, while
men find themselves defending obsolete and burdensome ideals of
manhood.

Aging potentially brings men and women closer as hormonal influences ebb and both beauty and physical strength are compromised, but there is always the risk that any change can be regarded unconsciously as a form of infidelity: How could the handsome man I married betray me by going bald? How could the pretty girl I married betray me by putting on weight? On the singles market, men are often busy trying to replicate their dating ideals of decades past, and women trying to recover their more recent and less idealized domesticity.

For me the associations of the word *dating* belong to the fifties, with sexual mores of seduction and defense, skirmishes about how far to go how fast, and both parties attempting to keep up an artificial front, a complex game to be consigned to the past. We now live in a culture in which friendship and collegiality are possible between men and women, women are expected to know their own minds, and sustainable friendships may seem more valuable than transient romance. Couples of all ages do find each other, but not necessarily through a reconstruction of long-forgotten patterns of dating.

I have one friend who, when her marriage ended, began by exploring a dating site on the Internet. I met Ellen Hall more than a decade ago when I was invited to meet with doctoral candidates in education at the University of Colorado. She was still working on her dissertation but had already established and was running a preschool called the Boulder Journey School, partly inspired by the approach to early childhood education developed by Loris Malaguzzi in the schools of Reggio Emilia in Northern Italy. Visiting with Ellen, I was totally enthralled by the sense of a school that reflected a world with something to discover and explore in every direction, a gentle unfolding of delighted curiosity and collaboration. Since then I have met with Ellen whenever I get to Colorado or she gets to the East Coast, read her current work, and become reengaged through her with trends in early childhood education.

Ellen is a slim, energetic woman, intensely focused on the issues of childhood development and their relationship to society. The daughter of first-generation Eastern European Jewish parents, she has developed her school as a place of learning for interns, teachers, and parents as well as for the children, studying, for instance, the children's concepts of their own rights or their empathetic relationships with pet animals.

When we first met, Ellen was married to a slightly younger husband and had her mother living with her, in a separate apartment designed for someone in a wheelchair. Ellen has had three children, two from her first marriage and one from her then-current marriage, which ended in 2008 after twenty-eight years. Ellen urged me to look at the dilemmas of men and women who find themselves single in their sixties not because of the death of a spouse but because of divorce.

"It's important for us as we age in the twenty-first century to know others feeling the same way," she said. "It's very different from becoming a widow or a widower. When I talk to friends who have had a spouse die, they talk about their happy memories. Someone like me who's divorced doesn't have that consolation. There is a whole culture of people my age, some looking for another marriage, some for another kind of lifetime commitment, or maybe just wanting someone to hang out with or travel with, maybe with no commitment at all."

In terms of life stages, Ellen is in Adulthood II. Her children have grown up, she has begun to delegate more of the management of the school she created, and she is focusing increasingly on writing and teaching about the approach to education that it represents. But to be alone at this stage of life is a violation of her mental model of how lives unfold. "Why aren't we sitting by the fire, talking about children and grandchildren and when and where we want to retire, looking back on our lives together? It's unnatural—inorganic. And dating seems inauthentic and awkward. At this point in the story you think you'd be enjoying the fruits of your labor. If there are worries they should be about the grandchildren and the kind of world they will inherit. To be alone is not for me a happy place to be. I have wonderful children and grandchildren and many amazing friends and an amazingly successful professional life. I should feel lucky, but I still feel an emptiness because when I wake up in the morning there's no one there and when I go to sleep at night there is no one there." Ellen's model of the shape of a human life, like that of Dan, who married in spite of his growing awareness of being gay, because "everyone marries," includes marriage as a matter of course.

By the time Ellen and I discussed these issues, she had turned away from seeking possible relationships through the Internet, troubled both by the sense of having been rejected and by having rejected others—sometimes in alternation. This may be a feminine point of view, but it struck me that a lifetime of different kinds of relationships with the opposite sex—as colleagues, teachers, friends, and parents of children in her school—made considering another human being as a possible "date" uncomfortable almost by definition. Meeting through a dating service makes it impossible to have a simple conversation without categorizing. Indeed, most of us learn early on that a friendship that has progressed to a romantic or erotic relationship cannot easily be restored to a more casual basis, which is one of the best reasons to be cautious about romance in the workplace.

Ellen also spoke about couples who stay together even though the relationship is imperfect, hoping that nevertheless they will "make it" to an "end-of-life companionship." But when trust is gone, and the future includes the possibility of being dependent on the other, that may become impossible. "It seems to me," I said, "that the Internet service was a first stage in your transition out of the marriage, and that now you have left it behind. There is surely a process of development going on that will change over time."

Another pattern that has emerged, however, is one in which a couple do not take up joint residence but go on vacations together. As with marriages of couples who have lived together for long periods, legal factors enter in, since an actual marriage establishes obligations that may interfere with promises made to children, who anyhow regard their parents' romantic relationships with suspicion, and marriage tends to involve one or both partners giving up familiar relationships. If you have a life of your own, it is easier to take a vacation from it than to close it down. Here sex differences seem almost as powerful as in youth, with women looking for stable relationships and many men preferring to remain uncommitted, and these differences seem to apply regardless of sexual orientation.

Generativity, the third of the crises resolved earlier in adulthood, also recurs. The children may have grown up and moved on, but the parents are still concerned to take care of them at a distance, to take care of the community, and to take care of the future, and still needing to find ways to contribute meaningfully to society. Continuing on the job, volunteering, engaging in social activism, and building new careers are the new resolutions to the recurring need for engagement.

The challenges that lie ahead at fifty and sixty are those that we encountered at sixteen and twenty-five: discovering who, finally, I am, who and what I am able to commit to, how to sustain that commitment, and how to invest my energy and my caring. Wondering whether I am still the person I have spent sixty years becoming and whether that is the person I want to be. Amazingly, after the passions and commitments of a lifetime, we have reached another threshold that calls for new or reaffirmed commitments, a new and more contingent sense of self.

One early morning when I was in my mid-sixties, I was alone in the house. I had been sitting in wordless prayer, watching the sun rise, when I stood up in a sort of trance and walked into the next room, where I had hung a cross on the wall, put my hand on it, and said out loud, "Yes, and yes, and yes." No more. And then a few minutes later I was wondering, What on earth was that, what have I said yes to? Joking, I told myself I had just handed three blank checks to God. And why three?

Repetition is more than emphasis. Three and seven are numbers that have had sacred meaning throughout the history of our civilization. Everyone can think of examples of their importance in scripture, myth, and fairy tale. Among other associations over the next few days, I thought of the angelic cry *kadosh kadosh kadosh* in Isaiah 6:3, which becomes the Sanctus of the Mass and echoes through all of Western music, and then of the words "What I tell you three times is true," which turn out, as I discovered when I Googled them, to be from Lewis Carroll, spoken by the Bellman in Carroll's poem "The Hunting of the Snark." But the particular meaning for me of these words that emerged from my unconscious is part of the larger question of what commitment means in the last third of life and why it reemerges as an issue, whether renewed or newly discovered.

Perhaps by coincidence, it seems to me that as we age we have not only to readdress earlier developmental crises but also somehow to find the way to three affirmations that may seem to conflict. Each can be recognized as related to an earlier affirmation, but the issues change and the earlier affirmations must be understood in new ways. We have to affirm our own life. We have to affirm our own death. And we have to affirm love, both given and received. As I write, I am uncertain of the order in which to discuss them because the relationships between them are so complex, but the logic seems to start with death, because if we live in denial of death, the other affirmations are undermined.

To affirm one's own death means to know and accept that it could happen at any time and to approach it with the sense of trust developed in infancy, recognizing that death is real and essential to the human condition, and perhaps beyond that with the hope of something more. *Yes.* Coming to terms with the idea of death involves practical steps like making wills and preparing health-care directives, clearing basements and attics, dealing with loose ends that would be burdensome and confusing for the next generation, giving things away and handing them on. Along with the attics and the basements, there are consciences to be cleared as well.

At the same time, affirming one's life means taking reasonable care of one's health, using the services that modern medicine can offer, exercising and eating properly, relaxing as needed, and staying busy and engaged. Affirming death does not mean courting it or refusing to acknowledge—and potentially to treat—symptoms as they emerge. *Yes.*

Affirming love means repairing relationships and building new ones, new experiences of empathy and reciprocity; even the closest of relationships shift as individuals take on new roles. Love for one's children changes as they become adults or it becomes suffocating. Love for one's parents may involve parenting them in turn as they need increasing care. Love for a partner may survive mutual aging only if it is transformed. Love for a family or a community may involve finding ways to contribute by doing familiar work in a new context, passing on skills or volunteering, or simply reaffirming friendship and helpfulness. Love for God and neighbor must change to include love for a self that is changing. Love includes both giving and accepting help gracefully. *Yes.*

Each of these affirmations is both old and new. Old because it is built on capacities and commitments developed in earlier years, new because each will play out differently in the last third of life. Each has a practical side and a spiritual side, and each is a challenge because of the new learning involved. Skills have to be developed to express even long-established commitments, and new commitments demand even more. Many late marriages fail—because habits and preferences are already formed—and no earlier marriage will guarantee the skills needed to make a new one work.

A long-established marriage also requires new skills in later life, new kinds of tact and support, tenderness and tolerance. Dealing with chronic illnesses is a whole new challenge. It is a challenge to engage with children and grandchildren (and sons- and daughters-in-law) without replicating earlier patterns. Experienced and loving parents need to adjust their relationships to adult children and remember that the disciplining of grandchildren is not their business; expressions of love at one stage may be inappropriate at the next, tactless advice may have an adverse effect. We cannot make ourselves into grandparents— our children do that for us, in their own time—but we can choose to learn how to be good and supportive grandparents and in-laws. As for serving others, whether as volunteers or as professionals, society is full of barriers to older people and even to their dedication, and well-honed skills need to be adapted to declining strength.

Whatever was taking shape that early morning, that threefold *yes* has become a useful way for me to think about these necessary affirmations, none of which occurs that quickly, each of which has to be explored over time.

When Erikson described the three stages of development that follow childhood, he set each against the pathology that results from a failure to resolve the crisis of that stage. Thus, the crisis of adolescence is identity versus identity confusion, whose emerging strength is fidelity. This is followed by young adulthood's crisis of intimacy versus isolation, whose emerging strength is love. Then comes the crisis of generativity versus stagnation, in the era of childbearing and fruitful and productive work, with the emerging strength of care.

Each of these resolutions needs to be reworked as old age approaches, for the dangers that Erikson described for each stage—identity or role confusion, isolation, and stagnation (expressed as a sense of uselessness)—are familiar problems of old age. What is critical in our era is recognizing that longevity creates both the need and the possibility for the growth involved in readdressing these issues, especially the reexamination and reaffirmation of identity. The new issue posed for identity is: Am I *still* the person I have spent a lifetime becoming, and do I still want to be that person? How can I affirm that identity and yet accept the knowledge that I will die? How will I learn and adapt to the new roles offered by the culture: grandmother (positive) or mother-in-law (problematic), wise elder or cranky curmudgeon, duffer or greedy geezer, sibyl or hag? How will I find a basis for fidelity in my awareness of transience?

Especially for men, whose sense of identity is most clearly linked to jobs and careers, role confusion is a hazard, but it is equally so for women if they are career oriented, child care oriented, or dependent on their physical beauty. Without reshaping the sense of identity, we die before our death by ceasing to be ourselves. Erikson argued that all of these issues recur in different forms throughout the life cycle but that at least a partial resolution is necessary at each stage in order to confront the next. If I no longer recognize myself and no longer know who I am, how will I love? How will I find the resources to care for others? How will I be able to act with love and conviction in the world?

Carolyn Heilbrun wrote about the period I call Adulthood II as the "Last Gift of Time."[15] It allows the active development of new skills and the expression of new commitments and kinds of intimacy that may have been denied during a busy adult life, but it is also a time for building on experience toward a sense of aesthetic unity, a time to recognize and complete—to re-compose—the pattern. Meanwhile, a striking number of people in this life stage joke about needing to figure out "who they want to be when they grow up," while others seek ways of returning that gift, as if enhancing a bodhisattva oath in the same life.

There are surely some people who can say that now, *for the first time,* they know who they are. Doctors, teachers, and even policemen enter their professions with particular kinds of work in mind and find themselves spending a lot of their time doing work that is quite different— filling out forms and writing reports, more with every passing year. These are the people who may have said in the past, "My job won't let me do my work." Often they cannot do what they see as their "work" in retirement either, because of issues such as insurance, but sometimes they can. I interviewed Father Cornelius Goggin, who lives in a retirement home for priests but drives several hours each way every weekend to help out in different parishes. Seventy-eight years old, he has to sit when he says Mass, and communion is distributed entirely by laymen and laywomen, but what he has to say when he preaches is always interesting. "I almost feel I'm more of a priest now I'm retired, because I don't have to worry about the church roof," he told me. "I don't worry about the parking lot on a snowy night. The last parish I was in, we had fifteen hundred kids in CCD [Sunday school], and three hundred and fifty teachers. I don't have to worry about that anymore. I just do what I was trained to do in the first place, administer the sacraments and preach. That's what I'm doing, and I feel that it's more rewarding now than when I was a pastor. . . . I feel more like a priest now than I did before."

As we spoke, he reminisced about studying in France, where he learned to love studying the Scriptures, and I could see him brighten with pleasure. He continues to subscribe to commentaries distributed by the Paulist Fathers, with a strong sense of the styles and emphases of the different Gospels and the awareness that many of those listening to his homilies grew up with little direct experience of these texts. I commented that he seems still to be growing as a priest three years after his jubilee.

Because it is a period of renewed freedom, Adulthood II can be a time of fruition and fulfillment. But always there are the premonitions of old age, slowly increasing changes in the body and the first few deaths of contemporaries. Then, as health deteriorates and true old age begins, different kinds of strength are needed, and the virtues developed in childhood are challenged one after another, reprised in reverse order. At first questions arise about competence—vigor and dexterity, intelligence and memory begin to seem less reliable, especially for those continuing professional work, so that their efforts to perform echo the concerns of Erikson's fourth stage, school age, when children have to prove themselves in relation to their peers. With formal retirement there is an echo of the third stage, play age, when the sense of meaningful purpose and responsible participation is challenged by the suggestion that retired people should devote themselves to golf or hobbies; play, which has been called the work of childhood, may now be proposed as passing the time for pleasure alone. Later many older adults find themselves in a battle of wills, insisting on their ability to hold on—to live alone, to handle their money and affairs, to drive a car—and a certain curmudgeonly stubbornness becomes an asset in resisting the need for supportive care as long as possible, relying on the strength of will learned as a two-year-old. Eventually, however, like infants, we have to entrust ourselves to the care of others, and more and more trust will be called for, along with an ultimate trust that can accept the losses of old age as well as the approach of death. Life review—remembering who we have been—offers a way of mining the past for the strengths needed in the present, a present which may seem all too grim.

As I reflected on this, I found myself thinking of a woman I will call Helen. Helen was the eldest child and the only girl in a devout Protestant family, which meant that from very early on she was taking responsibility and caring for others. She and her husband immigrated to the United States as young adults and raised their children in a handsome house in the Midwest, where they joined an evangelical congregation. He was a successful professional, and she was always busy in their home and active in the church. Their children grew up and married,

Helen's husband retired, grandchildren came, and Helen developed osteoporosis. In her late seventies she fell, breaking her leg in two places, and she fell again in the hospital, facing a long period of rehabilitation. Helen's husband, accustomed to a traditional division of labor, was quite unable to cope alone in their big house.

The family conferred and moved Helen's husband into an apartment in an assisted living facility with an attached rehabilitation and skilled nursing unit, where Helen could convalesce. Their two cars were given away, beloved items of furniture were moved into the small apartment where Helen would join her husband when she was able, and the house was sold. Meantime, Helen was forbidden to move from her bed without a professional caregiver to transfer her to a wheelchair, and the overworked nurses were often too busy to get her to the bathroom on time. She felt as if her entire life had been shut down and she was now totally dependent. The food, the care, all the circumstances of her life were unsatisfactory and decided without consulting her.

Helen's situation took me back to an encounter, many decades before, with my maternal grandfather, the first elderly person whose needs I had had to think about when I was a teenager. He had continued as a widower in his Philadelphia home after retirement, renting rooms to graduate students. The day came when they began to complain of faucets left running, pots burning on the stove, and doors left unlocked, and my mother asked my older cousin and me to go to Philadelphia and find a residential hotel he could move to. So Philip, who had a driver's license, rented a car, and we set off to research possibilities.

Bompa—my childhood name for my grandfather—was a retired professor of economics, ornery and domineering—a true curmudgeon. On a blazing hot summer day, we worked our way through a list of addresses, taking him to visit one after another, all of which he firmly turned down. We pulled up outside the last one, which had sounded good to me on the telephone, and I said, "You know, it's just not worth it, let's not even go in, let's head back." "Nonsense," he announced, "we're here, let's have a look." In we went, and I anticipated him with criticisms of everything we saw—the bedroom, the dining room, the management. "Forget it," I said, "this won't do." He told me I was completely wrong, triumphantly engaged a room, and we moved him in that evening. He grinned at me as we said good-bye and quipped, "You think you're pretty smart, don't you?" He remained there until his death, firm in his choice.

What I had been able to return to him, by letting him overrule me and assert his will, was his sense of agency, of being the master of his fate. This made him able to accept the help he needed even though he recognized what I was doing. Help is not always tactful, or it may move too fast, taking away all sense of choice.

But Helen's situation was more difficult. She told me despairingly over the phone that she felt "useless." Over the days that followed I found myself meditating on the ways in which aging often strips us of whatever has made us feel valuable and lovable. It struck me that taking responsibility and getting things done to meet the needs of others— being useful—had been central for her. Women often feel that without youth they are no longer attractive. Men feel the ebbing of virility. All of us feel a loss of energy and stamina, the need to attend to gradually increasing chronic conditions, and both men and women may find memory, concentration, and intelligence less acute.

I thought of reminding Helen of God's love and realized that because she felt useless she felt unlovable. She was assuming that others, including God, loved her for her busyness, her competence, her conscientious good works. I knew that her theology would have asserted, with Luther, that justification is by faith and not by works, but years of devoted service had somehow led her to feel that love has to be earned.

As I was praying for Helen during the following week, it occurred to me that living into late old age, living beyond the age of active wisdom into an era of passivity and helplessness, is the door to a wisdom of humility, the discovery that we are loved by God and by our families beyond the loss of those traits we value in ourselves and even beyond the point of active contribution.

But then it struck me as inadequate to speak about God without asking who—or perhaps which—is the Helen that the God she puts her faith in loves, for her unhappiness was flowing from a sense of herself as unacceptable. Eventually it occurred to me to say that although He surely loves her as she is in this moment, quite regardless of any work she might be able to do, He also loves her beyond time, in eternity— Helen is present to Him as an infant, as a serious schoolgirl, as a blooming bride, as a young mother, in her giving and in her discoveries and in her service, and is present to Him also as she will be when she dies, whenever that day comes.

This theological musing is congruent with the way memory works. Whether we look at ourselves or at others, we often layer the present on the past, but after a period of time, the deeper past comes to predominate. Thus, I have noticed that my memory of my parents has gradually shifted from my latest contacts with them, as death approached, to earlier periods of their lives and to images I remember from my childhood and youth. Today when I am asked for photographs of them, I provide photographs taken in middle age or earlier, at the times that connect with the work they became known for. If I develop dementia, I will lose the later memories first. In the meantime, I discover that I am still getting to know my parents and learning from them as I revisit their images at ages at which I am only now arriving. I know them better with every passing year.

Then I was reminded of couples I know who had had a youthful romance, met again twenty or thirty years later, and fell in love a second time, each seeing in the other both the present and the remembered beloved. I read a short story once about a woman who gives her husband a blue sweater to match the bright blue of his eyes as they were forty years before, never noticing how clouded his eyes have become, while he gives her a shawl to go with her red hair, which has long turned gray. In one way or another, each person I have interviewed for this book has affirmed earlier life stages as continuing to be present, not lost, not left behind.

An Israeli folk song started playing and replaying itself in my head, words from the Book of Jeremiah (2:2) set to music, in which the Lord says to errant Israel, "I remember for thee the kindness of thy youth, the love of thine espousals, when thou wentest after me in the wilderness, in a land that was not sown."

It's not easy and perhaps not very useful to wonder about the details of an afterlife—better to engage with this life as fully as possible. But it seemed to me that I had understood something useful to pass on to Helen, something that might take her beyond the self-disgust and loss she was feeling. The Helen whom her family love includes all of their memories of her, a radiance that surrounds her more vividly than her present distress. Artists imagining scenes from heaven paint men and women with "glorified" bodies—healthy and beautiful young adults. But perhaps in God's eyes we are always and forever all the ages we have been and will become, grown into a pattern as inclusive as the chambered nautilus that wanders the ocean, carrying with it all the stages of its life.[16]

CHAPTER V

Acts and Chapters

Tɪᴍᴇ, ᴀꜱ ᴡᴇ ᴇxᴘᴇʀɪᴇɴᴄᴇ ɪᴛ, is far from "like an ever rolling stream" as Isaac Watts described it[1]—or, if like a stream, it is far more varied than the simile suggests, sometimes wide and placid and slow-moving, sometimes racing through narrow gorges, sometimes scattered with boulders. There are landmarks and turning points along the way. The pace changes. Time has a structure, a variable cadence. Sometimes, indeed, the flow seems to stop. Contemporary thinkers discussing the process of evolution now describe it as "punctuated equilibrium,"[2] or, less formally, "punk eek."

The Eriksonian stages are impossible to specify for exact ages and may seem arbitrary, yet they reflect a reality in the way people experience their lives and in human cognition and perception, both of which depend on differences.[3] Thus, for instance, in speaking of colors, although there is no clear line between them, we name areas of the spectrum as if they were clearly distinct rather than varying continuously; in the same way we act as if night turned to day without twilight. We remember our lives in terms of periods, with beginnings and end-ings, and we think in terms of watersheds and transitions, turning points and critical moments. The ability to record and calculate time, breaking it into shorter periods, underlies the capacity to plan, to do first this and then that, to look both forward and backward.

Discontinuities—sudden growth spurts, sudden advances in learning and capability when everything seems to go into fast-forward—are especially clear in childhood. The same is true of aging, when, quite aside from the effects of any specific pathology, vitality may suddenly seem to ebb more swiftly, so one can speak as the French do of *un coup de vieux,* a "hit of old age."

The discontinuities in lives reflect discontinuities in the environment. For most human beings, the year is divided up into seasons characterized by different activities, like sowing and harvest, which are then marked by festivals, so that work does not continue at a constant pace. The concept of a Sabbath—not only the Sabbath that occurs weekly but the Sabbath that occurs every seven years (which exists today in the form of the sabbatical year that many academics are granted to refresh their thinking) and the Jubilee specified in the Torah, which occurs, with a remission of debts, every seven times seven years—is one of the great gifts of the Judaic tradition to the world, implying not only recurring events but recurring times of rest and reflection.

Punctuation may be essential to the examined life. For several years, I have been concerned that an effect of increased longevity has been to make adulthood, as we currently understand it, too long. As we look ahead to possibly even longer lives, we will probably need to invent some new forms of punctuation, new landmarks—if only to avoid the destructive trend to switch spouses as a way of measuring time! But even without a culturally shaped set of landmarks, I notice that, when people tell the stories of their lives, they tell them in terms of stages, eras, chapters, or acts, and mark these out with changes of career or location as well as with new relationships.

Because I have worked with life histories on and off since I first volunteered to be a teaching assistant in Erik Erikson's course on the human life cycle, I have turned to his model repeatedly as I have passed through different stages in my own life, both in search of understanding and in the effort to pin down and make available to my peers insights derived from research and from experience. I chose, for example, to study precursors of language in a set of filmed mother-infant interactions when I was pregnant and in my first years of motherhood. I wrote in middle age about the discontinuities in women's lives as I contemplated the discontinuities of my own life, some caused by following my husband's career, some by the interruptions of childbearing, and some by external events, like the Iranian revolution or the sudden death of a college president. I wrote a memoir of my parents when I was in my early forties, fairly soon after their deaths, for the death of one's parents, when one becomes part of the "older generation," is a watershed in many lives. Even so, I continue to feel that my understanding of my parents and of their choices has shifted with each decade of my own experience, as I learned what it felt like to be fifty, sixty, and now seventy, and empathized with them in new ways.[4]

The same thing is perhaps true of social or political concerns. It seemed fairly natural to me in my sixties to comment to my feminist friends that abortion rights might not be the most important issue for them to work on as they entered their sixties and seventies—the equivalent claim for control of their own bodies could be made for death with dignity legislation. Ultimately, however, it seemed to me that, instead of either of these issues, we should take advantage of our time perspective and the experience of social change during our lifetimes to work on issues with the future of children and grandchildren in mind. It seems probable that many careers that appear continuous actually unfold according to the rhythms of the life cycle. The title may remain the same, but the novelist explores different issues in each novel and the merchant begins to look toward slightly different products and customers.

Erik Erikson himself started his clinical career working with children and then began to work with adolescents and made his best-known contribution to the understanding of young adulthood and the identity crisis, illuminated by a study of Martin Luther's early years,

Young Man Luther. His next book, *Gandhi's Truth,* follows Mohandas Gandhi into adulthood, and *Vital Involvement in Old Age,* published in 1986 and written jointly with Joan Erikson and Helen Kivnick, dealt with aging. Joan Erikson herself edited a volume titled *The Life Cycle Completed* after his death, to which she added material on late old age and on dying.[5]

One of the women I interviewed for this project, Glady Thacher, who has been an activist all her life, has taken up new projects in the sequence of her own development and the assumptions about these stages that we share as members of the same culture. Glady and I met over the telephone, at the suggestion of friends, for several interviews, and then finally, when I came to San Francisco for the annual meeting of the American Anthropological Association, over tea in her living room, where we could look out toward the bay. It was the room of someone who loved the arts and whose imagination, like those of many Californians, had turned westward across the Pacific to East Asia.

Glady's early interests were in art; she studied studio art and philosophy at Smith College and, like many young women in that era, married in 1950, right out of college, and began having children. "I thought I knew what I wanted to be, and kind of *had* to be, in the tradition of the family, which was the arts. The legacy and dream were there," she told me.

"We moved out west in 1953, after Jim had had a little over a year in a big firm in New York. His father had started a law firm in San Francisco at the beckoning of a cousin and wanted to retire, so Jim had to make a decision whether to move out here and take over that small firm or stay in New York. By that time we had one daughter, just about a year old, and I was pregnant with a second child. We settled in San Francisco very near his parents' house, and we stayed there while he studied for the bar and then moved around the corner, where we've been ever since." Glady's husband, Jim, had died about six months earlier.

"That was a time when there was a lot of gestation and excitement in the San Francisco art scene at the California School of Fine Arts. Abstract expressionism was really in its flowering, so I went there, and I just loved it. It was a thrilling time. However, it was also a time of decisions. I realized I could not take care of two children when my mind was always in the studio, so I made what I thought was a very painful decision, and that was to close my studio. I felt at that time that I was giving up my personal life, my dreams. And when I found that life went on, I did the diapers, and then I just kind of gravitated to do some community work."

As the wife of an attorney, Glady was not primarily concerned with contributing to the family income, and she has ended up spending her life in the world of nonprofits. At first she worked for the United Crusade and then was asked to join the board of a halfway house for young people who had been institutionalized in the state mental hospital after mental breakdowns. "I asked the question, why were these young people so unempowered when their lives were strong and young? They didn't have any apparent disabilities, but they didn't feel they had any worth." On the advice of a psychologist working with the halfway house, she began studying for a counseling degree at San Francisco State. "It was an awakening, not at all part of the intellectual tradition I had had," Glady recalled. "I was surprised that even though the people with whom I did some practice counseling were of a different milieu, different cultures and ethnicities, I could find a way to empathize with them, and I became really deeply curious and interested in finding the real reason for the acting out and the disempowering of young people. Just a human dilemma.

"When I graduated, I thought of going on to Berkeley and starting a Ph.D. program there. But a couple of my own kids were teenagers by then, and I just decided to start this agency, called Enterprise for High School Students, that still exists. The seed idea was that their feeling of not being seen to be independent, not knowing who they were, separate from their teachers and their parents and their milieu, would be addressed by creating a kind of after-school matching service for sixteen- to nineteen-year-olds. I would train some mothers or people like myself in minimum counseling skills to listen to them and then kind of assess their skills and match them with summer or after-school jobs or constructive trips abroad.

"I'd never even kept a file. It was completely, you know, disorganized and pretty messy, but that disciplined me. I think life has its way of teaching you things you have avoided when you need to address them, especially if you have something in your mind that you want to do. What was brewing was a nonprofit, which was in my living room. We would go to the schools and say [to the students], 'Summer is coming, would you like a job?' Well, we went to one school, and about four hundred kids signed up that they wanted jobs. We were somewhat artful, I think, in realizing that if we asked 'What did you do last year?' on the questionnaire they filled out, we could harvest some of that. The ingenuity of some kids was amazing. They had found jobs working with the Coast Guard and with the Foreign Service as well as mowing lawns or babysitting, working for young parents with children or householders who needed somebody to come and fix this or that, or being a dog walker, or party help, and they wrote these up as responsible jobs with needed skills.

"My notion was that this was just an experiment: if we gathered the kids who had the motivation to want to do something, to express themselves that way and learn what jobs are like as they go through school, then there would be an equal number or more of people who would like to use a young person. I found to my great pleasure that the people who hired these kids wanted to help school them. There is this bonding when we invest in the promise of youth, and that moved us all. So anyway, it began to grow and grow in the house, and the living room was full of desks and telephones and a copier on the piano. Jim would go up the back stairs, and the kids would come home and say, 'Oh, Enterprise!'

"So then I had to raise money, and that's what started me on my begging career, which has been my kind of métier in the nonprofit world." Glady did not mention it, but one of the things that makes it possible to raise funds is recognizing that, just as some employers welcome the opportunity to help young people, some donors are grateful for the opportunity and the vision that give them a way to help.

"So that was one episode, but it was such a teaching episode. I didn't have any idea really that this was going to be a life path or that it would combine anything that I had left behind as an artist. I was so busy bringing up the children and investing in this that I just went on and got a federal grant to take the model into three high schools funded by the Industry Education Council, and that really brought me into the public schools, which were in turmoil."

The public schools in San Francisco were being overwhelmed at that time by the migration of impoverished African Americans from the Southeast and were failing badly. Glady realized that she wanted to move on from Enterprise, so she found funding for it, with a new executive director and its own quarters, and established the San Francisco Education Fund, which she then headed for eleven years. By this time, with four children, the youngest still in his teens, she was also involved in helping other communities with similar projects and had "begun to sense that a career path was coming together." She explained, "I had never imagined myself as a beggar or as what I call a plumber. A plumber is someone who manages to create a structure or a nonprofit that can go on and self-replicate. I had no idea I had skills in any of that." It struck me that studying counseling had given Glady a start in understanding her own skills so that, beginning with matching high school students with summer jobs, recognizing the potentials of others became for her a central theme.

"I didn't make such a big decision getting married or having children, you know; things were going along and it just seemed natural to do. But when I really had to give up what I thought was my whole identity, the identity of being an artist— when I said, All right, I'm going to let life just happen—it was like going over a jump with a horse. You know, you steer the horse between the wings and then over you go, and then, if you've made a good decision, it just melts behind you, it doesn't seem to be a barrier."

Glady went on to quote me back to myself. "I'm very struck by a passage that I read over and over, and it's so eloquent and insightful, I don't know how you've got all of it in one paragraph, but I just want to read it. You said, 'This is a book about life as an improvisatory art, about the ways we combine familiar and unfamiliar components in response to new situations, following an underlying grammar and an evolving aesthetic.'⁶ I was struck by it because this whole idea of combining the familiar with adapting to and living in . . . with weaving in the unfamiliar was . . . When I look back at when I was starting these nonprofits, I realize that, after all, it's like the snail that goes along and if it should look back, it could trace the curves in its tracks. When things began to come together, there was actually some kind of coherence, some kind of, I don't know, you call it a kind of aesthetic something that is underneath it all. It is certainly not anything that one *tries* to do. That was a real relief, because I realized that when I made a good choice, which happened to be giving up painting, serendipity came in, and one step in a direction would open up opportunities. So the work I've been doing in the community by organizing nonprofits just became a kind of métier. I never had to think, Oh, now that I've done that, what am I going to do next?

"I was privileged, because I had a husband who was making money and I had a little nest egg that had been left me, so I did have 'a room of my own,' chaotic as it was. I persevered because I found that somehow everything—different abilities, images, metaphors, ways of looking at the world—seems to be fully used when one is in a productive part of life. And then of course there were the transitions when you know (and you feel like throwing up), Uh-oh, you're going to have to change. But I felt during those years that I was really—what I was doing was productive."

Between the Enterprise project and the beginning of the Education Fund, Glady had been asked to sit on the Smith College Alumnae Association Board, and there she had recognized the same phenomenon of people feeling disempowered, so she created in 1963 what we would today call a network. "I realized that the alumnae of the college were getting advanced degrees, going to graduate school, having equal education with men, and then in the instinctive kind of traditional way were throwing that all back into the family, usually with a high-achieving husband, and kind of helping him in his career."

So Glady created Smith Resources, which worked by "getting women to send in their bios—where they went, what they majored in, what they'd done since, and how they could help one another. They could then talk to one another and help one another over that gap to where women were accepted in managerial positions and valued for their abilities to write, to think, and to lead. After this little pilot, when I left the Smith Alumnae Board, I started another organization on the same line as Enterprise and Smith Resources in San Francisco, for women helping women." This was called Alumnae Resources, and this time the ones who were listening and counseling were the women who came in themselves, seeking to understand their own potentials.

"Women are amazingly able to discover an affinity, and they are willing to help as human beings, but they need a way to know that they are helping," Glady explained. "So Alumnae Resources became very big, and despite its name it went on not just to liberal arts women but women in general and then men later on. Of course, they came in at times of transition . . . that emphasis on transition has been a secret of all the organizations that I have been part of starting. I left that in 1979, when my own career changed, but I took the same concept up later. I guess, as I have reflected on it and as others have, it was me going through these different stages of my life.

"I've been lucky in everything I've done in an entrepreneurial way in the nonprofit world because I've been among those who have sensed what is about to come, and in helping people find their own voice. There are many other ways of starting nonprofits or sprouting an organization, but it seemed to me that for me it was organic. It was like putting something in the ground, planting a seed as an experiment in order to see, Is there an unspoken need for this? Does this seed have a need to grow? Can it grow out of this soil and this particular community? If so, you're likely to be joined by other people and other organizations to help you iterate the words that need to be spoken. People can find a voice by joining a person or an organization they are comfortable with, that fits with how they feel and may be a sort of paradigm of their time. Then there are the forerunners of an idea. They may get battered down, they may be isolated, but they've made the first call. I think in the work that I've been doing, creating nonprofits, I've been lucky enough to speak up or serve a need when there was a groundswell for it. With Alumnae Resources, I found myself on a wave of sisterhood of the women's movement as it was just beginning to arise and be spoken in other parts of the world. We were very lucky to be so advanced in America.

"I guess Enterprise was the transition of young people who were trying to find their way and work themselves into adulthood. Then I saw that women like myself were also in a time of life when they were facing transitions. You talk in your book about the fact that a problem is also an opportunity to grow.

"I had a book by William Bridges, a very simple book called *Transitions*.[7] He was a successful professor at Mills College, and then in the sixties he decided he didn't want to do that, but he couldn't explain why. It was a time when people were starting various kinds of communes, not just youth communes that were acting out but communes of people searching jointly for new ways that they could get on together. He and his wife formed one up in Northern California, and he spent a year or so documenting what he was feeling and doing during the transition, and essentially the very simple model he came up with was that at first you resist the change and bang on the door that is closing, but then you realize that you can't go back. Then you go into kind of an abyss of unknowing and feeling very shorn and uncertain of who you are, your identity and everything. And then gradually, if you find some support and realize that other people are also feeling the same way, you realize that this is a growth period, a creative opportunity leading on to another part of your life . . . but you have to do some work on where you've been and exploring what you might want to do. That's why I started Alumnae Resources, to help people transition." The thread of continuity that runs through Glady's many ventures in the nonprofit world seems to be the creation of an organizational model for mutual support between individuals that allows them to begin to realize their potentials.

Glady spent eleven years working with the Education Fund. "We became a national model and the Ford Foundation took it on in a big way. It was both thrilling and absolutely exhausting, and I was overdoing myself, taking too much time from the family. But it was completely a good thing, this promise of youth and real investment— Well, anyway, I won't say more than that. I finished my tenure there after eleven years, and then I thought, Well, now what?"

Glady left the education fund in 1990. She had turned sixty and had surgery for cancer, and eleven years seemed to be enough. "But all this time another thing was incubating—you know how things do—here you are over sixty, but where are you? What's the next . . . ? You know? There's supposed to be retirement, but there seems to be no expectation about what that means, except that you not get sick and cost money to the taxpayers." Glady was also noticing what was happening to others her age as a result of downsizing during a period of economic downturn. "Aging workers who'd been there a long time were being kicked out under various guises and new technology was coming in."

For Glady, as she moved into Adulthood II, spiritual exploration became important. "I guess I needed a time for myself to kind of ruminate on where I was. I had been introduced to the Zen center in San Francisco in the eighties and Green Gulch [Farm]. That immediately became a spiritual home for me when I was doing the Ed Fund, so I'd get up very early in the morning and practice, and I used my vacations to go to Tassajara [Zen Mountain Center] and deepen my practice with the community. What that did was to make me realize that, at sixty-one or sixty-two, anything that I might start to help with a later-life transition needed to have a quality and dimension to it that acknowledged the need for purpose, that it was a time for many people after their first active careers to develop other ways of working, for profit or whatever, honing in on a kind of spiritual longing, to think, Well, I've lived this long . . . a need to find my own integrity.

"I had a vision of that when I was in the Sierras, walking with a group, going up a trail and suddenly looking down on this expansive landscape below and at the horizon. I was standing there alone, and it was like a reality shift. I saw it as a metaphor that life was final. I realized there was a finality in this landscape. It didn't mean that my demise was in the offing but that each of my steps down from the peak needed to be made with a sense of my own integrity. I needed to find myself. That stayed with me, like images do, and became the basis for starting what I call the Life Plan Center, which was for people of fifty or above, again a transition, with the same components of self-assessment, counseling, information on job finding, and workshops.

"There was another component, which became the Spirituality Workshop, that really put it out there that this was the ingredient that we all need in our life, a sense of meaning. I was trying to start something like right livelihood that expressed this urgency to incorporate a spiritual path in my life, and have people feel that they could talk about that, not in a religious way. Anyway, that survived for about six or seven years, and then it merged back with Alumnae Resources. Both organizations had to close in about 1999 because of the decline of the stock market, when companies and corporations were no longer using Alumnae Resources to recruit or find employees and people began to use the Internet to look for employment. Anyway, that moved me on again, luckily. Serendipitously. It was a bold step for me and opened up a larger dimension of thinking about life choices and life careers."

One of the keys to starting new things is the ability to sense what is happening or about to happen, to tune in on the ways people are beginning to speak about their experience. I found myself connecting with words and phrases that Glady used that had been landmarks in the shifts of consciousness taking place over the last fifty years. She used the words *empowerment* and *disempowerment* (and her own special twist, *unempowerment*), which were so much a part of the contemporary rhetoric of efforts for social justice, for instance, and she spoke of the need to "find a voice," which had been important in the women's movement.[8]

Glady's thinking about youth also seemed to fit very neatly with Erikson's stages and the need to develop a sense of identity as a precondition for making commitments rather than using commitments as a substitute for a sense of identity—a common problem for women in the past, when women were defined by their marriages rather than entering marriage as free individuals knowingly pledging their lives. And I found myself remembering the whole movement toward communes, a reaching for a way to express interdependence.

I also recognized in her use of the phrase "abyss of unknowing" a reference, perhaps unconscious, to *The Cloud of Unknowing*,[9] a work on contemplation written by a nameless fourteenth-century Christian mystic that has been seen as a bridge between Western mysticism and the Buddhist and Hindu traditions, especially Zen, to which Joan Erikson had introduced me several years before. In creating nonprofits that served the needs of individuals in transition, Glady was taking old and new concepts that were "in the air" and embodying them in organizations and ways of addressing problems, and she was increasingly aware that, in making decisions and moving from stage to stage, we are recognizing ancient traditions and also creating new ones, making new meaning.[10]

So often, creativity involves a marriage between the old and the new, but it takes a special talent to recognize a new synthesis taking shape, a pattern whose time has come, whether for an individual or for society. I associate this process of connecting meaning across time and its transitions, adapting and integrating new ideas, with the Lindisfarne Association, founded by William Irwin Thompson in 1972. I met Jane Fonda at a Lindisfarne meeting in Santa Fe, which she was attending for the first time as a result of her engagement with the Zen community there. Knowing I had been involved with Lindisfarne for over twenty years, she asked for some background. "I was trying to take notes," she said, "but I couldn't—something about a monastery on an island?"

Lindisfarne is the name of an island off the coast of Northumbria where a famous Celtic Christian monastery flourished in the late Middle Ages. William Irwin Thompson, a historian and poet, took it as the name of the organization that he created. The medieval monastery was destroyed but there is a Benedictine monastery there today. "Bill's background is Irish Catholic," I told Jane. "His concept was to create a residential community, initially at Fish Cove, on Long Island, a commune in which everyone was doing basically three things. They were doing productive intellectual work—writing, research, art; each one would have a spiritual practice; and each one would also be participating in the necessary upkeep and housekeeping of the community. This is a sort of echo of the Benedictine rule of monastic life, *ora et labora*, pray and work. But Bill also had in mind the role played by monasteries such as Lindisfarne in the Dark Ages, when they preserved knowledge, including the knowledge of Classical Greek, through a period of loss of literacy and documentation. Much of Greek philosophy was preserved by the Arabs also. And the monasteries also played a role when that knowledge began to be recovered and reevaluated, so that the wisdom of the past could serve the future. The great creativity of the Renaissance came partly from the rediscovery of that lost knowledge.

"Bill's view of the mission of Lindisfarne," I went on, "was that it would be a countercultural institution, exploring an alternative way of living. Part of its mission would be innovative thinking and creativity, but another part would be the rediscovery or reinterpretation of ancient traditions that have been lost or neglected in modern society, and for that purpose in 1972 he brought to Fish Cove a series of spiritual teachers, some of whom became Lindisfarne fellows. That's the group you're meeting here. There was a residential community at Fish Cove, and then there was a network of fellows that joined them once a year. The residential community doesn't exist anymore. They hadn't quite worked out how to pay the mortgage. But actually many of the people that were in the residential community are still fellows and are now part of the network. For instance, Richard Baker, at that time he was the roshi, the abbot, of the San Francisco Zen Center, and now he has a place in Santa Fe; he was one of the spiritual teachers that came and also became a member of the fellowship, so that's where I know him from. And Pir Vilayat Khan came, and a couple of people in the community decided that their practice would be a Sufi practice, while others said their practice would be a Zen practice. Brother David Steindl-Rast is a Benedictine monk who came and talked about Christian meditative practice. The fellows also included physicists and biologists and poets and social activists and philosophers.

"Now, I wasn't there for those early sessions. My involvement with Lindisfarne began in 1973, after my book *Our Own Metaphor* came out. But Lindisfarne was very important to me. There was an ongoing custom of a daily period of silent meditation in which I suppose people drew in different ways on what they had learned from these different teachers. That was my first experience of sitting and meditating in silence with a group who might have very different concepts of what they were about. But equally important was the fact that the fellows and other invited speakers spoke about their very newest ideas— discussions ranging from neuroscience to Pythagorean mysticism to microfinance—and it was a kind of annual wake-up call for me. Much of my intellectual life since then has involved continuing to learn with and from members of that group."

When the Long Island property was lost, the Lindisfarne residents were invited to move to a space associated with a disused church in downtown New York. The next stage involved a gift of land in Colorado, where Bill was able to begin an ambitious building program that included a beautiful meditation hall. That property was eventually transferred to a Zen community. There were also meetings held at Green Gulch Farm, a property of the San Francisco Zen Center, but over time Lindisfarne has survived only as a network of fellows, and even the fellows ceased to meet for several years, finally resuming in Santa Fe. "That's what you're seeing," I said to Jane, "a new stage in the life of Lindisfarne, or maybe a new incarnation."

Glady was certainly right when she spoke of serendipity. When I think back over the last fifty years, I see the constant formation of circles of conversation or activism created by individuals like Glady or Bill who have an instinct for the question that comes next, circles that dissolve and re-form into new constellations. Bill Thompson had visualized creating something as solid as a medieval monastery but instead created a configuration of minds, shifting and growing as ideas were absorbed into the mainstream and new ones developed.

Jim Morton, who is introduced in the next chapter, is one of the people I met through Lindisfarne, but he did not mention that example when he spoke of a kind of institutional crisis in our era, a weakening of trust in institutions that made the building of substantial institutions more difficult, even as acronyms and labels multiplied. It may be that the very fluidity that characterized the period was the secret of its productivity, yet I know of a number of creative thinkers from the sixties and seventies who are like Bill Thompson in wishing that what they created had been more substantial. Glady was a builder of virtual institutions, nonprofit corporations without buildings or campuses that served as frameworks for exploring different kinds of productive interactions. Lindisfarne has become a virtual association, a corporeal presence for only one week out of the year and for the rest an interweaving of ideas resonating back and forth and echoed in dozens of separate projects.

One of the roles I have played at Lindisfarne was in insisting that younger people be brought in. Some have been sons and daughters of the original members, some have been nominated by members from among their students and younger colleagues. The original group has already lost half a dozen of its number to death and many of us are now in our seventies, but we still treasure Bill Thompson's distinctive gift of picking up new themes of inquiry and creativity and inviting individuals who will both contribute to and learn from the work of others. Lindisfarne helped to turn me into a good listener, so that whenever I attend a Lindisfarne meeting I learn new things as the fellowship continues its process of metamorphosis, now in a new relationship with the Zen community in Santa Fe.

As a board member, I found myself urging against attempts for the Lindisfarne Association to acquire and hold a material base, yet urging in favor of keeping the relationships alive. There is no way of knowing whether this conversation will survive its founders, "though meet we shall, and part, and meet again, / Where dead men meet, on lips of living men."[11]

The rhythm of life includes death—multiple deaths, the deaths of parents and friends and the deaths of institutions. Exciting as it has been to see a new stage of the life cycle emerging in my own lifetime, it seems to me that the continuing punctuation of mortality plays a part in the search for meaning and in life's joys. Glady Thacher has created half a dozen nonprofits, each in response to the need of a particular time. Some will be dissolved, some will evolve to meet newly recognized needs. In the last year I have dissolved a small foundation called the Institute for Intercultural Studies,[12] which was created by my mother after World War II and which I have managed for over thirty years. By 2007 it was clear to me that we had completed the tasks for which I'd kept the institute alive, passing on the work of my parents and their colleagues to a new generation to debate and build on. Just as people die, so do most institutions, and only by asking whether they have fulfilled their mission can we fully understand what the mission was.

CHAPTER VI

Focusing Multiplicity

I MET JAMES MORTON at a Lindisfarne conference in 1974. He is a big, bluff, jovial man whose midwestern accent is overlaid by years at Exeter, Harvard, and Cambridge University in England. He had become dean of the Episcopal Cathedral of St. John the Divine in New York City two years before and was earning headlines by beginning a series of new programs. Jim has summoned me repeatedly over the years to talk to groups or to preach from the cathedral pulpit, and I have drawn him into conferences and onto the board of the Institute for Intercultural Studies, the small foundation started by my mother that I managed for thirty years after her death. In 1997 he retired from the deanship after serving for twenty-five years. By the time we sat down with a tape recorder to talk about his life and how it had unfolded since his retirement, he was seventy-seven and we had known each other for some thirty years.

Jim was one of the first people I interviewed when I began to think about how people compose their lives after retirement, because it has always struck me that he approached his task at the Cathedral of St. John the Divine much as I think of people composing their lives. As we spoke together, I had the sense of how he had drawn on experiences going back to childhood as resources but had at the same time been improvising all along, finding ways to integrate what he had learned, finding synergies that combined multiple, seemingly conflicting elements. Jim was sixty-seven when he retired from the deanship. How, I wondered, would someone with such a diverse range of experience and curiosity choose to focus his energies in retirement, when he no longer had the cathedral and its resources as a staging ground?

Jim's parents lived a gracious and privileged life, seriously interested in the arts, with influential friends scattered across the country. His father headed the drama program at the University of Iowa, which was one of the top theater departments in the country at that time. "This was before Yale had its drama school, mind you," he told me, "this is in the thirties. The Rockefeller Foundation was very interested in getting cultural stuff into other universities, and they put a lot of money into the University of Iowa, an aggie farm country university, so the Departments of Painting and Theater and Poetry all had very good people and buildings. A new theater was built, and the department had subdepartments of scene design and of lighting as well as directing and acting. . . . The man who was in charge of scene design required all of his students to make models of theaters, and I remember going down into the room in the basement where all these models were stored, and it just blew my mind. . . . Mr. Gillette gave me a model theater that he had cleared out, which I had with me at college. So . . . sort of theatrical-artistic-architectural stuff, all in a rather hands-on way. . . . I was a very happy kid."

Jim's mother had grown up in Houston and went from there to finishing school in New York, but she never went to university. Her father had given her a Steinway for her tenth birthday. "She was never a concert pianist herself but played and ultimately presided over all kinds of musical events that she organized, many of which took place in our home. Music was her world, which was great.

"So there I was," he told me, "as this little boy—an only child at the university." Only children often have a special entrée to the adult world, paying attention to adult conversations and concerns, as I did also. "My father's house was always full of his graduate students, and I was always in plays," Jim went on. "I took the little boys' parts in university productions, all the way until I went off to Exeter. I had to play the piano, too, from which I really rebelled. Oh, and another very important person in my life, through until I was about twenty-five, was my great-aunt, who was a painter. Aunt Virgie was the beautiful and rebellious one of four sisters—my grandmother being one of the sisters. One of my earliest presents was a small paint box and a little easel from her, and as a child of six and seven years old, I would go out and paint with her, which was fun. So the visual side of things has been very important to me."

Churchgoing was part of the family pattern also. "My father had been a choirboy at Trinity Episcopal Church in Iowa City. I have a wonderful picture of him at the age of, I don't know, eight or so, with his brother, in their cottas, in the boys' choir. So I always went with the family to church, which I loved, and I never went to Sunday school so I had no religious education, which I think probably saved me."

I laughed. "That was my mother's theory," I said. "You should take a child to church but not to Sunday school."

"Your mother hit the jackpot with me," Jim went on. "My life in that little church in Iowa City was just wonderful. It was very much a family thing, friends too. I sang in the junior choir, was an acolyte, got confirmed, but never any Sunday school, which was marvelous. It was a very organic kind of thing. It was not this sort of credal business at all. And it was . . . it was what we always did. I was just a very happy person in church, so that was very, very important.

"My father's family was from New England. His uncles went to Andover and to Exeter, and that was dangled in front of me, so at the age of thirteen, I took my first trip by myself and went and had appointments at Exeter and at Andover." As a child Jim was always building things and might easily have become an architect. "My interest in painting very early moved into more structural stuff like building a theater for marionettes. At the age of, I don't know, twelve, I was looking at stuff, Le Corbusier and Frank Lloyd Wright and Gropius and whatnot, and talking about studying architecture in college. One of my father's great pals, by the name of Dick Baldridge, said, 'Well, if you're going to be in Boston, check out the architecture school at Harvard. Gropius is the chairman of the department and you really couldn't do better than that.' So I wrote to Walter Gropius at the age of thirteen and got a response back saying, 'I'd very much like to talk with you, please come to Robinson Hall at eleven o'clock on Thursday' whenever the hell it was. So indeed I met with Mr. Gropius at age thirteen. We talked about Frank Lloyd Wright and about the Bauhaus, his own work, and whatnot."

Jim was welcomed at Exeter and Andover, but both schools had already allotted their scholarships for the coming year, so he continued at school in Iowa City for another year and went to Exeter the following fall, for his last two years. Considering how school and college admissions are handled today, the sense of privilege in this narrative seems to me astonishing, reflecting a world in which university faculty, although they were not often wealthy, were definitely upper middle class and formed a network with linkages to the arts and the professions. Much of what Jim did later at St. John the Divine had to do with bridging those circles, which have split so far apart in American life.

Already then, before Jim came east and before he started at Exeter, three key themes were established in his life: building, the arts, and the Episcopal Church. Already, too, Jim had become a performer. The next theme, social justice, was established at Harvard and developed in Jersey City and Chicago. The final theme, established after he came to the cathedral, was a new model of inclusiveness that took him far beyond the boundaries of the church in which he grew up and was ordained.

"So, off then to Exeter, and I did my senior paper on Ibsen's *Doll's House*," Jim went on. "I was in plays in the drama club at Exeter, but I also designed the sets for the plays—that was in the 'frustrated architect' department. I wanted to study philosophy, and I also, interestingly, wanted to take some religious stuff. I remember my father, once upon a time, had said to me, 'Have you ever thought of going into the church?' And I said, no, I really hadn't."

Harvard had recently instituted its general education program—the same one I encountered when I went there—to prevent students from overspecializing. Jim delighted in these courses, taking a famous course nicknamed "Rice Paddies," with Crane Brinton, Edwin Reischauer, and John Fairbank, which was his first real exposure to Asian culture. "Oh, also, in my freshman year, in my general education course, in which we read Marx, I became an atheist and so did not go to church," he told me. This, too, was part of the Harvard experience for many young people.

In spite of the effort toward general education, however, there were still people on the faculty (as there are today) who had very narrow ideas of what students should do, and this led to a crisis in Jim's sophomore year. "There was this man named Norman Newton—he didn't want students to study any history of architecture, 'Because,' he said, 'if you do that, you design like them.' In other words," Jim explained, "he had taken the Bauhaus reality and made a dogma out of it. There was no question I was modern, modern, modern, but I wanted to see it in a bigger context. And also, they didn't want any kind of philosophy or any of this religious stuff, except he did allow me to take a course on Plato, which I enjoyed, with Raphael Demos, and I took Social Relations I with Gordon Allport."

Gordon Allport was a psychologist who studied personality and was involved in the postwar effort to combine the behavioral sciences into a single multidisciplinary department, called Social Relations, which eventually deconstructed itself. In effect, the subtext of Jim's description of his Harvard experience was an effort to avoid narrowness and rigidity, an insistence on being allowed to cross boundaries and make connections between fields that was part of the intellectual history of the times and remained a theme throughout his life.

"It became a sort of crisis situation for me," he said. "It went into full bloom in my junior year. By then I had done all the mathematical and engineering stuff that was required, and Newton said, 'You've got to take the behavioral psychology course,' and I said 'I'm not interested in that.' I didn't take it. I wanted to do some history of architecture. Finally I was allowed to take a course, which I loved, with Kenneth Conant. He was very interested in the great church of Hagia Sophia, which was built by the emperor Justinian I in the sixth century"—the Church of

Holy Wisdom, I remembered, mother church of the Orthodox tradition, which was turned into a mosque for five centuries after the fall of Constantinople and is now a museum—"and in the monastery buildings at Cluny."

At this point Jim had a stroke of good fortune, for he met a professor of architecture named John Coolidge and asked his advice. "I'm at a kind of crossroads," he said. "I'm having a really difficult time in architectural sciences because Norman Newton is not allowing anyone to do any history of architecture." Coolidge said, "Oh, he's a very dogmatic guy. Listen, why don't you just shift from architectural sciences to history of architecture in the fine arts department, and I will be your tutor." Jim said, "You solved everything." He was still planning to go to architectural school but to follow a different route.

Jim acted in plays and sang in the Harvard Glee Club, and then in the summer he got a job in construction in Houston. "I was part of a building crew—doing very basic stuff, but it meant seeing how things are built. It was great." At the same time, he was taking a painting course. He paused in puzzlement. "Oh, I know what I was leading up to. Just for the hell of it, I thought I might go back to church in Houston. I had been absolutely overwhelmed at Harvard by Beethoven's *Missa Solemnis,* which I had sung with the glee club at Symphony Hall. And I went out and I bought the record, and I remember listening to that and sort of welling up, just listening to this music. . . . So I went to the Episcopal church in Houston and enjoyed it. And the very smart rector, whose name I do not remember, spotted me and said, 'Would you like to have lunch?' I said, 'Yeah, sure.' So I had lunch with him one day. So there was that. That and the impact of the Beethoven.

"One of my best friends at Exeter was a guy by the name of Andrew Norman. His mother was Dorothy Norman, the mistress of the great photographer Alfred Stieglitz, who was married to Georgia O'Keeffe. Dorothy ran what was really a salon in New York and also had a weekly column in the *Post.* She had built the first modern town house in New York—International Style, [William] Lescaze was the architect. That house on Seventieth Street was incredible. Artwork all over the house.

And she took me under her wing. 'I'm your godmother,' she said, and she would call up to Harvard and say, 'Come for supper, when can you get down?' and I'd say 'Sure.'

"The Normans had a big place in Woods Hole, so at the end of my freshman year, Andy said, 'Why don't you come up when you're finished with Houston and we'll go sailing?' " Jim was traveling with a couple of friends who were both painters, and the three of them stayed at Woods Hole and met other artists, as well as writers and political activists. Jim fumbled briefly for the name of Gyorgy Kepes, whose paintings explored natural forms and ecology, and found it by looking down at the bookshelf where books by and about Kepes were lined up, which gave me the link from Jim's interest in art to his later interest in ecology and the environment. "So Dorothy and my friends and I drove up from Woods Hole to Wellfleet and spent the day at the Kepes house," he continued.

"Dorothy and I became very close friends. This was my first time seeing the Cape, and I'll never forget her taking me around. I remember she stopped the car between Woods Hole and Sandwich, and along the highway there were tables selling seashells. She said, 'This is one of my favorite things, let's just see if they have any good shells.' What became so fascinating was her artist's eye making distinctions. Through her, I became an absolute connoisseur of rocks and seashells, as you can see." Jim pointed to bowls and baskets of shells along the window ledge. The room we were sitting in, like any room in which Jim spends time, was full of beautiful objects of art and nature, collected over the years, each one with a story.

"I buried Dorothy," he went on, "and I buried Andy. I introduced Andy to his wife, who'd been my girlfriend, and we buried her. It was a very close relationship." Talking with older adults about their lives inevitably involves memories of friends and family members who have died, an inexorable rhythm of loss, but Jim seems to have felt greatly privileged in officiating at the funerals of people he has known and loved, often people he married and whose children he baptized. All of the transitions of the life cycle are evoked, and for me at least there is the suggestion of ongoing development, for the burial service in the

Book of Common Prayer expands on the words of Psalm 84, shifting the emphasis from peace and bliss to continuing learning and growth, asking that the deceased, "increasing in knowledge and love of thee, may go from strength to strength in the life of perfect service."

"Well, now we've done the Houston business and the Dorothy Norman business, we're sort of in a good position," Jim went on. "We're in my junior year, and I was involved . . . I went back to church. I'd started doing that in Houston, and I never stopped. So all of my sophomore year I was at Christ Church in Cambridge and, you know, full circle.

"Then in my junior year, I went and heard Paul Moore speak at the Canterbury Club [the Harvard Episcopal students program] about his work in Jersey City. He absolutely devastated me. Poverty was the essence of Jersey City at that time, like the South Bronx ten years ago. It was really a desperate place, having done a complete flip in population. During the war, it became a terminal for the very poorest of the poor sharecroppers from the South who just engulfed it.

"Paul went back in that talk to having been shot through the heart and given up for dead at Guadalcanal. He didn't die, and the fact that he lived, he said, made him think about his life and that maybe God had something for him to do, and . . ." Jim gestured that he was skipping a long story. "So he'd go into seminary when he got out of the Marines. At that time it was the beginning of the worker priests in France and a big fascination with poverty at a deep level, Dorothy Day and so on, and also the beginnings of the civil rights movement."

I commented that issues of social justice had barely come up in his narrative until this point, and he nodded. "Not at all. Zero. This was the beginning of it. This is 1950. Then Paul Moore goes on to talk about the Gospel insistence on poverty and he tells the story of St. Martin of Tours, who was a Roman soldier, and the beggar calling to him from the side of the road. He hears the calling two or three times and doesn't pay attention, and then he turns back and gets down from his horse and goes and wraps up the beggar. All of the iconography has him cutting his cloak in half with his sword and wrapping up the beggar. The beggar still says, 'I'm cold, I'm cold,' and so he wraps him up some more and tries to warm him up, and then 'I'm cold, I'm cold,' and he lies on top of the beggar and blows into his mouth and the beggar becomes Christ. That's the story. And that's what he told.

"Well, that was not what we were expecting. It was very— It stuck. Then he just talked about the tremendous poverty of Jersey City and his ministry there. I really was smitten by what he said, though I didn't actually meet him. So I went over and took a couple of courses at the Episcopal Divinity School in Cambridge, and in the end I did two years' worth of courses at EDS for Harvard credit and meanwhile was doing heavy history of architecture with John Coolidge.

"Come senior year, Coolidge says, 'You have to at least do a senior thesis. Do you know what you'd like to do it on?' I had discovered that Germany in the twenties had the first modern church architecture in the world, so I came back and said I would like to work on that. . . . The great architect of the twenties in Germany who did the modern churches was a guy by the name of Dominikus Böhm, and he did wonderful parabolic stuff in concrete—it was fabulous. And there were two or three other architects.

"That was also the beginning of the modern liturgical movement, led by the Benedictines in Germany, so it became critical to make my thesis about the impact of this nascent liturgical movement in the Catholic Church on these modern architects. My thesis was a two-volume thing, and the second volume was all photographs, so it was very concrete. Well, the thesis was a hit, and I got a summa on it.

"So I got a call from the chairman of the department, saying, 'We're really very impressed with what you've done, and there are two Harvard-Cambridge fellowships and we would like to propose you for one of those through the Department of Fine Arts.' Lovely. And I won it. A fellowship to Trinity College, Cambridge. This was my senior year, two months before graduation.

"But—this is important, because this was the moment when I was finishing my thesis—I was reading and reflecting on a book called *Sacred Fortress: Byzantine Art and Statecraft in Ravenna,* by Otto G. von Simson, that came out in 1948. . . . The marriage of liturgy and architecture and mosaic was what that whole book was about. I remember reflecting on that as I was completing my thesis, and then whammo! I said, I could be a priest *and* an architect. I could be a *worker* priest! Then two weeks later I got this fellowship to Cambridge, which had architecture and of course a very important school of theology. When I graduated from Harvard, I went for the summer to the University of Marburg in Germany to learn German and to visit the churches that I wrote my thesis about.

"The day before I sailed, though, I went out to Jersey City for the first time. The Jersey City Ministry was started by three guys who'd gone to General Seminary, including Paul Moore, and a small group of Episcopal Sisters of Saint John the Baptist. And they were at this old church that was sort of down to seven old white ladies in a neighborhood that had become increasingly black, as had the city. So out I go to see this. Paul isn't there, but I meet one of his colleagues and I spend the afternoon, kids all over the place in the church. The open rectory was the symbol of that whole ministry. And then the next day I go to Germany—Marburg.

"At the end of the two-month language course, four of us decided to tour Germany together, and one of the guys had a jeep. And so we went around and I saw my churches and went to Vienna, and I went and stayed overnight with Dominikus Böhm, the great architect about whom I had written my thesis, and Rudolf Schwarz, and met them all in Cologne, and so went off to begin at Cambridge in October having really . . . It was a consummation of my thesis and architecture and theology and all that. And then I spent two years at Cambridge, reading theology. Michael Ramsey was the regius professor before he became Bishop of Durham and then Archbishop of Canterbury, he's the one who met with Pope Paul VI in 1966, which was the first time the leaders of the Roman Catholic and Anglican churches had met together since their separation in 1534. So I studied with him."

When Jim returned to the United States, he applied to study for the Episcopal priesthood in the diocese of New York, which required a single further year at General Seminary, during which he met and married his wife, Pamela, who shared his interest in inner-city work. During that year he finally met Paul Moore, who asked him if he would be interested in coming to Jersey City.

"I was just very smitten by that whole thing," Jim said. "Yeah, so in 1954 Pam and I are engaged, we drive to Jersey City in June, are married in December, and I'm ordained priest the same month. And Pamela and I live in Jersey City for eight years with Paul Moore and that whole crowd. So inner-city work is My Thing.

"Then at the 1962 General Convention of the Episcopal Church, there was a profound recognition that there was a racial crisis in America. So they said, what we need is an office of inner-city work at the national level, and I was asked to head that up. All of the other major churches were doing the same thing. And I mean white churches, because black churches didn't have big national things in the first place. So I meet regularly with the Lutheran man and the United Church of Christ man and the Methodist man, and a new Roman Catholic man. So this group of inner-city executives of the churches decided that what was needed was a national center to retrain clergy—not seminarians but those who were already sitting in various downtown places that were now surrounded by alienated brown people, while urban renewal was doing its stuff, often making things worse.

"Don Benedict, who was running the Chicago City Missionary Society, which was a United Church of Christ operation, said, 'I think Chicago is the right place to do it because it's a very, very black-white city, and a lot of churches have national offices in Chicago' (they don't now, but they did then), 'and I have a place for it to be, right by the First Congregational Church on the West Side, and you can have that free.' It was a great stone Gothic pile built around 1860, and the neighborhood around it had gone entirely black, and there was no congregation left. Next door to this huge church was a sort of mission hall with a lot of spaces for offices. And we all agreed that would be a great idea.

"So we create something in Chicago called the Urban Training Center. Jim Meyers from Jersey City was already laying the groundwork and working out a relationship with the University of Chicago Divinity School. At the last minute the guy who was supposed to head it was called to be bishop in Michigan, so they had to get a new person, and that's when they asked me if I would be interested. It was opened in the fall of 'sixty-four, and for the next eight years, I'm running the Urban Training Center." Jim was thirty-five when he went to Chicago.

Saul Alinsky was a key member of the group, and Ivan Illich was a frequent visiting speaker. "Archie Hargraves, who'd been one of the founders of the East Harlem Protestant Church in New York, was the one black on a staff of four," Jim explained. "I think out of the first group of something like sixty people, almost all men, there were perhaps two blacks. So Archie said, 'We've got to do something radical to shake them up. They've got to see something different from what they've grown up in and what they've been in professionally.' So he created—he suggested—'the plunge.' He said, 'They've got to plunge into the inner city.' . . . We sent them out for three days; they were given three dollars, and all they could take with them was their toothbrushes and their Social Security cards; no wristwatches, no wallets, no nothing, just the three dollars. And they couldn't come back to their Y room at night, they had to find a place somewhere in Chicago to sleep. Many of them went to all-night movies; a lot of them went to the obvious flophouses. They did all sorts of things—sold their blood, got day labor jobs, just roamed the streets. And then at the end of the three days we would meet at the bar behind the Y where they all were staying, and in the context of a Eucharist in the back of the bar we had supper and everyone preached a sort of sermon together, which consisted of the revelations they had experienced in their three days on the streets. All the staff did it. The openness was remarkable.

"Every person had a fieldwork assignment after the lectures, often in church agencies or community organizations. These were action assignments. Action-reflection as a mode of understanding was a sort of new cliché of that time," Jim explained. "Each one of the trainees—that's what we called them, not students, trainees—had to be part of an action-reflection group of fellow trainees, which would meet regularly and in which they would each in turn go through what they were doing in their action thing and then as theologians reflect on what that meant.

"Chicago was very, very hot in terms of action, and we brought the leaders in to be guest lecturers and on panels and whatnot. The stuff that you read about in the papers, and some stuff that you didn't read about in the papers, those were the actions on which people reflected, and those were what made the thing so exciting. It was—it had a very sharp sort of intellectual cast to it. Some of the best thinkers around came and spoke there, and it was also a sort of a base for the people in all of the agencies and community organizations who were working with the poorest people and involved in the sort of nitty-gritty revolutionary tenor of that time. So it was a very, very stimulating and exciting place."

Individual clergy and laypeople had been involved from the beginning of the civil rights movement, but institutional responses were slower. The Urban Training Center was created a decade after the Supreme Court declared school segregation unconstitutional in 1954. Rosa Parks had triggered the Montgomery bus boycott in 1955 by refusing to accept bus segregation, and the Southern Christian Leadership Conference was founded in 1957, the same year that Little Rock public schools were desegregated under the eye of the National Guard. By 1960 the focus had shifted to voter registration and a push for legislative change, with the March on Washington in August 1963, when Dr. King made his "I have a dream" speech. Resistance to voter registration and desegregation was increasing and came to a head in Selma, Alabama, in 1965.

"The staff and trainees of the Urban Training Center were there, staying in people's houses and joining in demonstrations. Then, later that year, there was a huge protest in Chicago about the racial segregation of the schools, and Dr. King of course was there, and our entire student body was with the Chicago protesters—we all got arrested, we all went to jail for about two hours; we got police records."

Jim was in Chicago for eight years. I commented on the hopefulness of that time. "I mean, there was a belief that it was really going to be possible to fix the things that were wrong."

"Absolutely!" Jim said. "That was before cynicism."

"We really believed things were going to be fixed."

"And then everybody got killed. There was a loss of courage and a loss of hope that things could change. The War on Poverty—that was a big sign of hope, hope, hope, and then the tremendous amount of internal graft and sloppy stuff—very few of those projects really did much good."

After the assassination of John Kennedy in 1963, a series of events began that gradually changed the atmosphere. Malcolm X was assassinated in 1965. Stokely Carmichael reframed the struggle in terms of Black Power in 1967. Lyndon Johnson did push through the Civil Rights Act in 1968, but that success was followed in April by the assassination of Martin Luther King, with nationwide rioting and whole neighborhoods burned in black communities, and then by the assassination of Bobby Kennedy in the same year. The black leadership became less welcoming of white participation, there was a backlash in the churches against activism by clerical "troublemakers," and at the same time the social conscience of the nation was increasingly focused on the war in Vietnam rather than on domestic social justice issues. Ironically, since then social activism has waned in the liberal churches, along with membership, and the lesson of political engagement has been taken over by the religious right, with a very different kind of focus.

I had been trying to get a sense of how these historic shifts affected different age-groups. Jim was forty-two when he went to St. John's, having had the experience of going from a privileged childhood to an awareness of issues of social justice and then seeing much of the enthusiasm dissipated. "A lot of people were in a sense orphaned," I said to him, "so they had to find new ways to be. New ways to express their commitment, new communities to work with, people who— I mean, you used the word *cynicism;* but all those people didn't just meet this transition by becoming cynical. There must be lots of people my age who remember what it was like to feel that they could repair things. And then lost that. And I wonder sometimes whether they could come back. I don't know that they'd come back to the churches. I don't know that they'd put it in religious terms, but whatever it is, to become less cynical."

"Oh, I think so," Jim said. "But I think this is an institutional crisis as opposed to just a church crisis. At times we had almost absolute faith in certain institutions, and that's changed. They still believe in the Spirit, maybe some of the forms are different, but that the Spirit is real and change is possible, and it's going to mean a different avenue. . . . I work with people like that, and they are some of the people who are in seminary now, but the ways it fuels them are different from twenty years ago. You've got to have institutions and structures to make things work, but our structures are so different now. I mean, my God, just think of the Internet. . . . You don't even have to have a degree; you can get what you need to know in other forms. So the stuff that's at our disposal is different. The vehicles are different."

Jim's mention of the Internet reminded me of his description of the importance of connecting action and reflection in the training program in Chicago. "My sense is that people's lives are organized in ways that give them less and less opportunity for reflection, except for those who have recognized that problem and taken on a meditation practice, a spiritual practice of some sort. I see people working terribly hard, on the cell phone all the time, logging in on their computers all the time, just caught in a constant flow of information, demand, expectation, and not having the time or not making the time to reflect on what they're doing."

In 1971, Paul Moore, the priest whose lecture on St. Martin of Tours had inspired Jim's original interest in social justice issues, became the Episcopal bishop of New York, and Jim became dean of the Cathedral of St. John the Divine the next year. As Jim described this transition, I could hear him struggling to explain why he wanted to leave the work in Chicago. "I loved being at the Urban Training Center, but I didn't see it as a life vocation, so to speak. I really was a very sort of faithful priest, . . . a tight-assed Episcopalian, you know, this was the true church. . . . So I was very excited about St. John's. It was a kind of coming home, a bigger and better home than I'd ever lived in before. This really makes me think. It was the frustrated architect in me. Here was the unfinished cathedral, right on the border of Harlem, and you could do all kinds of incredible stuff."

Jim approached his task at the huge, unfinished Gothic cathedral on Amsterdam Avenue with sweeping gusto and blithe opportunism, and it quickly became one of the liveliest institutions in New York City, stimulating sweat equity projects in Harlem through the Urban Homesteading Assistance Board and at the same time welcoming Sufi dancers and a homeless shelter, Buddhist monks and most of the Big Apple Circus, art exhibits and a tank of muddy water from the Hudson River to represent the sacred challenge of environmental stewardship. Among the artists in residence at the cathedral was Philippe Petit, the high-wire artist who had contrived to dance between the twin towers of the World Trade Center in 1974 and now brought his message of graceful balance to the nave of St. John's—a metaphor, perhaps, of the tension between the material and the spiritual. Peacocks came to live in the wooded cathedral close, and liberation theologians made their case from the pulpit.

Connecting things is for me one key meaning of composing, as women have tried to combine multiple commitments in ways that are not only workable but graceful. For Jim, the medieval cathedral was not a narrowly religious institution but reflected all the activities of the world around it—politics, economics, learning, and the arts—combined in a unified vision that gave meaning to life. I use the metaphor of composing in a second way as well, as musical compositions move through time, changing tempo and shifting themes, yet maintaining threads of continuity across multiple orchestral movements. For Jim, it seemed to me, the way a contemporary cathedral must address continuity across time is to find and affirm the threads that connect tradition to visions of the future.

"In architectural history, I really got to know the role that cathedrals played in the Middle Ages, and that to me was a fascinating thing," he said. "The cathedrals really started with the Silk Road and the beginnings of secure cities in the twelfth and thirteenth centuries. Europe was really rural in the Dark Ages; cities dwindled, and everybody lived in villages. . . . So when the new cities started growing, the cathedral was sized to be the center of the city. Cathedrals grew to be the centers of compassion and of culture. The arts, the intellect, politics. All that stuff.

"Now that holistic notion was what interested me. And also the notion of . . . here was this big monster cathedral, which had totally gone down in people coming to it."

Both Jim's experiences as a student and his early assignments seemed to link his priesthood with the city. The ritual life of a cathedral necessarily evokes attention to performance, which had also been an important part of his growing up, but I asked how that all flowed together with architecture and design. "Well, it doesn't—it really doesn't flow," he said, "but it explodes when I come to the cathedral, because that is the opportunity to be architect, complete the cathedral, make the cathedral the center of the city, the center of urban renewal"—he circled his hand—"and it's also there that I recognize that the city is not all Episcopalian and not all Christian. This notion of a cathedral—think of those windows—it's a cosmic notion. It's to hold an entire people. . . . My whole interfaith thing starts there—it wasn't part of Chicago at all."

I grinned. "You mean you weren't even an ecumenical Christian when you went to Chicago?"

"Oh, I was very ecumenical, but I was very Christian. That's what turned around with St. John the Divine. From the day I arrived, I realized the cathedral had to function on many different fronts. The social justice stuff really came out of Jersey City. It took the civil rights movement thing to blow that open. And the interfaith thing didn't develop until I came to the cathedral—I decided this is for the whole world."

During the twenty-five years that James Morton was dean of St. John the Divine, each of the themes that had become important in his earlier life was woven into the life of the cathedral. It became a center for the arts in New York City, a center for interdisciplinary scholarship, and a center for social action. Chapels along the nave were dedicated to poetry, to the environment, and to victims of the AIDS epidemic. Topical sermons were preached by poets and politicians, UN delegates and community organizers, Sufis and Buddhists, even anthropologists like myself. Work on the building, which had been halted in 1941, when the United States entered World War II, was resumed as a job training program for unemployed youth working with and learning from master stonecutters from England. There was a school and a homeless shelter and a soup kitchen. Children brought their pets to be blessed on the feast of St. Francis, and large animals—camels and even a small elephant—were included in processions. Waves of excitement and sometimes of disapproval surrounded St. John's—some people found it too inclusive or too daring—and cathedral events were covered by *The New York Times.*

As we spoke, I realized that even before Jim came to New York, the social issues being addressed in Chicago were beginning to be understood in global terms—that, as René Dubos urged that year at the UN Conference on the Environment, acting locally requires thinking globally. Jim had described a shift at the Urban Training Center during his last year to discussions of "white racism," and until I could tune my thinking back to that time, I was puzzled to understand why this was new. Then I realized that it had to do with a shift away from looking at race as primarily an American issue to an emerging awareness of a multiracial world. It was only after Dr. King spoke out against the war in Vietnam that African Americans began to think in terms of all people of color and to claim an identification between black Americans and Africans and Southeast Asians. Racism came to be discussed as a global problem and racial justice directly connected with the end of the colonial empires and the economic differences between north and south. All that came into focus in New York City because of the presence of the United Nations.

In 1975, Jim's third year in New York, there were two events as the cathedral connected with a Japanese Shinto sect called Oomoto, one of them as part of a weeklong celebration of the thirtieth anniversary of the United Nations in collaboration with the Temple of Understanding, an interfaith group founded in 1960.

"A Dutch dentist and artist named Frederick Franck, who had spent several years in Africa working with Albert Schweitzer, had become interested in this Japanese community. It was a kind of almost unitarian but deistic Shinto sect that had become a sort of center for maintaining the ancient traditions of Japanese arts and crafts. It was also related to a radical critique of the Japanese government building up the military in the twenties, so in the thirties Onisaburo Deguchi, the head of it, and all of the leadership were jailed. They revived after the war, and in the last two years of his life, after getting out of prison, Onisaburo, who was an extraordinary potter and calligrapher, made two thousand tea bowls. They look like Bonnard paintings, vivid colors, very beautiful.

"Frederick Franck heard about this revival, went to Japan, and wrote a book about them. The work was shown in four museums on the continent and ended up at the Victoria and Albert in London. It was a big deal, and Frederick Franck was in the midst of it. Well, at the show in London, the Oomoto group said, 'We would like very much to have it shown in the United States,' and Frederick Franck said, 'Well, I know someone in New York who has a big place and I think he's very interested in the arts, he'd be interested in this.' And I, of course, said, 'Yes, that would be lovely.' The exhibition was to begin with their ritual of purification, and they asked if they could do it at the high altar, so they had, at the high altar of the cathedral, this Shinto offering of fruits and vegetables and whatnot."

Jim was already running into some opposition at his "big place." "There were mutterings," he said, " 'This is pagan, this is terrible.' " Then came the celebration of the thirtieth anniversary of the United Nations. I was living in Iran at that time, but I had heard about the event because my mother, Margaret Mead, preached on the opening night.

"Oomoto was invited to come back for that," Jim continued. "So they do a thing, and we had Pir Vilayat Khan, the Sufi Muslim leader and musician who died in 2004, a very wonderful spiritual guy, doing his Cosmic Mass, which takes off from Père Teilhard de Chardin's notion. That was two Oomoto Shinto things in the cathedral in that year, one in March and another one in October, and there's a picture in *The New York Times* of your mother and me and one of the Shinto leaders, and that gets people talking about *what* is going on in the cathedral. So at the December meeting of the trustees, where we were accused of all sorts of things, there was an attempt to get me fired, but the trustees didn't buy it.

"Then the Oomoto people come back again, and say how much they appreciated being able to have their service at the cathedral because all of the shows of Onisaburo's art in Europe had been in secular museums, 'but we're a religious community,' they say, 'and this is a religious community, and you allowed us to have the Shinto service at a Christian altar.' Then the guy stands up, and he reaches into his kimono sleeve and says, 'We will be most honored if you next year would come to Japan and celebrate the Christian rituals in our Shinto shrine. Here are two tickets.' So in January of 'seventy-seven, Pamela and I go to Japan, and then we go to India, where we'd never been before.

"There was a real fusion of moments of wonderment and turning points for me. That was really the beginning of my conversion to an interfaith practice that is not in violation of who you are in your own tradition but is an opening to the experience of another tradition. That, I suppose, has been the major fulcrum in my professional life, but it started with a response on my part to their request to come and be a Christian inside of a Shinto shrine as they were being Shintos inside of a Christian shrine, and neither one of us died."

"No lightning struck," I said.

"No lightning. So my commitment to interfaith understanding really came out of that. That's also when I started having Sufi dancing at the cathedral. That was through Pir Vilayat Khan. People raised their eyebrows, but Paul Moore was very supportive."

Jim's first encounter with Hinduism had actually happened in Chicago, where he and Pamela and their daughters had an Indian graduate student living with them. "Mira asked me if I would do her wedding. I was still in my tight-assed Episcopal mode, and I said, 'You're Hindu, and that's fine, but I can't,' and she said, 'Oh, that doesn't matter to me, I can become Christian if you like.' I said, 'No, no, no. It doesn't work that way.' I got C. T. Vivian—Martin Luther King's right-hand person—to do the thing. Mira said to Pamela, 'The wedding will be in January, and it's very, very simple, all we need are palm trees and strings of marigolds.' We said, 'Well, yeah, but this is January in Chicago, there aren't any marigolds, let alone palm trees.' And she said, 'Oh, that's all right, just get some flowers,' so the entire apartment had chains of flowers, which were not marigolds but chrysanthemums. Then she said, 'We need fire,' so the hibachi was brought in, and the fire did indeed rise in the hibachi. They hang up a veil, you know, between the two getting married, and it's only after they've done their vows and so on that the veil is lowered. So that was marvelous, and the wedding was full of Jesuits because she was in a class with a lot of Jesuits.

"When Pamela and I went and stayed in India, seeing all the Indian theology at play in terms of the temples and the gods, that was the beginning of my fascination with the theology of a totally other religious tradition. The only other thing I had done was, when I was the counselor at a Jewish camp in my sophomore year at Harvard, I read all of [Abraham] Heschel's stuff and the Hasidic stuff and was deeply fascinated by the spiritual, almost Sufi-like aspect within Judaism. So there were these intriguing experiences with other religions. Hinduism through Mira, no Buddhism yet, no Islam until I got to the cathedral and met Pir Vilayat Khan and we started the Sufi dancers. The critical point was when the Japanese came back and said, 'Come and do the Christian ritual in our shrine, *our house.*' That was what blew me away. Just the possibility and the tremendous compassion on their part, and then doing it in Japan and realizing that there is something else."

"It seems to me," I said, "that most people assume interfaith communication starts from theologies and belief systems—"

"Which it did not for me."

"Maybe the key thing is not the language but the doing," I said, "the doing together mutually, the forms of worship."

"And at a very basic level, we begin with respect for the difference, as opposed to the denigration of difference," Jim said. I described the memoir of Leila Ahmed, who writes about what Islam meant to her as a child. She came from a fairly wealthy, elite Egyptian family, and what Islam meant to her as a child was the musical sound of chanting the Koran and the things that her mother said and modeled about giving to the poor. All that was linked in her mind with home and relationships and what she was learning about being a good person. "The theology isn't there," I said. "The authority structure isn't there. Islam is what is experienced by Muslims, young and old, male and female, literate and nonliterate. That's the door that has to be opened, I think."

I took us back to the narrative with a further question. "So Mira's wedding was the beginning for you, even before you came to the cathedral, and then you came pretty close to getting into trouble with all those offerings on the high altar? Not the last time you got in trouble."

"The other big turning point for me was the environment as sort of the largest issue that we have. I didn't even know the word *ecology*, and environmental concerns were nowhere in any of my education. It wasn't mentioned even in the study of the Psalms. . . . The wonder and splendor and all of that business is what the Psalms talk about, but that reality of creation was not linked to the current situation. . . . The environment just grew and grew as I met more and more people within that mode of study and action.

"I met René Dubos through a wonderful PR man we had at the cathedral who had read his new book called *Beast or Angel?*[1] about what makes us human. He thought it would be interesting to have Dubos have a dialogue with me as a priest. . . . At the end of it I said, 'I would love to have you preach at the cathedral.' I was organizing a series about poverty, and René Dubos gave this unbelievable sermon about lichens."[2] What we call lichens are actually a symbiosis of two organisms, a fungus and an alga, each of which gives up its separate existence. "They become glorious by diminishing themselves. That blew everybody's mind."

"But, Jim," I said, "how did you recognize that poverty, which was so important for you coming up, was a topic on which Dubos would have something beautiful to say?"

"He must have said something in our dialogue. . . . I knew that poverty was a central thing in my theology, in the church, in Christian life, and I think I asked him, . . . 'Is there a way in which what we mean by poverty has meaning to a scientist?' "

"In this context, holy poverty? Not poverty as a problem to be eliminated but poverty as spirituality?"

"Right."

"What fascinates me," I said, "is that the way people weave the parts of their lives together is also a kind of ecology: your interest in architecture, and the whole green cathedral project. It's such a beautiful marrying of concerns."

"Other issues came up as I learned that there was more to life than what I had thought about, things changed. The whole patriarchy business, and this song and dance about how it would be wrong to have women priests because Jesus was a male and that was God's plan. Well, that all went out the window."

"So where did getting out of patriarchy start for you? I remember there was a scandal about the *Christa*."

"The *Christa*. That was a big scandal, but the women's ordination thing was earlier." The *Christa* was a bronze sculpture of a crucified woman that had been created by the British sculptor Edwina Sandys for the UN Year of the Woman in 1975. It was at the cathedral during part of Holy Week in 1984, causing outcries of blasphemy around the world. Yet even St. Paul, no particular friend of women, said in his Letter to the Galatians that in the church, "There is neither Jew nor Greek, there is neither bond nor free, there is neither male nor female: for ye are all one in Christ Jesus" (3:28). This is what the *Christa* represented, at the same time that she served as a reminder of the ways in which women have suffered and sacrificed themselves through the centuries.

One more key element for Jim was added by another scientist, Lewis Thomas, who also preached at the cathedral. "It was in that middle period that it suddenly became very clear to me, with *ecumenical* and *ecology*—I love the derivation of those words, and they're very similar in that they're talking about a totality, which is what creation is all about, and *vive la différence*—that diversity is the essence of creation. I heard Lewis Thomas give a lecture in which he said, 'You know, there are no two cells alike. There are no cells alike any more than there are two snowflakes. There is nothing unique in being unique.' That was the perfect phrase. And uniqueness is the essence of creation. It really came through the greenness, and the greenness came from looking back from the moon, and the beautiful blue-green creation, and seeing that everything is on that little ball that you can blot out with your thumb. Totality, inclusivity, greenness, uniqueness, all of that was just a huge turning point for me. And that meant again a kind of intellectual license for having diversity of speakers, of preachers, of traditions and so on, celebrated. This is a Christian place, this is an Episcopal place, but our Eucharist was open to everybody, and whenever I had preachers of different kinds, I had them join the clergy and gather around the altar, even Muslims and Jews did this. It was wonderful."

Again and again, Jim emphasized to me that *interfaith* did not mean arriving at uniformity or even at a common denominator, that it meant finding ways to work together without blurring the differences and ongoing loyalties. More recently, I find myself preferring the word *distinctiveness,* to emphasize both difference and uniqueness combining in what makes a tradition irreplaceable.

Jim's twenty-five years at the cathedral expressed the holistic understanding that had developed through his childhood and earlier career, as architecture and performance, faith and social activism were braided together and matched to his concept of what a cathedral should and could be—much like what a life could and should be. Not an easy job to leave. Since his retirement, Jim has created a new institution, the New York Interfaith Center, that expresses one of the many themes of his lifework, the possibility that collaborative programs for the different faith communities in the city would both serve their needs and build trust and mutual recognition. Instead of leaving his work, he scaled down, focused in on the element that seemed to him most important among many, something he was uniquely able to do. Having gotten it established, he has now found an executive director for the center and has a modest office to one side, continuing as a member of the board as he works on his memoirs. On Sundays, Jim goes to an Episcopal church where he feels at home in the congregation, no longer onstage, and is careful to keep a tactful distance from the cathedral and from diocesan headquarters.

The Interfaith Center is not primarily a place where the leaders of the city's different faiths gather to debate theology. Rather it is a place where they gather sometimes to worship and sometimes to learn how to deal with the practical urban problems and challenges faced by their communities—the public school system, the health care system, the courts. The center has struggled to find a sustainable location. Most of its programs are fairly small, without a lot of newspaper headlines, but they are designed to have significant multiplier effects as the leaders of different religious communities are provided with the tools to guide and support their members in solving the problems of life in a new country. In a small way, but only a few miles from the United Nations buildings on the East River, the center is testing whether the global communities of Christianity and Islam, Buddhism and Hinduism can work together to address the problems of poverty, war, and environmental degradation, and the crises of epidemics and climatic disaster.

The Episcopal Church, like the other liturgical forms of Christianity, affirms that God touches human lives through the things of everyday life—bread, wine, water, oil, the material signs of the sacraments. Throughout his life Jim has been drawing out the meaning of material things given and shared to meet human needs and shaped into works of art. A very practical guy, this right reverend, not someone who believes that the "things of the spirit" should be separated from the concrete needs of daily life but someone who recognizes the sacred in both the curvature of a shell and the offering of a meal or a place to sleep. Moving from a "big place" to a little place, he continues to serve a holistic vision, using the experience and dedication of a lifetime to create a new model for mutual caring.

CHAPTER VII

Pleasure and Responsibility

WHEN I AM INTERVIEWING PEOPLE about their lives, I don't follow a set sequence or questionnaire. Most people seem to have an established pattern for thinking about their own histories, and these personal patterns tell me more than a chronology of dates and places, so instead of imposing a framework (which might be helpful in making comparisons), I let people frame their own narratives around the implicit plots or through lines that represent their theory of what the story is really about, what in fact their life has been about, a central passion or a recurrent challenge that acts as a landmark as they move from stage to stage. For some it is achievement, for others it may be victimization, while for others still it is continuing discovery and learning. Some connect the eras of their lives to demonstrate continuity, while others remember a series of interruptions and discontinuities.

Back when I first conceived of this book, I felt it would be important to include something about the ways in which gay men and women look at their lives in their later years and at the place of caring for each other and contributing to society in their choices. A colleague put me in touch with a gay couple, over sixty, one of whom at one time had been married and had living children and grandchildren, who were willing to talk to me about their lives and to appear in print without disguise, like others I have worked with on this book. So I flew to San Francisco to stay as a guest in the home of Dan Jepson and Michael Crowe.

Dan lives in Newark, California, a suburb of San Francisco, with his partner of more than a decade, Michael. They have a small house with a charming garden, carefully tended, in which they have installed a murmuring fountain that flows into a fishpond. Most of Dan's life has revolved around music. On the day I arrived, he and Michael took me to a choir concert in which one of their friends was singing. The following morning, Dan and I sat down to record in the shade of the garden.

Dan knew I had written sympathetically about the gay community in several contexts, including a book about the HIV/AIDS epidemic, coauthored with my biologist colleague Richard Goldsby, and he understood why I had been introduced to him in particular, so it is not surprising that, as he told the story of his life, he emphasized his development as a gay man. It struck me that this was what I have come to call a learning narrative, this one dealing with an unfolding understanding of his sexual orientation, what it meant to be gay, and how to live as a gay man in American society, a lonely process with no real guidance, which led to a lifelong concern with mentoring and heightened my awareness of how much learning is taken for granted when fitting in comes easily. At the same time, I heard another through line in his narrative, one of which he was perhaps less aware, a theme of taking responsibility that went back to his early childhood. The story began, however, with a note of rejection, another theme that recurred.

Dan started out as if he were creating a legal document: "I, Dan Jepson, was born about seventy years ago, April 6, 1938, in Douglas, Wyoming. It was not an easy birth. In a sense, I was rejected from the beginning. I was unusually large and my mother is very small, and at one point they gave the choice to my father and said, 'Which do you want, the mother or the baby?' And my father said, 'I didn't marry the baby.' This was all apocryphal. I wasn't there. So I came out . . . but I was a mess. They pulled me out with forceps, and they threw me on this other table and then worked on my mother, who was hemorrhaging like crazy, and it was only later that the nurse said, 'Oh, the baby's alive.'

"My mother didn't have a full uterus, and she had been told she would never have any children. She had three in the end, but all of us are missing minor things, like when I had a hand injury, they were going to take a donor area from my hand and restring it, and they discovered that, although everybody has two tendons that work their fingers, I only have one. The spare tendon is missing. And my sister had a very weak fourth finger, so playing the piano was difficult for her, though it wasn't hard for me."

The family was not well off, but they were rich in relatives (Dan had some forty first cousins), some of whom moved into the household at various periods. Dan's grandfather had lost his farm in 1933, and his father had had a car repossessed in 1936 because of a single missed payment. Financial concerns were increased by living in a small town where class was important: "It was very much a haves and have-nots kind of thing, coming out of the depression," Dan said. There was little work for Dan's father in Douglas, and in 1941 the family packed up, planning to move west, but ended up going only as far as Riverton, Wyoming, less than two hundred miles from Douglas, where his father got a job as a roustabout on the oil rigs. Eventually the family purchased a small house, which they improved over time, cultivating a substantial garden on adjacent land.

Dan and his brother went to college, but only one other cousin was able to go that far in school. Still, throughout his childhood, along with the anecdotes about his difficult birth, Dan heard comparisons made between himself and older cousins in the neighborhood. "This had some effect on me growing up," he said. "It's odd that one year of difference in development between kids can leave you sort of . . . For a long time I thought of myself as deficient in handling baseballs and hitting and stuff. When I turned out finally to realize I was gay, I wondered if that was part of it. I was always comparing myself to Larry and Jerry, and they were a year older . . ."

"And they kept being a year older," I commented. "It doesn't stop."

"And they were always . . . I mean, there are comparisons . . . growing up. There were a number of boys in the neighborhood who were, say, four or five years older, and they were doing incredible things, and I didn't realize how unusual this was until much later. They would dig holes in the ground to make these incredible hideouts or build tree houses. Then when we would try to do it, of course, our things didn't work very well. One of them, Jim, finally went off and became an engineer, ended up living in Sacramento. He was very clever and ingenious, and we just thought that's what older guys did."

Dan was his parents' oldest child and, because of his mother's continuing ill health, carried a great deal of the responsibility in the family. One of his early duties was bringing in coal for heating and removing buckets of ashes. The family had an old-fashioned icebox, for which they bought blocks of ice that slowly melted. "If you didn't drain it, it would run over," Dan explained, "and that was always a mess. You had to be very careful. So those were my jobs. I was doing this as a first and second grader. And I'm looking at kids now, and they don't seem to have that same responsibility. You couldn't just dump the ashes all over, and you were supposed not to drip the water. And it must have been fairly heavy. I'm saying 'must have been' because I don't have any sense of having been imposed upon to do this or being forced to labor. It was your job and you did it."

Later on, when the family took in two cousins whose mother had run away, Dan took over the laundry, with mountains of ironing, and the cooking, with his mother giving instructions from her bed. "My father was kind of useless on this kind of stuff," Dan told me. "It was no big deal. He wasn't really absent, but it was not his thing to do anything with Mother, I mean to talk about family and stuff like that. And later in life, I never really connected with my father. Not like we avoided each other, but we never did advice. But my mother would talk to me about her family and so forth because she had no one else to talk to." And Dan would take care of her as well as the house. "So this little boy was— I became her confidant a little too early, I think. It didn't seem to warp me exactly, but it left me with a little too much knowledge at an early age."

Dan had become excited about music early on and sang his first solo, "Beneath the cross of Jesus," in the local Baptist church while he was in first grade. "I had one of those amazing soprano voices. The church had a really good pastor and youth program. Religion was very important to me at that time, and I suppose I got saved and so on." Dan paused in the conversation from time to time to sing a few bars of a piece of music he had referred to, almost conversationally, now in a grown-up tenor. In fourth grade, he started piano lessons, which he paid for himself by delivering papers for thirty cents a day. In addition to music, he loved reading. At the same time, he was beginning to learn about his own body and its pleasures. "I became aware of my sexuality much earlier than I think most kids did," he said. "I was masturbating and playing games with the kids in the neighborhood, doctor and stuff, in third grade. I think I was precocious, because when I talk to other people, they say this didn't happen to them until sixth or seventh grade."

By seventh grade, Dan and another boy were vying to be substitute Sunday school organist, and the job went to the other boy, whose parents had made significant donations to the church. "That was my first hit of music and politics," Dan said ruefully. Later he took up the saxophone, working off the installment payments himself and joining the band. Between the band and the choir, participating in a lot of inter-school events in different towns, he told me, "you got an experience of doing really complicated music with the best singers."

When he was in college, Dan began to be offered scholarships and jobs using his music. After he graduated from college in Denver, his first job was in Kansas, running a chorus and teaching elementary school music. He was conjuring music from the children in the chorus and the band, which no one had imagined they'd hear, but at the same time he was feeling that, although he could work with what he had, he didn't have "the knowledge to build it." So he went back to school to find out what he'd missed, starting graduate school in Grand Forks, North Dakota, then switching to the University of Iowa.

As Dan told the story of his decision to go to graduate school, I realized that he had become able to critique his own training and was determined to do better with anyone he would teach. "So I'm there at the University of Iowa," he recounted. "I'm studying all this stuff and none of it makes much sense and I realize that I had started college in Denver with a fairly good, clear voice—I had a good, clear high A—and by the time I'd graduated I couldn't sing F sharp. The vocal training was just bad. My range had dropped, and it had come up from the bottom, too. I wasn't breathing right. It wasn't good.

"So I go to Imperial, Nebraska, and get away from that teacher. I do a few church solos, and the voice starts coming back. When I got back to just, quote, *singing*, rather than *trying* to sing, it worked. I didn't quite know what that meant, but I thought, Well, I'm really not a singer. Are you seeing that there's no real mentor in this whole thing? Just me sort of playing around with this. If somebody had grabbed me in freshman year and said, 'My God, what a voice, here let me do this,' I could probably have been a really good opera singer, a Mozart tenor, as they call it. I wouldn't have been a Pavarotti, but I would have been one of those people who could have done Donizetti or . . . But I didn't know and nobody told me and there was no mentor and I had this god-awful teacher who everybody said was okay who was destroying my voice. There's a lot of that out there. One of the people I knew had some recording equipment, and he recorded me and I listened to my voice and realized what was happening. Somehow after I got out of Iowa, when this guy had almost destroyed my voice, I suddenly had an interesting, good voice. This doesn't fit the picture, you know, because singers never know what they sound like. I had been taught to sing in a certain way, but it hurt. And 'just singing' was okay. And it sounds better.

"The other thing that I got into was suddenly realizing that I could carry emotion in the music, which nobody had taught me in Denver or in Iowa, nobody ever focused on What are you singing *about*? I know more about teaching now from having been abused and disabused and then abused again with my voice. Okay, so here I am in Imperial, Nebraska, and my voice comes back, and one of the things I did was the opening to the *Messiah,* you know, 'Comfort Ye,' and I could get through that really nicely, and I thought, That's odd, I couldn't sing this earlier and now I can sing it."

Ever since I was a dean at Amherst College, I have been intrigued by the process of teaching subjects that cannot be learned from books. These are the subjects for which teaching is hardest to evaluate, least understood by traditional academics, and most vulnerable to the assumption that, if you can do something, you can teach someone else how to do it. Teaching someone how to *do* something, to sing or to act or to play tennis, at a level of excellence is very different from teaching someone *about* a subject.

In the meantime, Dan had started directing plays at the little theater in town "at a thousand dollars a pop." He was also director of the choir at the Episcopal church.

Switching again to his sexual development, Dan described some of his early encounters with peers or with older men coming on to him, and the continuing difficulty of understanding what it all meant. The need for guidance, for good mentoring, was a theme that connected his remarks about sexuality with his accounts of his musical development. There is a widespread belief that homosexuality is a result of negative influences, but Dan was telling the opposite story, the story of a child born with orientations or potentials that don't match the models offered by an environment that neither refines nor develops them. "I'm trying to figure out," he mused, "where my wisdom came from." It would be overly facile to conclude that Dan's sexual orientation came from having to care for his mother and replace her at many "feminine" tasks, but his narrative made me think him fortunate for having learned as a child something that many men in our society never have the opportunity to learn, that loving someone means being willing to care for them.

At college Dan found an older man who became a mentor, helping him find a safe way into the gay scene in Denver, and even said to him, when he was a senior, "I don't know, you may not be gay." Meanwhile, he had met the woman he later married, assuming that, in spite of having fooled around with other men, this was the next thing to do. "I was really taken with her, and she reminded me of my mother," he said with a shrug. "Everybody gets married, I thought, . . . and I'd read that everybody went through this homosexual phase and then you move on to the next thing. We're talking about the fifties, remember. They didn't call it homosexual but same-sex phase or something. And I was able to function with her fine. It was just every once in a while I would fall off the wagon, usually when the marriage wasn't going real well. We were having some other problems and somebody else would pop into my life and it was never a satisfying thing because I never . . . It wasn't until well into my forties that I began to know how the equipment really worked. I think we should have seminars on this. It's like, when they brought out *The Joy of Sex* and things like that, I'd suddenly realize, Hm, well, that's a good idea."[1]

Sex is not, for human beings, simply a matter of "doing what comes naturally" but something that has to be learned, like walking—or like love, for that matter. Everyone has noticed the joy with which toddlers begin to walk, a satisfaction stronger than the falls and bumps along the way. Easy as it is to find examples of destructive pleasures, it is important to recognize that the capacity for pleasure is part of what makes human beings able to explore and to learn. Sexual pleasure also becomes a basis for fidelity and gratitude, and for responsibility to partners and offspring. It follows that, in human evolution, sexuality has played multiple roles, roles perhaps as important as procreation.

The capacity to experience and remember pleasure works as what the ethologist Konrad Lorenz called an "innate teaching mechanism," a reward that reinforces behavior, pleasure leading to repetition.[2] An example Lorenz used in a lecture I heard him give was a bird learning to build its first nest, gathering twigs (which is apparently innately programmed) and discovering that neither rigid nor limp twigs are useful but that flexible, elastic twigs introduced into the weave knit themselves together, which leads the bird to experience something like an orgasm, after which the bird seeks out and recognizes the right kind of building materials.

Freud's great contribution was uncovering the connections between human sexuality, including the experiences of early infancy and childhood, and other activities of life.[3] Erik Erikson took Freud's thinking further by showing how the bodily pleasures and modalities that emerge during development underlie the strengths we value most—the capacity to love, to hope in the future, to work, and to care for others.[4] In this sense at least, pleasure and virtue are not opposites but directly and naturally linked. There was a case several years ago when a woman confided in a health-care practitioner that nursing her baby gave her pleasure and excited her in a way akin to sexual pleasure. This was reported as an ominous portent of sexual abuse, and the infant was removed from her care and returned only after a long struggle. Yet we are all aware now that breast feeding, which is important for the health of the child even when alternatives are available, involves pain and discomfort at various stages and has to be learned. How logical that a woman's innate capacity for pleasure would become part of her learning process.

It seems probable that pleasure plays an essential role in learning and in other adaptive processes and that human sexual pleasure, even when separated from reproductive possibility, is part of what makes family life—and the labor-intensive rearing of human infants—sustainable. Pleasure builds the groundwork for responsibility, which raises the question of where transient relationships fit in, whether the responsibilities created by a given sexual relationship conflict with others, and whether they are or can be honored. And certainly it suggests that the coercive and exploitative use of others for sexual pleasure is a distortion of this basic potentiality of pleasure to build and strengthen human ties.

Marriage, in its many and diverse forms, has been the human institution in which the capacity for sexual pleasure serves individuals and society, not only through reproduction but in a variety of ways. When couples marry in their seventies, as is increasingly common, we don't look for babies, we look for contentment and trusting companionship and frequently find improved health. No one argues that adults who are unable or unlikely to reproduce should not marry, and only the bleakest of moralists would suggest refraining from intercourse during periods of infertility—indeed, reliance on these periods is the form of family planning approved by those who insist that reproduction is the only legitimate function of sex. This argument can be applied to same-sex marriage—true, same-sex partnership does not lead directly to reproduction, but it can lead to love and fidelity, to caregiving and responsibility in the same way as heterosexual marriage. The threat to marriage in our own society is not the inclusion of same-sex couples but the increasing failure to recognize marriage and family as the primary context in which individuals take sustained responsibility for the well-being and happiness of others. Inevitably, when same-sex relationships break down, we can see the same kinds of disappointment, anger, and irresponsibility that occur in heterosexual marriages.

Throughout history, there have been men and women struggling to live heterosexual lives, denying the sexual orientation that truly gives them pleasure and satisfaction, or struggling with loneliness or guilt for desires they have been told are sinful. Decriminalizing homosexuality was only a first step. We should be moving on to inviting same-sex couples to the same responsibilities that marriage represents to others—caring for each other in sickness and in health, sustaining the community, contributing to the development of future generations. And we should recognize that marriage is not an exclusively private matter, that long and happy marriages survive and benefit the community where kin and society approve and support them.

Critical to my approach to this subject has been learning as an adult that my mother was bisexual—and recognizing that a number of family friends lived with same-sex partners. But I grew up in the world as it was before the 1969 riots at the Stonewall Inn, only a few blocks from the house in Greenwich Village where I lived as a child. The Stonewall riots triggered the gay liberation movement when, for the first time, the

customers of a gay bar resisted what was then routine police harass-
ment. In those days, homosexuality was a matter for concealment that
could destroy careers and even lead to prison terms.

A decade later, homosexuality had been decriminalized but acquired
a new stigma as a result of the HIV/AIDS epidemic, which spread especially rapidly through a community that had been largely limited to
casual and transient sexual relationships, and was suddenly and flam-
boyantly claiming freedom. When I look around at gay men and
women of my generation, I have to remind myself that they did not
have the privilege I had in growing up of establishing early and stable
relationships of reciprocal caring, and that within the gay community
there have been perennial losses and traumas; because of the plague,
even death has a different face.

Those who stood up for gay pride in 1969 and are still living are in
their sixties and seventies, sorting out the meanings of aging and the
possibilities of participation and contribution as they grow older. Like
others who have grown up during struggles for "liberation" or against
discrimination, they have had the experience of learning to look differently at themselves and at their peers and have had to resist internalized
oppression as their own aspirations rubbed up against those of others
newly claiming a place in the sun.

By 1975, Dan's career in music education had run into a series of
obstacles, complicated by various kinds of sexual politics. He had married after college and had two children, a daughter and a son. The
pattern of the time had him making the decisions about where the family would live to fit the availability of jobs, and about returning to
school, but at the same time, Dan said, "It was a very strange thing
because our agreement was we won't have any kids until we get out
of school, but she had suddenly gone and stopped using her birth
control pill. . . . I like women, but I find that there is a major nesting
instinct that hits hard and wide." Medical bills were high, the marriage
was running downhill, and Dan and his wife, who had both read *The
Open Marriage,* a best seller at the time, were questioning their mutual
commitment.[5]

A job in Milwaukee looked like the solution, but "once again, she had no choice in where we were going." It was a two-year job with a possibility of renewal, but a politically astute soprano had been hired at the same time to teach on a temporary basis, and she got the continuing appointment. "I did some really good things there," Dan said. "I had some really good students, and I saved their voices. . . . It's one thing to get a job and another thing to hold it. You need someone who tells you, 'Dan, make sure that if you perform somewhere you put your programs in everybody's mailbox.' They don't tell you. I didn't do that, and later I realized they didn't know what I was doing." Dan told these stories with wry humor.

"One of the things I think happened at the university is one of my former students accused me of making a pass at him. I hadn't, but he wanted desperately to be a star. I tried very hard, but he just couldn't sing. He wouldn't listen to what I was telling him, but he had the idea of being up there in spangles and stars, and wouldn't that be wonderful? I think he complained, and what happened is the word got out that I was a—and oddly enough, to be hung for something you didn't do—I could have done it, you know, but I wasn't particularly attracted. I think that killed my academic career. But you could never prove it. And when there are too many people for too few jobs, any kind of taint on your record, you're dead." It was a very bad time to be on the academic job market. The expansion of higher education to accommodate the Baby Boom had overshot the need, so universities were in retrenchment mode, cutting back on hiring, and the turmoil on campuses during the sixties made hiring committees ultracautious.

"I'm sitting here in beautiful downtown Milwaukee," Dan went on, "and I have no job. You know, you have these great friends at the university, but if you're not there and you've been canned, it's like you have the mark of Cain. You have become invisible." While Dan was searching for a job, he was volunteering for a nonprofit, putting together a list of resources for survival for people in the same position.

When Dan got a job as a music teacher in the Milwaukee public school system, "It was a black high school, and the kids had been told they'd have a black teacher. I got there, and here's my honky ass; it was

1971, and I was in the wrong place at the wrong time. And they fought me the whole year. Okay, I failed at the university in a sense, because I wasn't retained, and then I went right out and I failed at this high school. They wouldn't let me teach them. I know they did this on purpose, because one time we were trying to do a few really simple things and I'm sitting there so frustrated, the basses just started singing their line and the tenors came in and the altos came in . . . they could do it without me, and they showed me, but they wouldn't do it for me. It was a real slap to my ego.

"That fall, I also decided to be a vegetarian. That was kind of dumb, because you don't just decide to be a vegetarian. I just started eating vegetables. I almost died. My body didn't make the shifts, and by Thanksgiving I was not well. I was supposed to be doing the Don Basilio part in a production of *The Marriage of Figaro,* and I couldn't—I lost my voice, got a cold, and couldn't sing. So somebody else came and did it. I didn't do many more shows.

"Then about that time, the marriage collapsed. One, two, three, the marriage collapsed over Christmas, the school transferred me, and the court said, 'Move out of the house, and you have to pay x amount.' It was all happening at the same time. What I should have done in retrospect, if I had been healthier, thinking things through right, I should have just packed the kids in the car, gone to Wyoming, established my residency, and divorced her there.

"She was in a funny space; she didn't want to be a faculty wife. She didn't want to show up and be my spouse at church, the choir director's wife. It wasn't that she had to *do* anything, but she decided she just didn't like that. Partly that was the female liberation thing, it was her consciousness-raising. I said, 'Look, I'm not asking you to be entertaining people in the house, all I'm saying is just be my wife.' "

Dan and I had talked about the role of spouses earlier. I had told him that both my husband and I have sometimes felt as if we are treated as appendages of the other. He has on the whole been less willing than I to go through the motions and even tends to take my absence for granted when in fact I might be interested in joining him.

In an e-mail he sent to me before we met, Dan had written, "I was married for 11+ years and the marriage did not collapse on the issue of sexuality. It was more of 'a funny thing happened on the way to Female Liberation.' I am probably one of those in the middle of the Kinsey sex[ual orientation] scale." Actually, in saying that he could have been happy continuing in his marriage, Dan was describing something that potentially made his life harder rather than easier, since there has been a tendency since Stonewall to regard bisexuality as a delusion and to insist that a given individual must be entirely gay or entirely straight.

"So now I'm up to thirty-five," Dan continued, as we sat sipping iced tea in his garden. "Thirty-five, professionally dead, not able to make it in singing, a liability of three hundred dollars a month for upkeep, no place to live. The house sold, and we got all of two thousand dollars out of it because we couldn't make the payments."

With his ex-wife in California with the two children, Dan decided to experience San Francisco. "I didn't know what I was looking for, but the people just weren't there in Milwaukee. I was trying to figure out what I was gonna do with my life, so I sat down and said, What I'd really like to have, I'd like to be living somewhere in the west with a partner, with someone—I didn't say male or female—with a partner, in a house with a garden and a fishpond and fruit trees."

"You got it," I said, looking around.

"I came out here, lived out of a suitcase, went to the baths. I discovered that it didn't snow here, and that was kind of interesting. I wasn't doing a lot of sex, and I was looking around, trying to do something, maybe music, while I was waiting, sending out résumés. I auditioned for some church jobs and didn't get them. I had this Christmas caroling thing, and I did an est [Erhard Seminars Training] course, and I got very interested in that.

"I was experiencing San Francisco a lot, just looking at it. I met a couple of men who were older. I had never met older gays who were fairly good looking and successful and not drunk. I fell in love with one guy, but he liked boys, like fourteen- and fifteen-year-old boys, and I thought, This is a disaster just waiting to happen, I don't wanna be there. And there was another guy who was just screwed up. So I'm in San Francisco and I'm looking around and I heard about a gay fathers' group, and I went there, and that's where I met the doctor I told you about, whose wife was a lesbian and he was gay and they had kids. And it was kind of interesting." By then I had noticed that, when Dan used the word *interesting,* it meant something like "appealing," rather than "odd." "There was another group at the time called G40 and although I was only thirty-eight, I went to this 'gay men over forty' group. It was the time of rap sessions; they'd do consciousness-raising things and they'd rap. So I got there and I met Ted, who died just recently. He was twelve years older, and he was a doctor, too. There were all these guys 'exploring their gay side.'

"Then I got a job with the Alameda County School Department, in a program for the arts in nursing homes. I was basically doing an exercise and music program for old people, a twenty-hour-a-week job. A couple of the nursing homes were really awful, but a couple of them were very good. One woman I remember was so upset one day when I went in; her son had just died. 'He was so young,' she said. 'He was only eighty-two.' Another woman had had five husbands. I got to know these women, but it didn't last very long. You'd go and suddenly one day they wouldn't be there.

"Anyhow, I got proposed to by Ted, so I was living in a very elegant address, high on top of Russian Hill. And it was a very nice existence. But Ted didn't— He was very clear that I didn't get a parking space in the building; I had to park somewhere on the street. There was a second parking space, but that wasn't for me. I could tell it was a very limited kind of relationship. But he provided me with a place to live, and we did a lot of things together. I made his life work. I understood then that rich people need somebody to manage their lives, so a rich man's wife or whatever is the one who stands there waiting for the people to come and clean the curtains or to pay the gardener, to pay the housecleaner or to find another gardener. All that takes time, which they don't have, and you end up doing this kind of stuff. Or, you know, going shopping for food. I did sleep with Ted, but he wasn't a very highly sexed person and he definitely didn't care if I did anything else, and so it was like . . . ookaay."

"What kind of emotional relationship would you have with somebody like that?" I asked.

"It was very stable in one sense. You know, you could care for him. It was a dependable thing. He had the same thing for breakfast every day. If you're in a chaotic situation, something that's stable can be very comforting. The excitement was outside, but you had this sort of stable core, you knew where you were going to sleep and you knew what you were going to eat. I moved into his place in August of 'seventy-seven and moved out the next year.

"That was a different world, San Francisco in the seventies. The plague hadn't hit yet. When the AIDS thing started, I remember they said some of these people have as many as a hundred partners. But I didn't, and I knew people who didn't. But there was a dark side to it. My ex-wife bought a house in Oakland with a small mother-in-law apartment, and a gay man had died there, but nobody missed him—that kind of thing happened to people you knew or heard about."

"People were breaking out," I said. "It was the middle of a revolution."

"It was an odd breaking out because it was done . . . It was a strange revolution, you know. Well, in the meantime, I met Paul."

Paul, I knew, had been Dan's partner before Michael and had left the little property we were sitting in to him when he died of blood poisoning, unrelated to AIDS. While Dan was with Ted, he was doing occasional house-sitting, and one day he threw a big party and Paul, who had just sold his place and was looking for somewhere to stay, turned up. "He was very shy," Dan said, "and had injured his leg. I said, 'Why don't you come and we'll cost-share with each other?' And so we sort of got together, in an apartment in Oakland, and I thought, Well, something like this may really work."

Dan had gotten a real estate license, but in 1980, after Ronald Reagan was elected president, the real estate business soured and interest rates were rising. Meanwhile the alternative energy projects Paul had been working on got canceled, so Dan and Paul both took a ten-week computer programming course at Golden Gate University and became pro-grammers. Paul was in a wheelchair most of the time, so when his grandmother died and left him some money, they bought the little Newark house, which was all on one level, where they lived for a year and a half, until Paul died.

"You probably had to take care of him a lot," I said.

"He required a lot of care, and I didn't mind," Dan said. "He was easy to take care of. You don't mind taking care of somebody who respects you, is light about it, and fun. He'd say, 'Oh, this is the best piece of toast I ever had.' And I would say, 'No, it can't be the best, you can't always be that happy.' Or 'This is the best piece of cake.' That was great. And he was very much into food, and he would read the restaurant reviews and we would go to the good restaurants and that kind of stuff. He was, honestly, just the best. He lived very much in the present in that way, and he was pleasant to be around. He said he didn't want a funeral, but he would have a memorial service if I wanted it, which was in his will. So when we were doing his memorial service, we asked everybody to share something about Paul's odd sense of humor. I still think fondly of it, the best memorial service I've ever been to. People *laughed*. They remembered him well, and then we had some music, an opera singer that we knew. Paul died in 1984. I was devastated. But I thought, You're conscious, you'll get over this, I mean, people die. Get a grip."

As often happens with gay couples, there was friction about Dan's standing after Paul's death. Paul had left the house and a life insurance policy for Dan, but he had stipulated in his will that $25,000 should go to his sister, and he didn't have that amount in cash at the time of his death. The family had not been aware of the relationship or who this roommate was who had been taking care of Paul, and although Dan kicked in about half the needed cash, that was as far as he would go. In the end, he was able to keep the house. By the time of our conversation, he had lived there for twenty-five years, with the yard and the fruit trees and the fishpond.

In 1985 Dan went back to a job he had been laid off from earlier, but the computer language he knew best was going out of usage, so he couldn't get programming work. For a while he rented out rooms in the house, and then he got involved as a volunteer with the Employment Development Department, helping other people get jobs, coaching them on how to handle interviews and what to put into résumés to avoid suspicious gaps.

"In Silicon Valley, jobs come and go like the wind," he said. "I had been raised with the mentality that jobs should last—you got a job and you retired from it thirty years later. I had never had a job last longer than three and a half years, and after a while I'd get so depressed if I lost a job that I'd cry. I'd go to all these job interviews—I mean, going out for sixty jobs, it's an incredible thing to do. And I was counting them."

Dan was in a good position to empathize with others looking for jobs, and ironically, after all this time, he found himself back in the classroom, teaching job seekers how to perform, how to "sing their own songs." This experience as a volunteer may have given him a new confidence in his ability to teach, for since that time he has had jobs as a trainer rather than a programmer, traveling around the country teaching people at corporations that have bought new computer systems how to program and use their equipment and software, always trying to keep ahead of the turnover in the industry.

Dan had referred often to his lack of mentoring, and it struck me that that concern might have helped him become an effective trainer. I wondered, too, whether that experience had been part of his willingness to talk to me about his life, for he had continued his connection with the gay fathers' group and was interested in my questions about his relationships with his children and grandchildren. Early on he had sent me an e-mail in which he wrote about having kept in touch with his ex-wife and their daughter, who lives nearby with her husband of seventeen years and a teenage daughter, and with their son, who is married but has no children so far.

"In 1985," he wrote, "my son at fifteen was having some issues about Daddy and his live-in partner, who had recently died of complications of blood poisoning. You might also guess that it is difficult for my son-in-law to have a gay father-in-law. A friend in the gay fathers' group that I was working with had a son doing a documentary on children of gay parents. It became *Not All Parents Are Straight.* We spent Labor Day weekend taping with my ex-wife and the two kids, and I thought that was the end of it. The thing spent a lot of time rattling around and finally got finished, and in 1987 it was shown at the Roxie in San Francisco. We went up there, thinking it would be a nonevent. We couldn't get in and had to wait for the next showing. It set records for the four showings that day. Sold out each showing. Later it went national and got some good ratings for that kind of show, and for the next three years it was all over the country. It was my fifteen minutes of fame. I was on the road a lot then and ran into it in Wyoming and in Wisconsin, where I was asked if I had been on TV the night before. Well, it was okay. I can talk about being gay, and it can be interesting. You go through a constant process of coming out and redefining yourself. It takes time to put it all together." Before I left Newark, I invited Dan and his granddaughter out to brunch and sat quietly as he tried to get beyond her teenage moodiness and encouraged her to engage with school.

Dan is still attempting to put it together. He still has not found the kind of mentor he was looking for but has begun to work with a life coach. He has had a number of training jobs, but the pattern of turnover in the industry continues, so the jobs that come and go don't fit his model of a career. "After I got laid off the last time, I looked around and I realized that at sixty-three I better try for retirement. A friend of mine was teaching autistic kids down here, and I looked in and said, 'Do you need any assistance with these kids? Could you use a musician?' I thought I'd probably just go down there, and we could sing. The first year it didn't work very well, because I didn't know how to get across to them or which songs would work. Then my sister gave me a book of songs for kids that were about that age, and as I got into it, it got to be kind of an interesting problem to look at and try to work with. Then I started bringing some of the other kids in there, and when you put the other kids in, the autistic kids would come along, and after they had seen what could happen, I could do the same songs with them even if the others weren't there. As I began to work more and more on this, I got into it. So I got to know a couple of the other teachers, and they're kind of fun. So I do this thing, and it's gotten bigger, and now I have all the third graders.

"Again, I'm not getting paid. I thought I should figure out something to do and maybe go back into the school system, where I could do something for money, but part of me wants to be able to say, 'Can't come in today.' And I don't want to have to answer to anybody's 'Are you teaching the curriculum?' Or parents who stand there and say, 'You know, my little girl really needs . . . whatever.' But the worst thing is filling out those god-awful forms. I don't think anybody has ever really calculated how awful the education system has got about filling out forms."

. Dan was obviously enjoying his teaching, but money remained a concern. "I think in retiring you really want to do something for money because if you don't do it for money you don't value yourself. I've sometimes given people voice lessons for free, and they don't listen to you. If they're paying you ninety dollars an hour, they listen. Same thing with massage, you give somebody a free massage, it's all right, but if you charge them—"

"That's what my husband is always telling me," I said, "stop doing things for free because people don't listen. They don't bother to learn from you."

"They don't care. I mean obviously, if it's free it's not worth much. It's valueless by definition."

I asked Dan whether he had picked up any more work singing in churches. "No," he said. "The thing about the church— When I was first with Paul, we were looking around for a church, and they got so obviously nervous that we would join them. I do not understand, but if you don't want me, then you don't get me singing solos every day. I'm not going to force myself on you. If you don't want my gayness—and it isn't that I'm hypergay, you know what I mean? I'll work in the school for nothing but . . . Never mind. Sometimes I miss it, but sometimes I don't. I guess a couple of things I have learned in my life, and one thing is, if people don't respect you, you don't need to give it away for nothing.

"So, the religion thing. Religion was very important to me early on, and it's still kind of there. It's like we're spiritual but nonchurchgoers. I meditate every day. When my mother was still alive, she kept lobbying for me to get back into the church, but she didn't push it."

Dan went on to talk about the importance of having friends, which is an issue for many older adults, and he began speaking about losing friends to AIDS. "You need friends that you can move on with. It happens to us all in the gay community and particularly in San Francisco. There've been I don't know how many out of my phone book from the first few years. I've never figured out quite why it was so virulent in the beginning, but I think that the virus must have been nastier then than it is now, because it doesn't seem to hit people as hard anymore. At first people would get sick and die within weeks, and they don't do that now." We spoke briefly about the "AIDS cocktail" and the progress that has been made in making it possible to live with the virus much longer, but only at the cost of taking strong drugs that are ultimately hard on the body.

Michael has retired from the National Park Service but gets called on for short-term consulting work in historic preservation, so both Michael and Dan have occasional paid work that follows an unpredictable pattern. Although they do not live in an overtly gay neighborhood, like the Castro in San Francisco, they socialize primarily with gay and lesbian friends and are thoughtful about the problems of isolation that others face and the ways in which aging affects members of their community.

As I think about Dan and Michael, my mind goes back to his one-time ambition, to live "somewhere in the west with a partner, . . . in a house with a garden and a fishpond and fruit trees." Dan has adapted and readapted to circumstances; he has not achieved the standard labels of success, but all in all he has an enviable and even admirable life. And he's kept his sense of humor.

CHAPTER VIII

A Time for Wholeness

THERE IS A STORY told of St. Thomas Aquinas that one day after years of labor he returned from Mass, simply stopped working on his *Summa Theologica,* and never resumed. When his assistant, Reginald, urged him to continue, he is said to have replied, "I can do no more. Such secrets have been revealed to me that all I have written now appears to be of little value."[1] "Mere chaff" was the translation I first heard.

Religious orientations, like other forms of human engagement, seem to take different forms at different stages of the life cycle, as ardor ebbs and flows or as time becomes more or less available for reflection. One of the most common versions of this pattern suggests a turning toward things of the spirit in later life, which does not necessarily mean toward formal religion and may or may not be valued by the community. Hinduism, for instance, affirms that after a man has passed through the stages of the student and the householder, he may withdraw from society to meditate and live as an ascetic or join India's mendicant holy men or *saddhus.* In the Islamic tradition, which calls for a once-in-a-lifetime pilgrimage to Mecca, this pilgrimage is often taken in late middle age, after which the returning *hajji*, deeply moved by the experience, is more devout and regular in his prayers.

The theme of spirituality in later adulthood is not limited to cultures with a belief in some form of afterlife or reincarnation, nor is it limited to individuals close to death. Rather, this deferral suggests that, during the first three decades of adulthood and child rearing, a preoccupation with material affairs is appropriate and to be expected, a long haul of necessary practicality before the period when "your old men shall dream dreams," but after "your young men shall see visions" (Joel 2:28), even as the adults of the society maintain its necessary rituals and institutions. It may also reflect cognitive changes, such as a wider and more inclusive perspective, greater tolerance for ambiguity, and even biological changes, such as decreased hormonal activity and greater congruence between male and female. Institutional or doctrinal concerns that once seemed important may become less so, while contemplation becomes more central. This story about St. Thomas Aquinas is especially interesting because it is the story not of someone converted in later life, like St. Augustine, but of someone suddenly drawn deeper into an earlier commitment. Such a story tests the notion of a through line in a given life story with an apparently abrupt shift; yet on examination one can see at least as much continuity as discontinuity.

In 2007 I was at a Lindisfarne conference held at a Zen Buddhist monastery, the home of the Prajna Mountain Buddhist Order in New Mexico, when I was approached by Jane Fonda, who has a home near Santa Fe. She told me that she wanted to interview me for a book she was writing on aging, and I laughed and said that I, too, was writing a book on aging, so perhaps we should interview each other. I find it interesting that, whereas I tend to use the life cycle metaphor of Erik Erikson, Fonda uses a theatrical metaphor, speaking of her years in movies and anti–Vietnam war activism as her "second act" and the years since she turned sixty as her "third act." In the story of her life, the third act has been a time of spiritual deepening.

Jane Fonda in her sixties is lithe and brisk. Her beauty seems a matter more of vitality than of sensuality, and she is clear-eyed and decisive. We spoke for only a few minutes that day, but the following spring, she came to stay with me in New Hampshire, where we sat together with two tape recorders running and took turns exchanging questions. The scene reminded me of the saying that, during the years of poverty and famine, Irish villagers survived by the women taking in each other's laundry. But I have learned that writers, including me, often interview other writers, finding them quick to understand the kind of material we want.

A wise friend had warned me in the meantime not to hand over all my best ideas and anecdotes, and had indeed suggested a way to plan for these sessions so that I would be following a script of what I wanted or did not want to share. As I prepared myself for our project, however, it became clear to me that it is more important to me to get my thinking into the cultural mainstream than to have my name on it. Like many women, I have had the experience of saying something in a meeting that is apparently ignored and then having some male colleague repeat the idea as his own half an hour later and get confirmation. I confess that, from time to time, when I want to get something done or an idea heard, I have explained it to some senior male before the meeting, saved myself the trouble of trying to be heard, and watched happily as the suggestion was accepted. You work with what you find. Jane and I will reach different people and put things together in different ways.

At some level, I do not believe that ideas are property. I believe they are bread to be cast on the waters. I write in the hope of having a significant impact on the culture and on the way we think, not only about aging but about making wise decisions in an endangered and dangerous world. I want to get these concerns into as many minds as possible, so that we will be working together toward solutions. I believe that my basic concept of composing a life has had a useful impact on many people, and it doesn't bother me when it floats back as "constructing a life" or "designing a life."

The best way to affect people's behavior is for them to take ownership of an idea or set of ideas, and in order to bring about cultural change, it is important that ideas seem to converge from multiple sources. Then, too, I try to avoid interviews where one person is getting something from the other without giving, so the concept of an explicit reciprocity was interesting, and I happily moved out of the role of neutral interviewer, exchanging experiences and aspirations.

Jane Fonda was a significant figure to me during my youth, often in the news as an actor and antiwar activist. Two memories popped into my mind when I met her. One was that at one time she had considered playing my mother, Margaret Mead, in a movie, and I had said that not only was she much taller than my mother but it would be hard for a tall person to play a short person who thinks she is taller than she is—too many layers. I did not discover until I met her that Jane herself is not particularly tall (she is five foot seven, an inch taller than I am, not five foot ten as I had imagined). That was my own projection. But she still has some five inches on my mother.

Fame is a paradoxical commodity. The other memory concerned Marlon Brando, the only other movie star I had met (I did meet Richard Gere at Davos in a small group discussing AIDS prevention in Africa, but only in passing). Brando had apparently confided in his psychoanalyst, an acquaintance of my mother's, that he had daydreamed of going to the South Pacific, especially Samoa, and wanted to meet her (his daydream may have led to his role in *Mutiny on the Bounty* and the purchase of a small Polynesian island years later). I was thirteen or so, and my mother assumed that I had a crush on Brando—I didn't, but some of my friends did—so she said she would be willing to meet him if I could come along. Off we went to an apartment he had in New York at the time, where there was a not quite party going on, a record player and a dozen people talking and drinking in a desultory way, getting up in pairs from time to time to dance.

It was a cold, drizzly evening. There had been four or five teenage girls waiting outside the building when we arrived, and it had felt very strange being ushered in past them as they stood there, wet and bedraggled, drooping with fatigue. So as the evening progressed, when Brando politely asked me to dance, I asked him instead to come to the front door with me and give the girls autographs. Astonished but compliant, he came downstairs with me, but they had given up and gone, and he then quizzed me for half an hour about why on earth I would care about them, with that extraordinary combination of curiosity and naïveté that actors sometimes show about the motivations of others, but without empathy for his disappointed fans.

When we met, Jane's antiwar history interested me more than her movies, for I had been involved in the antinuclear movement as a student, before the focus shifted to Vietnam. I knew she had been involved in feminist causes as well, which meant that she was yet another woman who had discovered feminism in the seventies and was now writing about aging. To me that made her an especially important person to talk to, for I had been wondering where all the passion and ideological commitment of the sixties had migrated and whether I was correct in believing that the activism of youth would reappear in combination with the wisdom and judgment of age. Jane remains engaged, passionate, seeking.

Gradually I learned that, although it fell into different chapters, Jane's activism was lifelong, growing out of a sustained conviction that her efforts could "make it better," whatever *it* was at a given time. At the point when we met, I had seen only two of her movies; she had read one of my books, *Composing a Life*. Our lives were lived on different tracks, yet it was no accident that we met in a Buddhist monastery and that much of our conversation revolved around spirituality. A year later, over three days of working together in New Hampshire, Jane and I built the foundations of a genuine friendship that was followed up again in Santa Fe and then in New York, where she was back on Broadway in 2009.

Jane Fonda was born in New York City, two years before me, in December 1937. She was drawn into acting as the result of appearing with her movie star father, Henry Fonda, in a community theater production. Her first film role was at the age of twenty-one and a whole series of roles followed, winning her two Oscars and five Oscar nominations, as well as a seven-year marriage to the French director

Roger Vadim. By the 1970s, she had become involved in the antiwar movement and married Tom Hayden. She married her third husband, Ted Turner, in 1991, and shifted her activism to women's issues, including teenage pregnancy in Georgia, where she and Turner lived. She went back to Hollywood after their divorce in 2001 to make *Monster-in-Law.*

All of this is easy enough to find on Google, but what Jane said to me was "I have been an 'award-winning actor' all of my adult life, but I'm realizing it's not who I am. I had defined myself by externals, praise, applause, awards, all those kinds of things. And I realized when I was entering my third act—I was still married to Ted for the first two years of my third act, from sixty to sixty-two—that I had to redefine my locus of well-being if I wasn't going to be miserable."

In our New Hampshire conversations, Jane expanded on this period of rethinking her identity, no easy task after such a public life. As she spoke of the extent to which she had been determined by the men she was with, it seemed to me that each of her marriages evoked different but intrinsic potentials, each expressed in a revised identity but each reflecting only a part of her. She seems to have been trying to find someone who sees her as she is—the verb she uses for this is *countenance,* with an idiosyncratic emphasis that goes beyond the dictionary meaning of accepting and tolerating, to genuinely recognizing and acknowledging the other, knowing and being known, no longer "through a glass, darkly; but then face to face" (1 Cor. 13:12). I found myself connecting the importance she gives to "countenancing" another to the issue of eye contact in interactions.

"The reason I know that an 'award-winning actor' is not who I am is because, if that was who I am, I would have been miserable when I had left my career to be with Ted," Jane explained. "I was also defined by how I looked, but moving on was not as hard for me as it was for other actors who have been very identified with beauty and youth and all that. I'm told that I was, too, but I never really owned that. You know, leaving the 'good old days' was not so hard for me because they were really so-so old days. When I was trying to inhabit an exterior that I didn't really own, that was hard. And as I was getting older, I was suddenly feeling that I could move back into myself. There's something to be said for having that happen later in life.

"Well, during my ten years with Ted, which reached from about fifty-two to sixty-two, I began to change. I knew that I was becoming much more internal, much more introspective and spiritual, which I had never been in my life. And I felt a need to begin to alter the way we lived to be more vertical than horizontal. We were skimming along the surface. I wanted to start drilling down more, and he couldn't, because his locus of well-being came from outside, and mine was shifting to in here." Jane touched her chest, indicating her heart. "I wasn't sure how I would answer the question Who am I? but I began to know how *not* to answer it, and I tried to tell him."

Turner was not receptive, and he responded to Jane's search almost as if it were an act of defiance or infidelity. "He is a man who doesn't like surprises," she said, "and this took him by surprise." Judging by Jane's description of his whirlwind courtship, Turner also seems to be a man who knows what he wants and goes after it, determined to possess it, and now suddenly Jane was revealing a side of herself that no other person could claim to own. Men are often jealous even of their own children and of the maternal devotion of their wives. "When you decide to move back and take up residence in your skin again," Jane said, "when that happens and you're conscious of it happening, it's beautiful. It's beautiful."

A search for the relationship between spirituality and age was clearly an important aspect of Jane's interest in her forthcoming book, and she began to ask me questions about my own experience and what I might know as an anthropologist about differences in spiritual development across the life cycle. I told her my story, describing my own history as having been both more connected to institutional religion than hers and more contemplative at earlier stages. I am not comfortable with the sharp distinction that has become common between "religion" as institutional and external forms and "spirituality" as personal prayer and meditation. I know that these are phenomena that can occur separately, but each seems to me now to be barren and easily corrupted without the other. I spoke to Jane about wandering alone in the woods in childhood, filled with awe and wonder but not knowing where to go with that experience or how to connect it to visits to museums of art, poetry read aloud at the breakfast table, or the occasions when I had been taken to church.

One of the things that my mother believed was that if children have shared the experiences of worship with a group of believing, engaged adults, they will have the capacity to empathize and participate later in life, so she wanted me beside her rather than in a Sunday school class, where I might memorize easily forgotten bits of doctrine with no connection to experience.

"So your mother didn't believe in indoctrinating children? That's no surprise," Jane said.

"No," I said. "But, you know, I've realized that there were quiet ways in which she made sure that I wasn't—how should I say?—culturally deprived, illiterate about religion. I think that makes a lot of sense. It makes sense that children should participate in the events and processes that adults feel are significant. I believe in taking children to the polls to see adults vote, and to funerals. That's actually one of the things that concerns me about some of the spiritual communities that have sprung up in this country, that some of them don't have a model for how children are brought in. It's like the relationship between Islam and Sufism. Islam is the religion of a full community, and Sufism is for a minority of self-selected adults who want to follow a particular spiritual path within Islam. The gateway is through the wider tradition that you meet as a child, that you may leave behind but you never fully reject. When I look at spiritual communities in this country, of the kind that grew up in the sixties—let's say Zen communities—I can see that they came from the more specialized parts of wider traditions, and I don't think they always do a good job of figuring out how to include children. Because, of course, they tend in this country to have couples, to have children growing up.

"Incidentally, that's one of the things that I like about the Vietnamese Zen Buddhist teacher Thich Nhat Hanh, that he reaches out to the children of the people that come to hear him. Now that doesn't mean that those children will grow up to follow that particular path, but it does suggest that, if you want to think of the life of the spirit, you have to think of a full lifetime, not something that only adults pursue. And heaven knows, the sense of wonder that you have as a child is something you would like to preserve into your adult spirituality."

"Do you think that in the last third of life there is a special role for spirituality?" Jane asked. "This is something I feel, but maybe it's just my personal experiences because this has happened to me later in life. Somehow, the slowing down and the deterioration of the exterior along with the proximity of death encourage us to go inward. And the going inward changes how we view things. Have you experienced that, or do you feel that's a part of the third act? Ram Dass [a spiritual teacher and author, born Richard Alpert] says the role of elders is to move away from ego into soul."

"I'm not sure," I said. "I mean, yeah, many traditions do specialize spirituality in old age. But, looking at the way Erikson spoke about the search for identity and idealism in youth, these are spiritual issues, too. I think we fail to offer access to spirituality to a lot of adolescents, but they're struggling with spiritual issues. Surely the soul develops at other stages, too. I think childbearing— Well, I've given birth twice. My first child was premature and died. And my whole spiritual sense about those experiences and about breast feeding and so on was very power- ful. Breast feeding has been for me a kind of model for self-giving. I think it changes the way you feel about the ownership of your own body when your body is nourishing another being. So, I think there are probably forms of spirituality that are appropriate to every stage of the life cycle. But we may not have our educational system and our child- rearing patterns set up in a way that nurtures that. Think of the Native American vision quest, for instance; that's an adolescent or even pre- adolescent experience, built in by culture.

"That said, I think it's fair to ask whether there are kinds of spiritu- ality that make more sense as you get older. And I suppose one would ask about solitude versus being part of a group, or about healing and advising. I have time on my mind a lot—whether we can contribute a long-term perspective. I also think Erikson is right about a greater inclusiveness of vision. That's a very important part of where we're trying to go."

I realize as I review the transcripts of our conversations that sometimes I was lecturing to the tape recorder. But Jane's attention and curiosity were intense. There is a real similarity between actors and anthropologists in that both try to inhabit multiple worlds and to understand the experiences and motivations of people living different lives. Jane's academic education consisted of two years at Vassar before she dropped out, but it was clear from her many references that, when she takes on a role, she both tries to meet with people who have lived the kind of life she is going to depict and also reads widely. Method acting, in which she was trained by Lee Strasberg, involves intense interior search—a capacity for introspection that a mystic might envy. Her activism is also based on an intense effort to understand the people she is concerned with, whether they are Vietnam veterans or teenage girls. In her autobiography she says, "I've learned over the years that for me to want to study, it can't be the generic liberal arts approach. I have to understand *why* I am learning, *what* I am learning for, have to feel the *need* to learn because it relates in a palpable way to my life, to what I am *doing.*"[2]

I had been drawn to faith earlier than Jane, but my sixties were also a time of return. I had chosen to be baptized and confirmed in the Episcopal Church (my mother was an Episcopalian, my father a determined atheist, institutionally at least) when I was fourteen. My mother believed that children should have some exposure not so much to doctrine but to worship and to the accretion of awe and devotion around ritual forms that would provide an empathic basis for recognizing and responding to faith later in life. This seems to be part of a larger principle that has been important to me, that instead of standing on the sidelines and studying, the way to learn is through participation.

I had grown up going to church from time to time with my mother and more frequently with her close college friend, whom I called Aunt Marie and with whom I spent many weekends in my childhood. She taught me the Lord's Prayer. More important, I knew that my mother had grown up in an unchurched family and made her own decision to be baptized just before turning eleven, and that she had maintained her membership in her childhood parish all her life. I also knew that my father had specified, when I was born, that I not be baptized. My mother had told me that the choice was one I should make myself, however, whenever I was ready, conveying to me her own seriousness and the sense that the choice was an important one. As a child, I developed a wide-ranging curiosity about religion, going to different kinds of services with my classmates and choosing topics related to religion for term papers, so apparently I had understood that this was a responsibility that lay ahead. There was a small reproduction of a Raphael Madonna and Child, in a gilt frame, on a bureau in my bedroom, which my mother gave me for some early birthday. After my parents separated and my father remarried, he brought his father's art collection from England and hung a watercolor by William Blake, *Satan Triumphing over Eve*, on his living room wall. Satan, the fallen angel, still beautiful, wears a look of deep sadness.

Still, I had only the vaguest idea what Christianity was supposed to be about, as I discovered with some surprise while dutifully reading a set of books in preparation for baptism. I knew the stories of Jesus' life and sayings, but I had no notion of how these beautiful and moving stories (like the music and ritual of Sunday mornings) were supposed to be connected to the lives and choices of people today, or how Christians have struggled to understand who Jesus was and how His fate could have established a new relationship between God and humankind. I had become used to hearing the term *Son of God* and the words *redemption* and *atonement* without ever having struggled with their meanings. So I had homework to do. I suppose I was as serious about the whole thing as I was capable of being at that stage of my life.

Two years later, I went on what was intended as a two-week visit to Israel with my mother, who had been invited as a consultant on the assimilation of immigrants, and I decided to stay for a year, learn Hebrew, and complete high school there. I noticed the disappearance of church from my life at Christmas with a pang of homesickness, but I was deep in the study of the Hebrew Bible and Hebrew literature for my Israeli matriculation exams. The old curiosity about anything to do with religion stood me in good stead as I worked my solitary way through fat commentaries and visited in households with differing relationships to Judaism. *The Book of Job*, the poetry of Haim Nahman Bialik, Hasidic tales, and the longings of the Diaspora haunted me for years and are with me still.

My curiosity was still there when I returned to the United States for college at Radcliffe, which by then shared all Harvard classes. I studied Arabic and Islam and Rabbinical texts and wrote my general education papers on related questions, but put Christianity on a back shelf for five years. Eventually, after I graduated and was married, with a husband for whom Christianity was an important part of his Armenian identity, I decided that I had to figure out what, if anything, this church membership that I had chosen as a teenager might mean beyond pleasant customs shared at Christmas and Easter.

I have no idea what triggered this process—perhaps it was the fact that Barkev asked me to make sure that, on the morning of our wedding, I took an hour to get away from the hullabaloo and sit in an empty church. Perhaps it was adopting the prayer said in Armenian by his family before every meal, a custom we carried into our marriage. What I decided to do was start where I had left off, with the Episcopal Church, and explore what would happen if I behaved "as if" I believed, going to church, taking time to think and read, and experimenting with prayer, as if I had faith in someone listening. Some instinct or some echo of my mother's belief that participation was the place to start made me begin with practice rather than theology.

So while I was working on my doctorate and in my first year's teaching at Harvard, I went through what I think of now as the real process of conversion. Going through the motions gradually acquired deeper and deeper meaning. I became actively engaged, working with the student chaplain at Harvard and tending toward "high church" or Anglo-Catholicism in ways that made my husband fairly uncomfortable, but even so we began to go together to the Episcopal church in Peterborough when we were in New Hampshire.

In 1966 we went to the Philippines, where I taught at a Jesuit university, and while there I fell into the habit of attending the campus daily Mass, had long conversations with Jesuit friends, and organized a retreat for women faculty. By the time we left, I was very close to becoming a Roman Catholic. One reason I did not was that the rector of the Episcopal church in Peterborough, Al Kershaw, whom both of us liked, had become rector of Emmanuel Church in Boston, a once wealthy but now dwindling church that he was struggling to reinvigorate. That opened a door to a church commitment that the two of us could share.

We went to live in Iran in 1972. On Sundays I took our daughter, Vanni, with me to the Episcopal church there, but without the music and invigorating preaching at Emmanuel, Barkev had no interest, so the compromise that had taken us to the same church in Boston, albeit with differing understandings of what and why, didn't carry over. Weekdays, I found my way from time to time to one of the two English-language Roman Catholic churches in Tehran, St. Abraham's, run by three Irish Dominicans, one of whom was also bishop of Isfahan, his diocese including all of Iran, the other being mostly American military families. In 1976 I went to St. Abraham's and asked to be received into the Catholic Church.

I took Vanni with me because otherwise she would have had no religious context at all. I did my best to explain to her what was happening, but she was six, and we were in a Muslim country, where the differences between Christians simply did not loom large in people's minds (and why should we emphasize them?). I did not see the transition as a rejection of a false or invalid form of Christianity. For me it was a movement from a side stream into the main flow of the river, deeper, more universal, but the same water of life. Because I felt that, on balance, I had benefited from the fact that my mother thought it important to give me some experience of church in childhood and then let me find my own way, I never pushed it with Vanni. As time went on, it seemed to me that those experiences simply didn't "take" for her or that she had rejected them or found them irrelevant.

In 1978 Iran was swept by revolution, and early in 1979 I came back to the United States with Vanni, while Barkev stayed on for another year as I tried to find a job and resume our American lives. I found a job as dean of the faculty at Amherst College, and Vanni and I moved to Amherst, Massachusetts. The story of what happened next, as I lost that job in our third year there, after the sudden death of the college president, Julian Gibbs, is told in *Composing a Life*.[3] But another part of that story is that, on the day before Julian's death, I rolled my car on an icy turn on the way up to New Hampshire, and after my dog and I had crawled out, basically unhurt, and I had inspected my bruises, gotten a passerby to call the police, and sorted out towing, I realized that at no time in that sequence had I turned to God either for help or in thanksgiving for my safety. This seemed to me to prove that I had never believed in Him at all. I think I lost faith not in God but in myself as someone capable of faith. I told myself I had been deceiving myself and others, and without discussion I simply dropped out. There is a fallacy in taking one's own psychological state as either a proof or a disproof of faith, but I didn't notice it.

Right after that, the roof fell in, my job at Amherst fell apart, and I had let go of sustenance I needed at the worst possible time. I was away from the church for more than twenty years, often longing to come back, sometimes beginning to pray, and then saying to myself, "Who are you kidding, you can't possibly mean this, come off it." And quite unable to talk about it.

I did fit into Jane's model in the sense that one of the threads of my life that came back into focus as I grew older was my faith, which I had thought totally abandoned. As the twentieth century wound down, I had taken one small step toward return by starting to attend Quaker meeting as a way of spending that hour on Sunday mornings in the presence of God and open to whatever clarity might come. I was dipping my foot in the water, rereading things that had been important to me years before, revisiting the Episcopal Church, beginning tentatively to pray, becoming more and more clear that I would come back but not quite knowing where or how. In 2006 I went for surgery to remove a colloid cyst in my brain, and I thought surely I would be asked for a religious preference when I checked into the hospital and a chaplain would turn up and I would have a chance to figure this all out— hospitals used to be more leisurely—but instead I was on some kind of conveyor belt to the OR, finding my own words of faith and contrition as best I knew how. And then, after the surgery, still procrastinating.

Finally, five months later, at the age of sixty-six, I met with one of the Jesuit religious counselors at Boston College, where I had a visiting scholar appointment that was about to expire. I chose that course, and indeed had embraced the connection to BC, because of the Jesuits I had known in the Philippines. Welcomed and reconciled, with a sense of the gentle but firm working of grace over a long period, I felt my understanding of what had happened and what I had been doing in the meantime shifting like tectonic plates as I regained a lost sense of underlying continuity. I also realized that my return must include a new degree of engagement, engagement in a parish community.

When Jane spoke in more detail about her own journey toward Christianity, it seemed clear that for her the relationship between an internal pilgrimage and a supportive community had been hard to establish and was still in flux. "When my second marriage ended, my friends all said, 'Stay busy.' I knew that that wasn't right," she said, "and really for the first time in my life I was intentionally quiet. I kept working out because I knew the endorphins would keep me from completely going under, but I couldn't eat, I couldn't move, I could hardly speak above a whisper. If I moved, it was very slowly. So I was very still, and one day, I remember it very clearly, I thought, If God wants me to suffer, there's got to be a reason. It was like, Who? Is that me? And the complexion of my pain began to change. I felt strongly that I was being called to go through this, and that there was a reason for it.

"Then what began to happen was what I could only describe as coincidences. It was like pieces of a puzzle coming together, you know. A person that I had never met before that I absolutely needed to know would come into my life, or someone would give me a book, or . . . Bill Moyers quoted Einstein as saying, 'Coincidence is God's way of remaining anonymous.' And I thought, I am being called to accept God.

"Right then I met Ted, who brought me to Georgia. I had never lived in a place where people practiced a religion, ever. Only some of my Jewish friends in Hollywood went to temple and celebrated the Sabbath and so forth, but other than that . . . it was not part of my life, not part of my culture."

"Illiterate," I said, referring to the loss of contact with any religious history and tradition that has become common in American and European society and that I had been protected against.

"Yes, I was illiterate," Jane said. "And now I find myself in Georgia! I wasn't feeling the presence of God, but it became a sort of an intellectual thing. It was hard to feel the presence of God being in Ted's presence because he drowns everything out—he is an atheist, or at least he was until recently. But I was being exposed to people that he knew in his business world, and I began to talk to them and ask questions. Then, when I was about fifty-eight or fifty-nine years old, I started to feel a call to faith, and it felt very strong, and it was this— I had this feeling of being guided.

"I talked to different people, and I just . . . I wanted a container for it. That's when I asked this woman, Nancy, who was the wife of a Turner Broadcasting executive, 'to bring me to Christ,' although I didn't really know what that meant. It happened too soon, and it was not the right context; fundamentalist Christianity was not what I was looking for. Nancy has a very large Bible study class, about four hundred women, huge. I went to it later on, and I had to flee. So I've done everything backwards."

"We've both done some things backwards," I said, "but can you tell me the story again? We were talking in the car, and I don't think we got it on tape."

"Okay. I've written about it, too. I was realizing that I believed in

God, and it was hard for me because my father was so opposed, but I knew that this was becoming something that was important to me. I asked Andy Young to have breakfast with me, and I told him the story, and he said, 'The Greek word for saved is *whole*, and you are whole, you have been saved.' It felt facile to me then, that answer. Then I asked my friend about it and told her the story, and she said, 'What being saved meant to me when it happened was taking the next step.'

"Well, you don't say that to me. If you are offering me to take the next step in just about anything, I will do it, just to do it." One of Jane's most striking and enduring characteristics is her decisiveness. As a young woman protesting the war in Vietnam, Jane threw herself into action, going to Hanoi, occasionally doing something she eventually regretted, like posing beside a Vietcong antiaircraft gun without considering how the picture might later be interpreted, so her swiftness can sometimes be a problem, but how much more powerful it is than the tendency to dither that overtakes some of us as we get older.

Jane continued her description of asking her friend to bring her to Christ. "So I said, 'Okay, help me take the next step.' And she gave me the Gospel of John, which I found extremely moving—and that was it. I read that, and then she brought me into the chapel at the Peachtree Presbyterian Church. And we knelt in front of the altar and I was weeping, I was very moved.

"By now Ted and I have split up. He was very angry about the Christianity. He said to me once, 'If you had to choose me or your faith, what would you choose?' And I said, 'My faith,' and he was very angry. I don't blame him, because I hadn't discussed it with him. I was so fragile in terms of the strength and depth of my beliefs, I knew that if I did, he, who was the head of the debating team at Brown, would talk me out of it. And most of what he would say I would agree with, that religion has been the cause of wars and deaths and hypocrisy and all those things, and I completely agree. And yet there was something happening in me that I treasured and I didn't want him to tromp all over, so I did not discuss it with him. So it was a fait accompli, which was not good for him.

"Anyway, I didn't like the group Bible study class, so I began to go once a week to this woman's house and do Bible study with her, under-lining passages and homework and charts; it was— I felt myself go dry. I felt the reverence evaporate, and I told her I had to stop.

"Meantime, the man that had driven us to the church that day went on a national radio show and said that he had 'brought Jane Fonda to Christ.' Then, before I knew it, Cal Thomas (the right-wing Christian syndicated journalist Doubting Thomas) was writing articles saying that he had a hard time believing that Hanoi Jane would become a Christian and so forth. It was really horrible. You know, I was not in a position where I could defend my faith, and yet I didn't want to say, No, it's not true. It is true, and I do feel born again, but I didn't want to be associated with what those words have come to mean. And it was all over the place. I must have gotten a dozen Bibles in the mail, and peo-ple would come up to me in airports and give me little slips of Scripture and letters. It was amazing, but where I was coming from was not what they were assuming. I went with Cal Thomas to the National Prayer Breakfast in Washington, and I thought, I don't feel at home here.

"Okay, I thought, I've got to figure out what my home is then, because I don't want to renounce this. I said, I'm going to have to go back to scratch and study. . . . I had not even read the Bible in full. That's when I enrolled in the Interdenominational Theological Center in Atlanta. Not for long, because I got a job to do a movie called *Monster-in-Law*. But I was there for part of a semester and did my homework, and I loved it, just loved it. I want to go back there. The problem is, I travel so much that it's hard to get any kind of consistent study. I began to read Elaine Pagels and Karen King, and the Gnostic Gospels.[4]

"So I'm a work in progress, and I've sort of moved, although they don't seem to be contradictory to me, from prayer to meditation. Ted and I split up on January 3, 2000, and I moved with my dog into a little house my daughter has in a nongentrified part of Atlanta, while she was in Paris, a little guest room that had no closet. I was very sad because I had wanted the marriage to work, and yet I knew that it was right that I didn't stay. I knew that I could have stayed and not had to work and died married, but I wouldn't have died whole. I felt myself becoming . . . moving back into myself. I was conscious of it, and I knew that what I heard myself saying again was, This is God. This is what we are meant to be, and it's what Jesus preached, it's what he taught. Wholeness. Not perfection. Wholeness."

"Very different," I said. "You know, in Hebrew, the word *shalom*, 'peace,' comes from the same root as the word *shalem*, which means 'complete.' It's another one of these linkages like *holy, holistic, whole*, where you can follow the track of people's understanding unfolding in the connections between words and yet the words get debased as people use them without thinking about their meaning."

"They get ironed flat," said Jane. "Now my Bible study teacher, the woman who saved me, would say that what I'm experiencing in [Zen] meditation is— I don't know, she's a very wonderful woman. She wouldn't say it's false but that it doesn't count in a way, but I— It's a somatic experience for me. I feel a lot of the time now the way I used to feel only when I was by myself at the top of a mountain or in the woods. I feel the presence of God. I feel reverence, humming within me. And I feel it when I'm meditating, and I feel it when I'm reading Scripture, when I'm trying to sort out my religious feelings. There have been times when I thought I should be an Episcopalian. I like the ritual. And other times when I felt guilty about that, because I don't have the depth of understanding of what it means and I don't stay anyplace long enough to really get into it, so I'm a little bit confused, . . . which seems ridiculous at seventy, but . . . I should have it all straightened out by now."

"No way," I said. "The divisions between the denominations of Christianity are all wrong. They are competing versions of one truth, and we ought to be able to think in terms of that one truth and not go around with one little sect saying to people in the other little sect that they're going to Hell. It has a lot to do with issues of power and control and competition and all that. And it's obscene."

As I have thought back over Jane's story, I have been fascinated by a word she used, that she was looking for a "container" for her developing spirituality, a context in which to plant and cultivate the beginnings of faith. I took this to mean that she understood the need to situate herself in a community and in a historical tradition. But her early efforts had confronted her with rejection rather than affirmation. I could see why the Episcopal Church attracted her.

"The great strength of the Episcopal Church," I told her, "has been what is called the Anglican compromise, though recently that's looking pretty ragged. After Henry VIII broke with Rome, things went back and forth for over a century, sometimes violently, with martyrs and countermartyrs and general hatefulness in both directions. When Elizabeth I became queen, she reasserted the authority of the crown over the English church, but in the Act of Uniformity of 1559 she affirmed norms of governance and liturgy that eventually provided a viable long-term model for coexistence, with a prayer book that carried on the tradition and the structure of ordination, bishops, and so on, which became the Episcopal Church in the United States, with a sort of acceptance of local variation and of the fact that people might have different preferences and understandings. You couldn't standardize the thing. I think that's critical, simply knowing that when people said the same words, they didn't mean the exact same thing to everybody. Now, for me it's self-evident that they can't mean the same thing to everybody. But in spite of the possibility for conflict that's always been there, it's been pretty resilient.

"For a while Barkev and I had our own version of the Anglican compromise and went to Episcopal churches, he coming from evangelical Protestantism brought to the Armenians by Congregationalist missionaries, and me being what Episcopalians call high church. And there was room for both of us. But it was really because of a particular priest. Al Kershaw was a southerner and a superb preacher. He'd won money on *The $64,000 Question* on the subject of jazz, and after he did that, he thought he would go and be in a small country parish and not be in the city. He was a real scholar of jazz and brought musicians from New Orleans to play in Peterborough."

"Here?" Jane asked.

"Here in New Hampshire. Inspiring and funny and paradoxical.

And incredibly expressive. You know, people would come out of church and he would hug them and pick them up and swing them around. So we both loved him dearly. Eventually he left Peterborough and came down to Boston, where he at Emmanuel Church created the best music program at any church in the city. So while the theology wasn't of so much interest to Barkev, the preaching and the music were important to him. And Al was also very much of a social activist. He was going to take this blue-blood, WASPy church that was dwindling in membership and get it involved with urban renewal and social change and generally shaking things up. We were both involved in that, leading discussion groups and so on. Barkev was on the vestry for a while. Vanni was baptized there.

"But it really depended on that one person. So basically, after we left Boston to go to Iran, Barkev was not interested in going to church and began to get annoyed that I went. But there was that period when we had our 'Anglican compromise,' where I could find what I needed and he was finding what he wanted, and we were doing it together."

"It's interesting how you describe it," Jane said, "because when I was going to church in Atlanta, I tried many churches, and the only church I felt comfortable in was the black Baptist church. They have a fabulous preacher, also, with a lot of social engagement and great music. And that's where I went, until the reporters discovered I was there, and then I couldn't go anymore because reporters would come. But I liked that. It seems . . . the faith that comes from oppression seems to vibrate with me more."

Each of us, apparently, had had difficulty in integrating personal experience into a larger community. But community is an ideal that has always been part of the Christian tradition, in spite of all the schisms and divisions. If Alfred North Whitehead is right in saying that religion is "what an individual does with his own solitariness,"[5] a quote often used to argue against organized religion, then what we are called to do with that solitariness is to let go of it and realize that we are not solitary, to weave the threads of personal experience, including experiences in different contexts, into the fabric of community even as we embrace the knowledge that we are not alone.

Jane continues to be interested in acting, and philanthropy is important to her as she continues to work through her foundation with programs for teenage girls, based on the conviction that population can be stabilized if young women are educated to have a sense of their own value and ability to contribute—a basis for hope. In 2009, she was back on Broadway, in *33 Variations,* a play in which she starred as a musicologist trying to understand why Beethoven wrote so many variations on a single theme. The playwright, Moisés Kaufman, was clearly inviting the audience to make a connection between themes in music and the thematic structure of lives—the lives of the composer and the musicologist, the place of creativity and selection, the ways in which an individual, looking at his or her own life, can play with multiple alternative interpretations, as in variations on a theme or the looser structure of a rhapsody. My husband, perhaps responding to the way the play overlaid two different historical eras, commented that Bach fugues "work" as music if they are played backwards. For Jane, a return to Broadway was a return to an earlier period of her life, though not a period she was particularly nostalgic for. But she played the role from her heart, and I found it full of echoes. We compose our lives in time, improvising and responding to context, yet weaving threads of continuity and connecting the whole as we move back and forth in memory.

CHAPTER IX

What We Pass On

E ACH NEW GENERATION of adults inherits a way of being from the previous generation and passes one on to the next, with changes large and small occurring at every step. The handing on of accrued learning and experience takes place in many different forms, not only in relation to biological children but in relation to students and others whom we teach and guide, sometimes specifically preparing them to replace us. In the days when skills were transmitted primarily through apprenticeship, part of the obligation of the master craftsman was handing on his skills. In the modern world, however, there is an increasing gap between the practitioner of a craft, whether it be fashioning machine parts or crafting legislation, and the training of someone who can follow in his or her footsteps, for alongside every type of master craftsman there has emerged a group specializing in transmitting those skills, teachers for whom transmission is more important than but does not necessarily exclude practice.

One of the key issues in conversations with older adults concerns legacy—not only the material or monetary legacies they will be leaving, but the values and commitments and skills they have striven to model and pass on that constitute a nonmaterial legacy, to kinfolk as well as to the larger society, often rooted in contributions made through lifelong participation.

Some of the people I interviewed for this book, including myself, inhabit the academic world, in which everyone is expected, to varying degrees, to function in three ways: to do original scholarship; to transmit knowledge both new and inherited to the next generation; and to participate in the governance and maintenance of the scholarly community (this last is often referred to as community service). But individuals vary greatly in which of these activities they regard as primary, some pouring their energies into committee work that might lead to a departmental chairmanship or even a college presidency, some resenting every obligation that takes them away from original research, and some focused almost entirely on their students and on improving their own performance as teachers. I once commented naïvely to a colleague that surely we were there to serve the students, that was the whole point of the enterprise, wasn't it? "Not so," he said, "they are here for us"— which I took to mean that being employed as teachers created the opportunity to be scholars. His was a minority view in a competitive liberal arts college that required publication and original research but on the whole regarded these activities as necessary to support the quality of teaching, not as ends in themselves.

On the other hand, there are professions in which practitioners do not think of themselves as teachers—or may begin to think about teaching only when they become concerned with preparing their successors or finding a way of "giving back" in retirement, for instance, as mentors of troubled adolescents. Hank Lawson, for example, was very clear that teaching and guiding the young was part of his role as a parent, but teaching was probably not defined as a part of his job at the boatyard, although I suspect that his conversations and explanations were helpful to younger workers as well as to the owners of the boats he worked on. His retirement is notable not only for the transfer of skills and standards of workmanship to a different scale and different materials but also for his capturing and extending his potential as a teacher.

As I listened to men and women telling the stories of their lives, I became aware of the great variation in the importance given to teachers and other sources of guidance and learning in their narratives, going back to their student days. In some cases this was probably accidental, depending on the flow of a given interview and the mood of the day, but Dick Goldsby, who lost his father when he was five, consistently emphasized his debts to his teachers and mentors over several days of conversation, whereas Dan Jepson mourned the lack.

When Dick and I, at his suggestion, wrote a book together about the social implications of the HIV/AIDS epidemic, we chose a double dedication: he proposed a dedication to a high school biology teacher of his, Luke Ponder, in Kansas, where schools were still segregated, and I proposed a dedication it to a math teacher, Josephine Horner Belknap, at my all girls' high school.[1]

Dick had described his public high school education as superb, partly because teaching was one of the few jobs open to highly educated African Americans. "Not a tough upbringing," he said. "But Luke Ponder was exceptional. He was a biology teacher with a master's in zoology from the University of Kansas. He made an enormous amount of difference, not just because he was a good teacher but because of what he was willing to do over and above his teaching duties.

"He started something called the Guide Right High School Fraternity. He was a Kappa. That's one of the black fraternities. Kappas and Alphas, another black fraternity, some of them have chapters in high schools, where they will take kids in who are fifteen, sixteen years old, and they will be sort of junior fraternity members for a period of time. Which means that you have people kind of looking after you and urging you on, complementing what your own family is doing. And in addition to that you have twenty other boys who are doing the same kind of thing, so you're not out of step if you're trying to achieve, you're very much in step. There's a great deal of social pressure and a great deal of social cohesion in terms of a group of young men trying to make it and being encouraged to do so." Dick and I had spoken about the fact that in many schools today the effort to succeed academically is nonconformist and isolating behavior for minorities.

Luke Ponder's influence and guidance continued after graduation, when he arranged for Dick and some of his peers to be dining car waiters during their summers as college students, and Dick counted off their names and later careers. "All of us who got on that dining car had very good lives afterwards. And we made a lot of money. We're talking about the fifties. I would live off my tips, and still I could save fifteen hundred dollars in a summer, and I am not a particularly thrifty person."

Dick's father ran an insurance agency, and his mother had been a schoolteacher. "He had asked her to retire from that," Dick told me, "because he didn't think it was proper for a woman to work—a man ought to support his household. Like many middle-class blacks, he tried to emulate what he saw as the way whites behaved. Terrible mistake for my mother, because even though he got off to a good start, he was ungracious enough to die when he was forty-three, and even though he did leave insurance for her, it was really very tough for her to raise two boys and put them through college. She reconfigured the house, and we rented rooms and there was a social security check and also a veteran's check, and she was an extraordinarily good manager."

Even in high school, Dick had jobs in which he was encouraged in useful ways, including a summer job as a maintenance man at a swimming pool. "We all wanted jobs working for the city," he explained, "so you got a city check *and* you were at the swimming pool, and all your friends would come and swim. As a maintenance man, I would get my work done very quickly in the morning, just had to mop floors and clean things up. So I could bring my chemistry books, and study some before the pool opened at ten. I remember one morning the supervisor of the city pools, who was a teacher in the white high school system, came, and there I was reading my chemistry book, and he wondered if I had done my work. After I told him I had gotten everything done, he looked at my book. 'What are you reading?' he asked. And I said, 'I'm reading chemistry.' He came over and he looked at it, and he said, 'If I can get you anything else to read, let me know.' So again, a situation of encouragement, essentially every way I turned. No one tried to hold me back or anything. Just everybody participating and helping me go forward."

This was true at home and with relatives as well. "I barely remember my father," Dick told me, "but I missed having a father around as I grew up, and I envied the boys who had fathers." His father and grandparents had died, but he had a maternal uncle in Chicago and spent summers shining shoes in his uncle's barbershop, starting as a twelve-year-old. "Glen Walsh. He was an extraordinary man, a guy with a poor fifth-grade education, who had a seven-chair barbershop and met a payroll every week. His sons worked in the shop. One son became a judge in Chicago; another had a law office. He treated me very much like a son.

"As I look back, I remember what a great manager he was. He hired two porters in his barbershop, and the job of a porter meant you kept the shop clean and you brushed people off when they got out of the chair. They would give you a dime or fifteen cents, or you shined their shoes, and they would pay you fifty cents for the shine, and maybe they would tip you a quarter or so. Well, when I came up in the summer, another person coming in, it cut into the income of the people who were there all year, so my uncle did two things, one of which I didn't learn about until after I left. He supplemented their income during the summer when I was there, gave them extra money. And secondly, he gave me some of the dirtiest jobs to do around the shop. I had to clean the spittoons and I had to mop the floors. I resented cleaning the spittoons; I didn't resent mopping the floors because that seemed like heavy work and I was trusted to get the floor clean. He was a great manager, everything being orderly and clean, so I was kind of proud to be chosen to do that. Cleaning spittoons wasn't any fun."

"Good thing you didn't know much biology then," I joked.

"He was a figure I could look up to as someone who had accomplished and who had very high standards. He was uncompromising and a person of great physical courage," Dick said of his uncle. When labor organizers tried to pressure his sons working in the barbershop into joining, he refused to let them. "So he would bring his shotgun to the shop and put it in the corner. Now the unions were run by organized crime, and they could have taken him out just like that. But I think they figured it wasn't worth the trouble. He was willing to put things on the line that way. He was that kind of person."

"Barbershops are very important community centers in the black community, right?" I said. "I mean, people would have known he was doing that, and it would have influenced them." That twelve-year-old boy was certainly impressed by the quiet presence of that shotgun, but he was equally impressed by the quiet determination behind it and by the order and cleanliness of the barbershop.

As Dick moved on in life, he mostly encountered fairness and, especially, helpful teachers and mentors. At the University of Kansas, where he majored in chemistry and graduated in 1957, he was placed in a scholarship hall, the first black to be so admitted, and was elected president of the hall in his second year. Although his teachers were expecting him to go to graduate school, he initially took a research job at Monsanto in St. Louis, and there again found someone to admire, Bob Redoux, who had gotten his master's degree as part of a Monsanto program. "He was just terrific, just a wonderful person to work for and with," Dick said. "Probably the most gifted person I have ever seen in a laboratory. It was like watching a very skilled pianist. You would just watch the way he handled reagents and glassware and the way he moved—he had this towel he put over his arm. It was a performance."

Dick married his first wife, Barbara Ann, in St. Louis, and then in 1958 went on to three years at UC Berkeley, where he shifted into biochemistry. He grinned. "Chemists are smarter than biochemists, just like physicists are smarter than chemists and mathematicians are smarter than physicists. It's a different order of abstraction. But biochemistry gave me a chance to show that I could do quite well at Berkeley. Then the second semester came along, the preliminary exam. The preliminary exam at Berkeley was different from what it was in most places. There the first question was, 'Tell us about your research.' And that was the most important question you were asked during that examination. This meant that from the beginning you had to find a lab you thought you could work in and get going on a research project. And they expected results. You didn't have to have a paper published by the end of your first year, but you would come and work in the lab, and after a while you kind of knew what you were doing. They preferred that you work alone. Every emphasis was put on doing real science and real problems. That's what turned them on. This is the way almost everybody does it now, but that was unusual at that time.

"I worked for a person who really would let you go on your own. He was brilliant, Melvin Calvin, who won a Nobel Prize for photosynthesis in 1961 that wasn't shared with anybody. He could have gotten it for inventing homogeneous catalysis, he was the first person to do that. He could have gotten it for a collection of other things." As often happened in our conversations, I took us on a detour so I could understand what Dick was saying—surely, I thought, photosynthesis was not discovered in the nineteen sixties! "Oh, people had known about photosynthesis since back in the 1700s. But they didn't know how you get from carbon dioxide in water to glucose and amino acids and things like that."

"Did they have the role of chlorophyll then?"

"Yes, they knew it was important in capturing energy. And Calvin wasn't the one who figured out how it did that. That came later. What Calvin figured out was how you get from carbon dioxide and water to sugars and other compounds plants need to grow and maintain themselves. And it turned out to be an extraordinary pathway. For example, the familiar sugar, glucose, has six carbons. Carbon dioxide has only one. So everybody tried to figure out how you got from carbon dioxide with one carbon to glucose with six. Many tried to get there directly, but the actual pathway turned out to be much more complicated. In a flash of insight, Calvin realized that three, four, five, and surprisingly even seven carbon atoms formed a complicated web of reactions that allowed plants to make useful and complex sugars, such as glucose and sucrose. And all of that came to him as he was waiting for his wife at the supermarket. He went home and he wrote it down. He was right. Calvin could do that.

"Calvin was known around Berkeley as the meanest, orneriest, nastiest person in the department, if not on the whole campus, to everybody outside his own laboratory, which had about sixty people. To people inside . . . I remember I got a call, 'This is Genevieve Calvin, I couldn't reach your wife, so I had to call you. Could you come to our house for dinner? I know how busy you are but . . .' It meant a great deal to me. I was one of his TAs . . . just a grad student." Dick paused as tears came to his eyes. "Sorry . . . I didn't expect to have this kind of reaction.

"Well, I would grade papers. He didn't grade the papers, but when time came to assign the grades—there were perhaps two hundred students in the class—this guy a few years away from a Nobel Prize would sit down and go over every student's grade. Now and then he would raise a student's grade because this student had shown enough of an upward trend. He'd be doing this maybe about ten thirty or eleven at night, and then he'd drive everybody home.

"He was a good person. It's a terribly important thing to do all through your life, to associate yourself with people who will help you *on* your way, rather than standing *in* your way, people you won't have to get around but people who will help you get over. And I have come in contact with a lot of such people during my life." He shook his head ruefully. "I didn't expect to get this kind of reaction. I've never gotten this kind of reaction in talking about the support I've gotten."

"It happens to me, too," I said, "when I think about some of my teachers." Josephine Belknap, the math teacher whose name stood next to that of Luke Ponder in the book Dick and I wrote together, saw that I was ahead of my high school class in math and suggested that I be released from attendance and from the daily assignments to burrow into analytic geometry on my own, on two conditions: first, that I keep up with the class and take the exams, and second, that I tutor a classmate who was having difficulty and make sure she could keep up. Like Melvin Calvin, she encouraged me to go ahead on my own and at the same time taught me a lesson in caring for others. The two conditions were closely related because, as is often said, the best way to learn a subject is to teach it.

"It's over now," Dick said, of the way his memory had affected him. "I'm back."

Once again, after he got his doctorate from Berkeley, in 1961, Richard took a job in industry rather than an academic position, this time at

DuPont, another industrial giant that supports highly competitive research. Eventually, however, Arthur Galston, a Yale professor of botany who was a consultant for DuPont, told Dick, "You really ought to be at a college. You ought to be teaching."

"He stole me away to Yale," Dick said. "And I spent a year at Yale. I enjoyed it a great deal, and then somebody rubbed me the wrong way by telling me I'd be lucky if I got tenure. Tenure! I said, I don't have to stay here. And I went back to DuPont. Totally selfish, thoughtless. So this guy, Art, who had brought me to Yale at great risk to his consultancy at DuPont, remained my friend, and they took me back at DuPont with open arms. I stayed at DuPont for a year then decided, No, I don't think I want to be here. I would like to go back to Yale. Art could have discouraged me, or he could have discouraged the people at Yale, but he did quite the opposite, and I came back to Yale in 1966.

"Art really taught me how to teach. He was an artist at teaching, a truly gifted teacher. He knew how to set topics up so students would learn things, building courses so that students would become progressively interested in topics. He did pedagogy as a science, so to speak, and spent a great deal of time doing it. He sort of brought me in there as a protégé, and saw that I got this very good teaching assignment so that I had a chance to succeed. I wasn't very good when I got started there. He was very much a mentor, a very patient one, and he developed me into a very good person in the classroom, taught me how to listen to students."

Dick went on to tell me about Art Galston's history, the anti-Semitism and hazing he had faced as a student, and the senior scientists—George Beadle and Linus Pauling—who had encouraged him. "Art was kind of a wunderkind, a Jewish kid who grew up in New York; his father lost his money during the depression. The first year he was teaching at Caltech, George Beadle, who won a Nobel Prize, said to him, 'You're going to teach with me; any jackass can lecture, it takes talent to run a lab, so *I'm* going to run the lab and you're going to have the job of giving the lectures.' Imagine somebody doing that for a young assistant!" When some of Art's research provided clues that led to the development of Agent Orange, this disturbed him greatly and led him to an interest in the ethics of how science is used. In later years Dick brought Galston to Amherst to lecture on the ethics of science. As Dick spoke, it struck me that the laboratory bench is one of the places where apprenticeship continues.

Dick always emphasizes the centrality of basic lab research, but I could also hear a theme running through his life of communicating with the public and with students who were not going into research. While he was at Yale, he wrote a book on elementary biochemistry and a biology book called *Race and Races*, which went into the small ways in which human populations differ, yet made it clear that these unfamiliar differences, like the more obvious ones, are insignificant in relation to the unity of the species (different textures of earwax, for heaven's sake!).[2] This is a book that he plans to revise when he retires from teaching and lab work. The book he and I coauthored on HIV/AIDS was intended for the general public, and he and his wife Barbara Osborne coauthored a textbook of immunology.

As Dick described individuals who had been important to him, he tended to mention the ways they composed their lives around this balance between different kinds of work, such as physicians conducting research or teaching but also keeping up with clinical work, because, as he quoted John Littlefield, a senior medical researcher at Harvard, in whose lab Dick spent a year, "If you're not seeing patients, you're not really a doctor. You can't with any kind of confidence teach medical students once you lose your clinical edge, and you've got to practice to keep it going." Of one research colleague he said, "For a month every year John would come to the office around five o'clock in the morning, get through his administrative stuff that had to be done, and go out on the ward to take a swing at clinical bat."

It seemed to me that as he spoke Dick was discerning patterns in his work that he had never spelled out before and experiencing their emotional meanings in new ways. At one point he said, "Right now I do three different kinds of teaching. First, I teach immunology—there I feel is an opportunity to take a bunch of very able Amherst undergraduates and they by and large are able to do it. So there I get a chance to actually teach people at something that approaches a graduate level.

"Then I have students who are basically liberal arts students. That's interesting because you get to wake people up. People have these stereotypes of what science is. They think science is dull; they think it's all written down somewhere. They are surprised to find that, as a working process, science is about checking and sometimes disproving earlier results, about finding out something new, and that what we think is right today almost always turns out not to be the case tomorrow. Most of the students, these very sophisticated students I have in class, are really surprised and enlightened. They are also surprised by some of the people I have come in as guest lecturers. And they're surprised about bioethics and that scientists care about things like this, I mean really care.

"Then of course, you get, not so much to reproduce yourself as much as to develop people who will go beyond you. In most cases, the people I have had as graduate students had no idea they were as good as they are. Barbara tends to get the people who come in acknowledged as the best students entering U Mass. By and large, with one or two exceptions, the students I have gotten from U Mass have been students who are second or third tier. Students somebody has written off, students who in some cases had almost written themselves off and when they finished had real confidence, got out and fared well." Dick described a student who seemed to be "just kind of biding her time and not billing herself a whole lot as a scientist or an intellectual," whom he and Barbara hired to work at Hematech and who "became an extraordinarily good scientist." Dick and his present wife, Barbara Osborne, had been involved in creating Hematech, a biotech company that developed techniques for producing human immunoglobulin in cows and was subsequently sold to a company in Japan.

"I take what people think of as very ordinary material, and they make much more rapid progress than expected. Part of it is you can't hit them too hard initially so they lose confidence in themselves. They have to have time. You have to give them a problem that is interesting and important scientifically, but it's much more important to get a problem that will work, so they get some data and they have some success they can show other people, because how your peers regard you and how the faculty regard you has a lot to do with how well you're going to make your way in our business. It's funny, what you find is that they become much more ambitious as they gather strength. They themselves will make their problems more demanding by going deeper, and that's been one of the very bright spots."

There are many professors who regard research as their real work and teaching as a part of their job that interferes with their real work, something that the stars can often avoid completely. When Dick was considering accepting an appointment at Amherst and Barbara was looking at local institutions where she might work if they moved, they were both concerned about teaching loads and reluctant to compromise their research. Dick said, "Now I look at what my wife is doing— and Barbara is now a star, a real honest to God star. Barbara teaches even though she complains about it, says she hates it and so forth. She is the honors coordinator, which means she has fifty advisees or honor students. She cares. She knows these people. She writes letters for them. She's also taken a couple of junior faculty people under her wings, and she cares about them. When they get their grants, it's like *she's* got the grant, that's the kind of joy she feels about it."

I commented that teaching is only one of several ways of supporting the next generation. "The big researchers may be putting their energy into mentoring the people that work in their lab or, true enough, they may just be exploiting them."

Dick shook his head and began to speak about the next semester, when he would be on sabbatical at MIT. "You have probably the best scientific technical institute in the world, with the best faculty in aggregate in the world to teach. And these people are so powerful and they are so well connected that they could stop teaching in the middle of the class if they wanted to and nobody could stop them. They would not think of doing that. That's not the culture of the place. The culture of the place is one that believes they're supposed to teach."

"But, Dick," I said, "I think you're talking about places where people are teaching their heirs, they're replicating themselves, they have superb students, which is different from teaching biology in a place where nobody is going to become a biologist, nobody is going to—"

"People at MIT feel they *ought* to teach, because, they say, why would you get some of the best undergraduates and graduates in the country to come to MIT and then stick them with people who are inferior teachers? At Harvard they seem by and large to be untroubled by those sorts of concerns. At MIT, of course, everybody had to take biology. Econ majors, political science majors, engineering majors, physics majors. So maybe some of it is, they're teaching themselves, but the bulk of that class out there is people who are never going to take any more biology. And a fraction of them hate it.

"At the University of Maryland, where I was on the faculty for ten years, you got an extremely broad spectrum of students, particularly at the time I was there. I had a lot of premeds, and of course you had people who were in nursing and so on. And chemistry departments are notorious for failing students, for discouraging students, and for demoralizing students. Chemistry is really sadistic. They're a little like musicians—chemistry is something you kind of can do or you can't, and they generally have very little patience for people who can't do it. Well, at the University of Maryland, they would teach introductory chemistry for close to two thousand students each semester. That's a lot of people. And they had a reputation in the seventies for failing maybe twenty or thirty percent of the kids.

"Then a physical chemist, a successful and very good researcher, took the job as chairman of that very large department—they had more than fifty faculty members—a routine, tough, state university chemistry department. And he said, 'This is ridiculous.' So he went to the School of Education and said, I think we need to worry about science *education,* and he got a woman named Margie Gardener with a degree in education, who joined the chemistry department, supported by both departments financially, and her job was to show them how to teach chemistry. Eventually they realized, 'The problem is, we expect people to learn it too quickly; all we care about is to get them through the semester.' So, instead of an up or out system, a one chance only system, they adopted a mastery system. You take the exam, and if you fail the exam, they don't let you go to the next exam to fail that one, you retake the one you failed a week later. This time you still don't do so well, just a little better, and so two weeks later, you'd have to take that exam again. Guess what? The majority of the students could finally get to the point where they could answer seventy percent of the questions. So they were giving Cs to almost everybody who finished elementary chemistry, and they actually knew that much chemistry. They just changed the way of teaching from 'you're too dumb to learn this, go away,' to 'we can teach you this and you can do it. We'll help you and we'll give you time to learn it. We're not going to reward you the same way we reward people who get a hundred percent the first time around, because that gives everybody the wrong message, everybody.' " Dick made a sweeping gesture. "It's the way to teach."

"That sounds like Home Depot. 'You can do it, we can help.' "

"If you get the right leadership, you know, you see that sort of thing happening. Amherst College has decided to adopt what they call intensive sessions in economics and chemistry. . . . The chemists are actually doing better than anybody else right now, even though they've got the most difficult subject. The kids have more class meetings, they have more little quizzes, they have more exercises to do. They have all the lecture classes with the other students who are taking chemistry, but their sections are called intensive sections because there's more drill involved, and they also have labs for these special sections. We do more work, too; it takes a lot more time. The special sections are run by senior faculty members. It's for the students who come in with lower math SAT scores, haven't had the same education as the other kids that are there, and just get overwhelmed by it, get discouraged. About half of these students are black or Hispanic and half are white, but a lot are kids who are there because they play hockey well or some other sport, from an urban public school or a Catholic high school, and a solid working-class background.

"Comparing somebody who's gone to a wealthy suburban high school to somebody who went to high school in a big city? Very different. Very different educations. The kid from the suburb is our kind of kid. He's easy for us to teach." The issue is not so much one of intelligence but of the attitudes that students bring to learning. "I get kids," Dick told me, "who come to biology class with their Bibles . . . very rigid in terms of moral beliefs. . . . But they're now doing these intensive sessions at Amherst and it's working, to the extent that kids who ordinarily would not have scored in or around the class average now are."

I listened in a sort of wonder. Dick had told me that minority students do not seek him out and that he is not part of the "black scene" in the Pioneer Valley, and I suspect he is regarded as a tough grader. But I have listened to him patiently laboring to explain a difficult concept.

There is a big difference between, on the one hand, supporting programs that will systematically strengthen the skills of students who come in with poor preparation so that they graduate on an intellectual level with their peers and, on the other hand, cutting them slack so they are held to lower standards. Having taught for a semester at Spelman College, a historically black women's college, I have learned that giving easy grades is no favor—upholding high standards and supporting real effort is.

I'd also noticed the reference Dick made to the way Melvin Calvin might boost the grade of a student who was showing an "upward trend." A highly competitive institution can guarantee distinguished graduates by its admissions. But the real question is how an institution both challenges and supports students so they can develop further in school as well as after they graduate. That same balance applies in rearing children. We talk about legacies—but our legacies are not only in the help we give to those who come after but also in the demands we put in front of them.

Partly because of the glamorous progress of genetic research in recent years, American society is beginning to tilt again in the direction of genetic determinism, which made it especially reassuring to me to hear a biology professor talking about drawing out potential so that a student who had not seemed particularly promising could be successful given a second and even a third chance. We have made huge progress in enhancing the prospects of children born with disabilities, but we continue to be willing to write older students off for lackluster performance and to condemn those who have gotten into trouble with the law as unredeemable instead of noticing how much learning and change is possible, even rather late in life. What Dick had to say about the importance of teaching and about what he had gained from his own teachers was especially powerful as he reflected on his earlier jobs and marriages, looking back on himself as demanding and self-centered.

Dick is an example of someone who managed to go a long distance by being smart and then grew into real wisdom and a talent for happiness, but he was amazingly open in speaking of earlier failures in his personal life. In working with life history material, I have made a practice of focusing on individuals whom I truly admire and of letting them decide which parts of their lives they wish to share and which they would like to leave behind. Sometimes this means hearing only one side of the story. When I wrote *Composing a Life,* I understood that people have difficulty discussing the losses and failures in their lives, and that this is something which must be respected. But it gradually became clear to me that such experiences need to be shared, along with the triumphs, both for the teller and for the listener. We compose our lives from both pleasant and unpleasant materials, but the painful materials are harder to talk about. One way of addressing those lacunae was to include in that book the story of my own unhappy experiences as dean of the faculty at Amherst College.[3]

A conversation I had with my daughter, Sevanne, drove this necessity home. I mentioned to her that I had received a letter telling me that I had not been awarded a grant I had applied for, and she looked at me in amazement and said, "But I thought you always got whatever you applied for." If there is one thing necessary to survive as an actor, which was Sevanne's chosen profession, or indeed as an artist of any kind, it is the ability to handle rejection. Yet parents are often reluctant to offer their own struggles with rejection or humiliation as possibly useful models, especially if they have survived and succeeded in other ways. Parents, inevitably perhaps, feed off of their children's assumption of their omnipotence and withhold the stories that make them feel smaller.

Thus, African Americans who grew up during the civil rights movement tell their children stories of the great demonstrations that led to change and of the excitement of encountering figures like Martin Luther King or Malcolm X, but speak much less of the nagging fear under Jim Crow of going out at night or the shameful anxiety about finding access to a toilet when traveling or about asking for directions.

This set me thinking about a whole landscape of untold narrative and therefore of unshared learning, learning that might seem of little value yet had perhaps made survival possible. For those who survived the Holocaust, it was often decades before the stories of survival could be told; these were humiliating stories that included eating insects or vermin and even betraying others, or that required admitting to disabling fear or despair.

Even on minor issues, who of us tells our children, who seem to us so extraordinarily beautiful, how we agonized as adolescents over zits or extra pounds or other blemishes, or about having no friends to join in the school lunchroom? Chances are, they are having comparable experiences and need to know they are not alone. Then there are the times when we may have behaved in ways hurtful to others but may have acted without a full understanding of the consequences, which we regret quite as much as we regret missed opportunities and undeveloped talents. Only our stories can arm our children against doing thoughtless damage.

One thing that young people need to know about their elders is that they have not lived perfect lives, that some of their wisdom comes from the experiences they hope the next generation never has to share. These are the very stories the next generation may not have the privilege of hearing.

When Erik Erikson spoke of "the acceptance of one's one and only life cycle as something that had to be and that, by necessity, permitted of no substitutions," he associated that acceptance with integrity, and spoke of despair as its opposite: "the feeling that the time is now short, too short for the attempt to try out alternate roads to integrity. Disgust hides despair, if often only in the form of 'a thousand little disgusts' which do not add up to one big remorse."[4]

Yet many of us do find ways to try out alternate roads to integrity, if only by articulating the problem. The years of relative health and energy that have been added to life expectancy often represent a second chance at adulthood, an opportunity to compensate for earlier mistakes or omissions, as people realize that, although time is indeed short, it is not as short as they expected. The decisions that people make about how to spend their atrium years must inevitably reflect negative as well as positive experiences, a chance to re-compose.

In interviews I have sometimes heard people say, "I should have gotten out of my marriage years ago, but it's too late now." Yet there has been a striking increase in recent decades in both later life marriages and later life divorces. Grandparents sometimes speak of building a kind of relationship with their grandchildren that they missed with their own children at a time when they were preoccupied with building careers. People in their seventies may begin piano lessons or take up watercolor painting or pursue a new academic degree, turning their steps to the road not taken, however differently it lies. It has become a cliché to say "It's never too late to . . . ," a cliché that, like the old promise to women that they could "have it all," is more nearly true than ever before but still not entirely true. Nevertheless, there is indeed time now for more. The critical question about regrets is whether experience led to growth and new learning. Some people seem to keep on making the same mistakes, while others at least make new ones. Regret and remorse can be either paralyzing or inspiring.

Some of my interviews with Dick Goldsby were joined by his wife, Barbara Osborne, and revolved around years of domestic happiness combined with professional collaboration, but when we met separately to discuss the earlier stages of his life, Dick described his first two marriages very much in terms of his own inadequacies and limited understanding, the mistakes of a very young man. Barbara is Dick's third wife. His first wife was named Barbara Ann, and his second wife Ann, a sequence of names that made for confusing listening, so although he often refers to his first wife as Barbara, I have consistently included her full name for clarity.

"One of the biggest mistakes I ever made in my life was to choose the woman that I married first, a terrible mistake for me and for her," Dick told me. "I had never had sex before and was desperate to, and she seemed available. So the wedding night came along. She hadn't grown up enough, and I hadn't grown up enough either. I was absolutely overbearing, totally dictatorial. She eventually turned out to be an extraordinarily strong person, but she let me treat her that way for eight or nine years. I wanted her to work, but she never really developed a skill that would allow her to hold a job for long, and then, for godsakes, I had three children, one right after the other, and how was she going to find the time to go to work? Marilyn was the fourth child; she came in 1966. These children were all born without our intending them to be born. I was a terrible husband, not a bad father but a terrible husband. And it was a very bad marriage. I was truly abusive. I didn't beat her up or anything physically, but I beat her up emotionally and verbally all the time."

I listened in amazement as he said these things. The Richard Goldsby I know and have known since 1982, now in his seventies, is unremittingly gentle and considerate, and his present marriage seems fulfilling both for him and for Barbara. And ours is not a casual relationship within which a superficial view would be possible. As dean of the faculty at Amherst, I was involved in hiring him and was in some sense his boss; we later coauthored our book on HIV/AIDS at his suggestion; and he and Barbara once rented the apartment my husband and I have in Cambridge when they were both on sabbatical. All these relationships had a high potential for friction. We continue to get together frequently, as individuals and as couples.

One point of contrast that struck me immediately was that, after two failed marriages, Dick married a professional colleague and peer who evokes a level of mutual respect that was missing from his earlier marriages. Growing up in Kansas City, Dick had been fortunate in finding mentors who encouraged the drive and circumspection necessary for an African American child to realize his potential, and I often noticed a preference for ambition and striving in his descriptions of others. Barbara Ann was clearly highly intelligent, but as a young woman she'd lacked a sense of direction. Dick told me, "I was disappointed in the fact that Barbara Ann didn't seem to have the kind of focus it took to get anything done. As an outstanding high school student, she had been selected to go to St. Louis University to integrate the place, and she had slept through her classes the first year there. Her mother had then sent her to Lemoyne College in Memphis, where she also slept through class. She reentered college when we were out in California, really didn't have the follow-through to pass her courses. When I met her, she was doing absolutely nothing. But she was very interesting."

Dick's mother had been a schoolteacher before she married, but his father, who was running an insurance agency that served the black community, asked her to stop working.

This was a version of domesticity that was still strong in the fifties and early sixties; one that was replicated for Dick and Barbara Ann as he progressed through a series of jobs and eventually joined the faculty at Yale. "Her life was to a large extent taking care of children, taking care of a house, having dinner ready at the time I insisted on, keeping things as clean and as neat as I thought she should have kept them. That was basically the way I saw her life," Dick told me. "Now, she was interesting to other people, and so she would develop friends every place we lived, and they would interact with her and sometimes rescue her from this existence she was in. But she always met them through me. We would be invited out to dinner, the wives would meet, they would call each other and they would come over and every now and then she would go over to their houses, but most of the time they would come to our house. That was true in California, it was true in Wilmington, Delaware, and it was true in New Haven. Everything was almost exclusively through me. She had very little life outside, and at the time I didn't think there was anything unusual about that.

"I didn't spend much time thinking about her or her needs, but I was good at pointing out to her what I perceived as her inadequacies! I was an absentee dad and husband. When I was around, I interacted strongly with the children, and they enjoyed the interactions and so forth, but I wasn't around a whole lot. And often when I was at home I was working on a lecture or a book, and when I was doing this, I told her I had to have absolute quiet and privacy, and my wife made sure that I had those things. She surely did. She developed some backbone about the ninth or tenth year of the marriage and began to come into herself and talk back to me.

"When we got divorced, I left her with four children and went off to Harvard to do a sabbatical there. They were in suburban Woodbridge, Connecticut, for almost a year, and then she moved the children back to St. Louis, into an all-black inner-city ghetto where they were perceived as talking funny and acting strangely. The kids got beaten up in school all the time. She realized that what she had to do was to impose absolute discipline on them or they might not survive in that neighborhood. And from a distance I would sympathize with the kids when they got whipped because they had said the wrong thing or something. I can see now that she had to be strict to raise four children in that situation without anybody getting in trouble or getting arrested. Not easy, especially for our son or for any black male coming up in St. Louis at that time.

"Barbara Ann got very much involved in politics. She was known around St. Louis as a tough, kick-ass community leader. People didn't mess with her around there. She led all kinds of boycotts and that sort of thing. Got herself a job as a court bailiff and retired from that job with all kinds of honors and people saying nice things about her. If I had had the kind of obstacles put into my path that I put into hers, we wouldn't be having these conversations now."

I asked Dick what had ended his marriage to Barbara Ann, and he replied that a chance to make some extra money allowed him to get away. "I had my first sabbatical from Yale coming up, and I was able to make a triple salary that summer. I made a salary on my grant, I had my academic salary, which was paid in twelve installments, and then I had the extra bonus of working in a summer enrichment program for black kids at Yale. I had my exit door—enough money to maintain a family and a separate existence in another city. We never had any money to speak of, not because we didn't make a good salary. Yale paid very well. I was just a poor financial manager.

"I hardly dare tell you how I left. The day before I was going to leave,

I took my wife out for dinner and a movie, I took her home, and I told her I was leaving. It was just an incredibly terrible, terrible thing to do, to lift somebody up and then do that sort of thing to them. . . . I was a nice person to other people, I've always been pretty nice, but I was self-centered and unthinking and uncaring.

"I had no doubt that I would continue seeing the children, I loved them and I cared about them, I just wasn't going to live with her any-more. That's all. I thought that's how it would play out. Well, it didn't play out that way. I didn't see that I wouldn't be an integral part of their lives and they of mine. The first month, I lived on campus at Yale until I could take up my sabbatical tenure at Harvard, at which point I lived in Adams House. That was 1968–69."

Barbara Ann eventually died of diabetes after a series of amputa-tions. "She lost one leg and then the other, and she gave up. I remember talking to her when she first knew she was going to die; she had heart failure, she had diabetes, and she had incredibly high blood pressure, she knew what the outcome was likely to be and she was still spirited. Then she had that first amputation, that really took the heart out of her, according to the kids. Then when she had the other leg taken off, she stopped being the strong and powerful figure they were accustomed to, and they were surprised to find that their mother was a human being, too."

Dick's second wife, Ann, had been a schoolteacher. This marriage lasted only about a year and a half, with no children. "You know, I didn't really want to marry Barbara Ann, I tried to call it off and didn't have the guts," Dick explained. "And then with Ann, I really knew from an early point this wasn't a good idea but was so infatuated, I went for-ward with it. I was just incredibly mad about her, and she did not love me. And within six months of being married to her, I stopped loving her, and had we stayed together, one of us would have killed the other. It was an ugly, poisonous relationship. We were unfaithful to each other, me very early in the relationship, she later on. She was an alco-holic, and I probably would have become one had I stayed with her. . . . I couldn't bring home checks fast enough. I had signed a book con-tract with Harper and Row, a very nice advance for the book on race, and it was almost gone before we got it. Like that." Dick resigned from Yale, pulled out of the marriage, and took a job at the University of Maryland.

Barbara Osborne and Dick met in Maryland. "She came and joined my laboratory," he told me, "and that was my salvation, to be with somebody who had the same core intellectual values and somebody who had a great deal of common sense as well. I mean, you know, she doesn't want to go out and buy something just to show it off. And we love each other."

Barbara is a white woman from Pennsylvania, fourteen years younger than Dick. Unlike him, she had been involved in the idealism of the sixties and had campaigned for Eugene McCarthy. With no children of her own, Barbara has made a sustained effort to engage with Dick's children, and one or another came to live with them at different periods. More recently, Dick's grandson Charles has spent time with them in the summer while his mother, Marilyn, who is in the military, has been away for training. It took time for Dick to work out his new role as a grandfather both with his daughter and with Charles. In the beginning, Charles got along better with Barbara than with him.

"In the early days," Dick said, "the way I thought I could do it was by making decisions about what our grandson would do and then announcing to his mother what was going to happen. To some extent this was because quite often we would be sending a check. That really didn't work very well."

"What a surprise," Barbara commented.

"Marilyn has a very strong will; we don't know the situation as well as she does, and so forth. What's worked much better is just to respond to some request. And even," he said wryly, "actually talking, discussing with her what she thinks ought to happen, has turned out to be a novel and useful approach."

Barbara nodded. "Charles called me Grandma until he was about eleven or so, and then he started calling me Barbara, which is fine. He really bonded with me in the beginning. He called Dick 'the napkin king' because Dick was always telling him to use his napkin and then giving him orders on how he should behave at the dining room table and how he should cut his food. He was afraid of Dick."

I laughed. "This guy has really mellowed."

"I know he has." Barbara laughed. "Exactly. But not totally. At first he was pretty directive about the way the child should behave—he's five years old, for godsakes. And secondly, for his whole conscious existence, Charles had been with a mom and no dad around, and at that point Marilyn was dating guys, and he didn't like her dating. So men were competition for him. He used to call Dick 'that man who claims he is my grandfather,' all this stuff. . . . There was tension between the two of them, and Dick was, you know, 'the kid can't like me, why do I have him living here with me? This isn't working.' As Charles has gotten older, he still cares about me and we are buddies, but he would much rather do things with Granddad, because they want to see the same terrible shoot-'em-up kinds of movies, with boobs falling out, and things that I'm not at all interested in doing."

"They do guy things together."

"I would say that even now Charles is really in fact closer to Barbara than he is to me," Dick said. "But we've gotten much closer."

"In 2006, when we took him to sports camp on the Amherst College campus," Barbara said, "he grabbed my hand and he said, 'You know, I'm a little bit scared, Grandma.' Here he was, sixteen years old, starting to drive, and he grabs my hand and says, 'Do you think they're going to like me? There are no black kids here.' I was Grandma that day. And I said, 'You only see a few kids, there might be more black kids, you don't know.' 'I'm just a little scared, maybe I should go back home.' And of course within hours he was an integral part of the place. We picked him up three weeks later, he didn't want to come home . . . he wasn't inter-ested in having us visit."

"To put it differently, he was otherwise occupied," Dick added.

Dick and Barbara have had the geographical problems that attend professional marriages, each receiving offers that would separate them, but have ended up at neighboring institutions, he at Amherst College and she at the University of Massachusetts, Amherst, sometimes collaborating in their research and sometimes working in tandem. Recently, in exploring family genealogies, Barbara discovered with glee that she has at least one line of black ancestry, what used to be called "a touch of the tar brush," now greeted with pleasure.

Selling Hematech, the biotechnology company they had founded, meant that Dick and Barbara had the resources to think ahead, which led to a conversation about different kinds of legacies and appropriate ways to pass on resources. "I think it's enormously satisfying to be able to talk to somebody, to say, 'What would you like to do?' " Dick commented, "and then when they say what they would like to do, to be able to enable it, like sending Charles to Japan with the Experiment in International Living."

Barbara described a conversation in which a young woman had asked Charles about his college plans. He was saying he wasn't really sure yet what he was looking for, and she'd said, "Well, you've got to find a good state school that you can afford to go to."

Barbara had joined in and commented, "He doesn't have to worry about that; he got a part of the company when it was sold and he's got quite a good nest egg," and Charles had said, "Yeah, that's right, I can go wherever I want." At that point, Barbara added to me, "He really enjoyed the fact that he could choose—he also pointed out that it would be nice if we let him keep that money and we pay for college."

"I've thought about this," Dick said, "and wondered about it a bit. So many of my choices—what to do after going to graduate school, where to take a job, and that kind of thing—were made fundamentally looking at money. That's been until very recently a critical feature in my decisions. I would like to try to take some of that kind of pressure off him. I see how it's driven me to certain decisions that I might not have made otherwise, but on the other hand, it's a powerful motivating and focusing influence. I kind of admire rich kids who do very well in school more than I do the poor ones, because the rich ones have other options. I think it's more difficult maybe to really buckle down when you don't need to. The poor kids don't have a choice. I sometimes wonder whether it would be a good thing for Charles to have no feeling of financial pressure at all."

"You know, some young people are going to make career decisions that don't earn them much money, and I would like them to have the option to make those decisions," I said. "When I see them working hard at what they care about, doing something worthwhile and creative, it doesn't bother me that they aren't earning a lot. Scholarships are okay, because they press you to keep up standards and they don't mortgage your future the way loans do, but Charles wouldn't be eligible for any kind of need-based scholarship."

Barbara nodded. "I think he has enough to get through college comfortably and not incur debt, but he's going to have to get out and get a job and do something. I think he should feel that he's got to become gainfully employed. If he wants to go to graduate school, I would be willing to help with that as well, and I would be willing for him to know that, but I want him to feel that at some point he's got to support himself and the money is not unending. I think he knows that. But then once he is established, we could give him enough to let him buy his first house, whatever it takes to ease his progress."

Since the selling of the company, Barbara had started research on a protein called "notch" (because mutations affecting it cause notches in the wings of fruit flies), which is essential to embryonic development but also promised interesting connections to her earlier work on cell death and to the development of tumors and the amyloid plaques of Alzheimer's. I've been interested for some time in career patterns that move in zigzags rather than straight lines, so when Barbara described her shift of interest, I asked her about this. "You pick up a clue, something connects with it, and off you go in that direction," she said. "It partly has to do with what different students are interested in. You let them into your lab because it seems to connect, and it turns out to be really productive in its connections."

"If I asked you," I wondered, "leaving financing aside as an issue, what questions you think you might want to work on, looking ahead as long as you can, how would you frame those questions?"

"I think it would be very hard for me to frame the questions, because what I've learned about the way I do science is that I cannot predict what I'm going to be doing five years from now. If I find something interesting on the way that takes me off on another path, I'll go there. It's partially because I like following where the clues lead me and partially because in that way I am forced to learn a new field every three or four years." For a scientist, there is always something new to be learned. "I didn't know anything about this notch protein. I'd heard of it, but barely. And it's become fascinating. I suspect that five years from now I probably will still be working on it, but I will have another thing that's interesting to me as well and I will probably be veering in another direction. I won't have solved any big question that way, but I will solve a lot of little questions. I'm a meanderer."

"Barbara is a scientist," Dick said. "She is interested in the questions that really don't have answers yet. What I enjoy more than anything else is taking something and making a tool. I like the craftsmanliness of it. It's very different, more engineering than science.

"The styles are so different in science. Look at somebody like Melvin Calvin and look at Linus Pauling. Calvin wanted to figure out how photosynthesis works, and he essentially worked on that for most of his career. If you look at Linus Pauling, for one or two years it was this, for another five-year period it was that. He was really all over the scientific map."

"Yeah, I am more the Linus Pauling type than the Calvin type," Barbara agreed.

"Much more. But very significant things come out of going places where people haven't been before."

"I guess there are two things I would say about five years from now," Barbara went on. "I will be working somewhere in the immune system, almost certainly, because it's a place I feel comfortable; it's home and I know the players, so it's a comfortable place to be, just from a collegial point of view, and I know the experimental system. But I wouldn't necessarily say I'll be doing x in the immune system. I will be following where my nose takes me. I tend to like, and I get turned on by, going to areas where people haven't been before. When I found this interaction between our cell death protein and notch, nobody had even thought about notch in the immune system. I really like that, because I think that gives me a little edge when I'm not competing with a million top guns in the field."

"Well, but just until they notice you're onto something interesting," I said with a laugh. "Then they all swarm in, right?" This is where the nature of legacy in scientific work is so different from what it is in the humanities. The names of those who make major scientific discoveries may get remembered, but the original papers reporting on research go quickly out of date as work gets replicated and elaborated, is integrated into broader understandings, and opens up new mysteries to be pursued. "How about you, five or ten years from now, Dick?" I asked.

"I know you think you're going to be dead," Barbara cut in, "but you've been telling me that for twenty-five years. You won't be. So what do you think you will be doing?"

"Whatever," he replied. "One of the things I have learned is that when people think they know what they're going to do in five years, they almost never do it." Dick's wisdom.

Mine: "One of the things I have come to feel, looking at the revisions that people make in their plans as they go along, is that if you think you know what you're going to be doing in five or ten years, you're wrong. But if you don't have an opinion on it, you're in trouble. In other words, go toward the future with a plan that you're willing to let go of."

CHAPTER X

Shaping the Future

D ICK GOLDSBY HAD URGED ME to meet with Ted Cross, who had endowed the chair at Amherst College to which Dick was originally appointed, specifically to explore the question of legacies. I had explained my project when I made the appointment with Ted, and he had clearly prepared for our meeting by thinking about various kinds of legacies that are passed from parents to children. The term had a barrelful of meanings for him, ranging from property to the obligation of caring for aging parents, from positive values like social service to prejudices like racism and sexism, from genetic characteristics like intelligence or skin color to community membership, and going on to values that might get passed on to the greater society, from tangible economic values to social and ethical values. The legacy that particularly concerned Ted was a journal he had founded in his late sixties and the archive built in the process, the products of Adulthood II, after a successful business career and family.

Ted, who is white, came from a middle-class family that had been hit badly by the depression and had had to struggle to give him the kind of education his parents had had. He has had a long-term interest in race relations and particularly in African American access to education, an interest that was born when he was general counsel for Sheraton Hotels in the early sixties. "There was a strike against one of their hotels in California, two hundred black kids arm in arm in the lobby protesting because no blacks were employed there. They paralyzed the hotel," he said. "The police couldn't move them—they didn't have enough prisons for all these young blacks. So I was sent out as a lawyer for the hotel chain to negotiate some sort of a settlement. I worked out an affirmative action deal with the mayor and the hotel, in which the hotel would hire two blacks every year.

"Then, on my way back home—it was the time of the second march on Selma—I had to stop in Chicago, and I was watching this horrible business at the bridge on TV, and instead of going home I went to Selma, and I was in Selma for a week. From then on, I just had an interest that I really couldn't control in this whole situation. Maybe it was because my teachers had put me in an inferior category; I didn't like people put in categories. So in terms of what became of me, I developed a very strong interest in the black situation."

Ted continued his career in law and also developed with his brothers a successful niche publishing company that was sold in 1980. "And then I said, Well, what next?" He was sixty-eight. "That was the beginning of the work leading to *The Journal of Blacks in Higher Education*," he told me. "We measure progress, evaluate individual colleges and universities—which ones are committed to advancing blacks, and which ones aren't. Which ones have black faculty in large numbers, which ones don't." Ted's focus in Adulthood II has been the creation and maintenance of the journal, tracking academic affirmative action and hiring policies across the country.

Ted explained that he still had no succession plan to maintain the journal, which he works on full-time. "It's really a problem," he said. "Probably, as I look back on it, it's more important than anything else I've done. We have established a history, an archive that is irreplaceable, on what's happened over the past fifteen years—in the elite schools, the

Ivy League schools, the smaller colleges, the public universities, we've got it all there. It's been a tremendous amount of work. And looking back on my life, except for my years in the Navy, this is probably the most important thing that I've done. I'm now eighty-three. I do a tremendous amount of work on it every day. One choice would be to take it to Harvard. I guess I could place it at Princeton. But the journal is highly political, comparing and publicizing the successes and failures of major colleges and universities. This will never happen if the dead hand of academia sets the policy."

"One more boring journal of academic papers," I said.

"Let's say that the important news is that Yale has a very poor record on minority issues, which is in fact true. This story would never get reported if the journal were published by a university. And we're getting into a big situation with the superiority of black women. That is such an incredibly important subject. There is a collapse of black men. Have you seen the figures on college graduations of black men? The women are racing ahead, doing better than white women. Can academic people be counted on to publish something that is so politically incorrect? Harvard Law School has far more black women being admitted than black men. How things have changed. Nobody likes to tell the truth about the very serious decline of black men in higher education. If this trend continues, there will be no more black men in college. It used to be that very few black women held Ph.D.s or did graduate work. It was black men. Now it's completely reversed. It's all black women. You know the statistics that we report; there're now a million black people in four-year colleges. Incredible, what has happened over the last fifteen years. It's really shot up. But it's all women. And that's the story that has to be told. If the journal was in academic hands, it would not happen. I don't know what to do about it."

Ted went on to speculate on the origin of his interest in racial justice. "My grandmother always said the reason for my interest was I was born on Lincoln's birthday. You'd have to go to a shrink for maybe five years to find out what really was going on. The standard stamp in those days was a three-cent Lincoln stamp, and my grandmother used to send me thousands of canceled Lincoln stamps. She always said—I think Mother said, too—that maybe there was a reason why I was born on Lincoln's birthday. Maybe I thought of myself as an emancipator. You know, a twentieth-century emancipator. Who knows what lies within if you delve down deep enough?"

I laughed. "When I was a child, the Roosevelt dime came out. I had ten cents a week allowance and this card that had a place for putting Roosevelt dimes in that you could save up until you had five dollars' worth and could open a first savings account. In 2004, Gerry Ferraro and I both gave talks at Hyde Park, which is set up now as a Roosevelt memorial, as part of our Granny Voter project, and I realized that my whole feeling about Roosevelt had been carried by dealing with these dimes and by the tone in people's voices when they talked about FDR. Roosevelt's death is one of my earliest memories. Lincoln was obviously further in the past but is a very important symbolic figure."

"People still send me information about Lincoln. What a man he was!" Ted exclaimed. "But a very racist man. As human beings, he believed blacks deserved equal treatment, but nevertheless he had a distinct feeling they belonged to a subhuman species with inferior intelligence. He was going to ship 'em off to Africa. It's amazing. His position on slaves seems to be in large part driven by a desire to hold the Union together. Who knows, really, what is the real story? But there are plenty of examples showing that he held racist views. Everybody did. At that time almost all whites were racist."

Ted went on to talk about other kinds of succession. "I think most chiefs, whether it be college presidents or corporate CEOs, want to have qualified successors. But you often get a cynical thing in the corporate world, where people want a weak person to succeed them, to emphasize their own strengths. To have a strong person follow them demeans their accomplishments."

"And the new person has to prove that he's better than his predecessor, so he starts tinkering instead of waiting and learning," I said. Increasingly the corporate world is concerned about the loss of knowledge as a result of retirements, creating a niche for those interested in participating part-time, often as consultants, as Ruth Massinga and Michael Crowe continue to do.

"People of accomplishment naturally worry about what lies ahead in their own lives after retirement. CEOs think of politics as a way to go. They think of the foundation route. They start giving money to important social causes. This is important to make their lives full. I think of these goals as a kind of tripod—government service, involvement in academia, say a college trusteeship, or philanthropy, a board seat on a respected foundation. They start off with money, and they ask, What the hell does all this mean? How do I really establish myself as a person of achievement where people will say my work did change the world in some way? They are convinced that they are as good as they need to be.

"I often think of the enormously wealthy Boone Pickens, who has made huge fortunes in oil. He is approaching the end of his life, so he announces that he's going to pile lots of money into clean energy. Some people may, you know, fund new buildings and insist that their names be on them, but they're extending their own lives in many cases, aren't they? So there's a selfish aspect to it, and then there is an idealistic aspect, where it's 'Gee, I've got to do *something*.'

"I think the factors are: 'I'm not going to be bored by golf for the rest of my life; I've got to do something new; I don't know what it would be.' There's a boredom factor, plus extending their lives, plus somehow transmitting to the next generation something of value. Also, I do think the religious thing is a factor with many people, even if they don't go to church—the Day of Judgment. Maybe it's not about going to hell or heaven, but that there will be some sort of a judgment made on your life. 'What did your life mean? What did you do?'

"Going back to legacy effect, what are we about? Maybe your idea of legacy has a profound basis in biology. If we're just another animal with no function in the world except to transmit genes, is that the story of what we transmit? My values will not necessarily pass on to my children. My children have no serious interest in what I'm doing. They say, 'Dad, you're a good guy.' But they quickly go to sleep if I raise issues about blacks in higher education, the nature of justice, the loss of bird habitats, or the future of higher education—things I care deeply about. I'm not transmitting anything but a general attitude toward life and what one does in life other than eat donuts and go to dinner parties. They have their own agendas—goals that may be more important than mine." Ted's other consuming interest is in birds, where a variety of altruistic behaviors have been observed that play back in his thinking about social issues. "In these huge colonies of murres up in Newfoundland, I've seen birds that have adopted three little chicks that don't belong to them. This has nothing to do with transmitting their genes, yet they do this."

"Your kids like your hobby," I said, "but that's how they see it, it's your hobby." On reflection, it struck me that it would be more accurate to say that they *respect* Ted's work and he respects the choices they have made. At one point in the conversation, when he was speaking about how often the children of wealthy families become playboys and contribute nothing to society, he described his family as all engaged in doing things that he regards as *worthy,* a description that has stuck in my mind, shorthand perhaps for *worthy of respect*—including the possibility of goals more important than his own. Ted is married to Mary Cross, a talented photographer, and they have a blended family of five daughters. One is a psychotherapist who also teaches at Yale. Another, who was widowed fairly young, majored in mathematics at Harvard and founded with her cousins a successful data storage and information delivery company, in addition to serving on nonprofit boards. Of his stepdaughters, one is a nurse practitioner, one is a lawyer, and the third has just finished her Ph.D. in psychology. Although his main focus has been on racism, he referred frequently to the barriers women have had to overcome and has clearly given thought to the problem of sexism.

"You know, the theory of [Richard] Dawkins is that we're only here to transmit genes,"[1] he said. "It's a most powerful biological legacy, yet there is an overlay consisting of the values or social capital we pass on."

Looking at the transmission of values and ideas to a wider community may become critical in later life, since the genes will have been passed on some time ago, with unpredictable results. "Actually," I pointed out, "biologists are beginning, when they're talking about social animals, let's say a herd of deer, to look at the question of why some deer survive beyond their reproductive capacity. Because if the only thing that's critical is passing on the genes, and it only takes a year for a fawn to be an adult, then why don't the older deer just die off at that point? The older animals may have knowledge—for instance, of where to find water or grazing during a drought—that is critical to the survival of the entire herd, and of course the herd has many genes in common. The older animals contribute to what's called the herd's inclusive fitness, and so do birds that adopt parentless chicks.* As for humans, we transmit certain traits genetically and we transmit other traits by teaching."

"It's not only teaching, but the images a parent displays to a child will influence that child forever," Ted elaborated. "I remember my mother—what she read to me, what she said to me in terms of ambition and belief in myself. Those images are totally controlling. She kept reading *The Little Engine That Could* to me. She always said, 'You're a lot better than you think you are. You got a C plus? Well, you're better than that.' Mother would take us over to the Perkins School for the Blind, and we'd do work there. She was very strong on seeing that her children helped others. She always insisted that I have a job in the summer helping people. And Mother had a tremendous influence on me in terms of the importance of bringing something to your life other than economic success.

"Later on, I was in the Office of Economic Opportunity in the Nixon administration. [Donald] Rumsfeld was head of OEO but had bigger aspirations and went to work in the White House as counselor for Nixon. He then put [Dick] Cheney in charge of the OEO, and I worked with them. Few people today believe me when I say how dedicated Rumsfeld and Cheney were to the programs I was developing for inner-city economic development."

*See chapter I, reference 3, on page 253.

Ted had recently reviewed figures showing that in many black families that had made it into the middle class, children were not growing up with the values that would have carried that gain into the next generation. "Why would one group, where so many have achieved middle-class status, not be transmitting their achievements? And why is this failing to happen at a disastrous rate? I would like to know if it's happening with Hispanics or other groups. And how about women? Does it make a difference if the parent is a college graduate, and does that accomplishment get passed on?"

"I think we underestimate the cultural lag of any social change," I said. "You often see parents who've gotten into the middle class but are still raising their children as they remember being raised themselves, so the children grow up without the middle-class values. And how much does one get from one's peers, and who are the peers with whom these kids are associating? I think you have to ask that, too."

Ted asked me how I would define the difference between heritage and legacy, and I took a stab at it. "Heritage is looking back, legacy is looking forward. So you have Black History Month, and that's about heritage. Black legacy month would be about the future."

"There's wanting to pass a legacy on to your children to give them the advantages that you've attained," he said. "I might make sure my kid has enough money to go to college, or to buy a house, all that kind of thing. This can be a quite selfish way of making your life more important because you're passing on an advantage. But a legacy could be a big disadvantage, too, say in some Asian societies where the social security system is based on the children taking care of their parents. I don't know if it's a legal obligation in China, but it's a very profound social obligation, isn't it?"

"That's the tradition," I said. "And that incidentally is the thing that was hardly ever mentioned in the debate about Social Security, that if Social Security deteriorates, it's not only seniors who will suffer but the young people who are trying to get themselves established, who may feel obligated to fill the vacuum. So Social Security is not a program that just looks after one generation; it affects the entire household."

"Going back to the Chinese system that imposes obligations on children," Ted mused. "An individual child may say, 'My God! My whole life I've got to support my parents.' Or somewhere in Africa, where the youngest unmarried daughter has to take care of the elderly parent—sort of a reverse system of primogeniture."

"That's why many women aren't getting married in Japan now; they don't want to take on that job, which falls on the daughter-in-law." This is typical of cultures where the bride goes to live with her husband in his parents' home. Although this kind of direct caregiving is less common in the West, the next generation may inherit the tasks of dismantling a household or managing an intellectual estate, as I managed the intellectual estates of my parents for thirty years after their deaths.

"I've always been interested in the conflict between the merit system and the legacy system," Ted continued. "What is the function of the biggest legacy system of all, which is primogeniture? Theoretically, its purpose was to eliminate disputes. Even in this country, someone like Malcolm Forbes dies and he's got five kids who want to run the empire, so what he wisely did was designate one person, who he thought best qualified, but sometimes there's a rule that the firstborn gets it."

"It's to prevent the breaking up of estates," I said. "If you look at agricultural societies—look at Ireland, say—you've got a family living on enough land to support a couple and their children, and if each one of them marries and has children and all want to live on that land or divide it up, they've got to be starving. Primogeniture avoids disputes and sets it up so that the division of agricultural land into separate holdings remains at a level that can support a household. And the others may emigrate or find some other kind of work.

"Now, in Islam the rules of inheritance theoretically divide the inheritance among all the children, and this can be a major problem, because holdings can get smaller and smaller and scattered around. You can do that with sheep and camels if the land they graze is essentially common land, because the heirs start off with a certain number and they will propagate. But if it's land that you have to farm, you can't start off with a small piece and have it propagate!"

"Inheriting a white skin has been a legacy advantage and a black skin was a big disadvantage," Ted commented. "Today, having a black skin may be an advantage in applying for certain positions. Being a woman has an important advantage in becoming a college president! Affirmative action has shifted the biological disadvantage to advantage in some contexts. I think that's good. Who would dream that this could have happened?

"It's difficult to sort out good and bad in these legacy advantages and disadvantages. Does the legacy system always interfere with merit? Are legacy and merit always at war with each other? Now take a typical situation where, say, the head of IBM wants his son to be president. Now that's in direct conflict with the merit system. People who rise to positions of power (a) want to hold on to them and (b) want to control where they go next, whether it's property or wealth or influence. In college admissions, the merit system is overturned by the legacy advantage. They even call the kid who is admitted under the system a 'legacy.' "

" 'Unto every one which hath shall be given; and from him that hath not, even that he hath shall be taken away from him,' " I said, quoting Luke 19:26.

Ted was pleased at the fact that in recent years the extent of scholarship support at prestigious academic institutions has increased dramatically, to the point of no tuition if parental income is below a certain amount. But the lifetime advantage of that kind of education has declined, and graduates of state universities are getting the top corporate jobs. "It's very strange. Harvard recently said no loans. Princeton is free. But it didn't seem to have much effect on black admissions. Large numbers of blacks at Harvard don't need scholarships. It used to be that the blacks at the strong colleges were so-called ghetto kids, poverty kids. Not so anymore. Now they are sons of engineers and doctors. A lot of them are preppies. Remember the effort way back in the sixties? But again, it's not always a question of money. There may be social factors which stop a blue-collar kid from Detroit going to our elite eastern schools."

Ted has been an education watcher but not an educator. He is now a life trustee of Amherst College. "I can go to any board meeting, but I prefer not to," he told me. "They don't want old fogies up there, sounding off and asking questions. I always want to talk about the GI Bill and how that transformed Amherst. The GI funding of higher education created a nation where fifteen percent of the kids went to college instead of six percent before the war. What a legacy for the nation! When I went to Amherst, there were freshman kids with four or five sport coats, expensive furniture, everything but slaves. The GI Bill brought in all these wonderful blue-collar kids from working-class families in Lawrence, Lowell, Springfield. They had never considered Amherst before. Thanks to the GI Bill, Amherst was free. These kids, they came to Amherst and radically altered the demographics of the campus.

"Amherst today has the highest percentage of blacks of the most prestigious colleges and universities in the country. And Amherst is working hard on the low-income thing. President Tony Marx has adopted a no-loan policy, with no tuition for kids under fifty thousand dollars parental income. But think of a bright kid from Detroit, where his father works on an assembly line. You post this huge tuition or sticker fee and you send an elitist message to these kids. They don't want to go to school with kids whose fathers are earning half a million or a million a year.

"My kids know how I value opportunity, equality, equal treatment, decency, and civility, but sometimes I think the only thing I passed on is that they'll say, 'Daddy saved our ass during the war, when he was in the Pacific fighting the battle there for two years.' I can take credit for that legacy. It's an important thing I did. Your life was at risk for two years in a war that's probably the only war we've fought recently that one could justify. So I passed that on to them. They're still alive, not living under a Nazi or Communist regime, so that was a legacy. But also, I passed on the values that they know I believe in because of the work I do with the journal and with blacks. But what I give isn't specific, I'm not transmitting a skill like an electrician might transmit a trade to a child. That's not going to happen, nor would I expect it.

"Businesspeople do often want to transmit a position. They want to bring up their kid to eventually head the corporation. You know, IBM, McGraw-Hill; there are thousands of corporations where the objective of the CEO is to transmit the job to his son, and maybe today to his daughter."

Ted paused. "There's something more called for. At some point you introspectively look at your life and say, What has it meant? And think about the thoughts, not just think but think about your thoughts."

That phrase, "think about your thoughts," struck me—the need for self-observation and the need not only to look at particular thoughts or actions but to place them in a larger ethical frame of reference. In anthropology we emphasize participant observation, but in recent years we have been increasingly careful to include, as part of that, reflexivity or self-observation. "Do you think if you knew why you were doing what you do, it would be easier to pass on? If you had a rationale for it?" I asked.

"No, no, no. I don't think so. No, I think you pass on a legacy by example."

"One of the things that I've been interested in," I said, "is that I know a lot of people who were raised in religious households and don't go to church anymore, but some of the things that they grew up with, including the notion that you help the poor and the unfortunate or you work for change, get carried on, maybe by starting nonprofits that are doing real service. Religious values get passed on without the beliefs, and it's not clear to me how many generations you can do that for."

"Well, a lot of Christian values are pretty bad, too," Ted said. Actually, the issue is not so much whether the values passed on are religious or not but the level of abstraction, because the specifics change. It is one thing for members of a family to see Dad contributing to his alma mater and to continue to do so; it is something different if they have absorbed the idea that education is important and they contribute to the institution that seems to need their support in the present to improve quality or access. I grew up hearing about the "poor starving Europeans" at the end of World War II, but the principle involved is that no one should starve, and that may involve giving to relieve famine areas in Africa or Asia. Ted's concern with birds might involve struggling against climate change in the twenty-first century. Or one of his children might carry his concern for black education into a concern for children with disabilities. The example that he sets, of commitment, is important, but in order to be followed, his commitment has to be translated to the needs of a new era. This is why Ted's recognition that what his daughters do is "worthy" makes sense, even though it leaves him concerned about what to do with his own ongoing work.

Ted returned to the meaning for him of having served in World War II. "Many men my age have nothing to look back on that makes them a good person except maybe that they went to war. Like manning a Navy ship when I was eighteen years old—just totally incompetent, but you grew up fast. Then to have to go back to Amherst and wear little beanie hats and fraternity rushing, so absurd! You know, after you'd seen people die, seen people lose their heads because of a big gun that backfired . . . If you're interviewing older men who were in World War II, the war experience would be very important for you. They're all my age, eighty-three, eighty-four, eighty-five, dying like flies. Read the obituary pages. I think it's important to know their attitudes towards war and whether war is for them a proud memory of having done something important."

"Do you think that the kids that are in Iraq now are having that same experience?" I asked him.

"I don't think so, because I'm sure most of them hate the war. They think the war was a fraud. The other war was quite different. When Pearl Harbor came, no one, *no one,* thought of running to Canada."

"It was the 'good war,' " I said.

"I tell my children, Why don't you write me a note on VJ Day and say, Thanks, Dad? You know they don't. A lot of men have no legacy but having protected the lives of future children. Most men hate their jobs, a lot of them don't like their wives, have no respect for their children. All they have is the war, only the memories, the glories. I think if you talk to older men, the war is a very important thing. To have fought in World War II, that is a helluva thing to bring your children, even though you feel the evils of war."

Ted Cross was the only person I interviewed for this project who had seen active service in World War II, because my primary focus was on the choices that individuals make as they enter Adulthood II, which for Ted seems to have coincided with the founding of his journal fifteen years before. Ted used this period of life to create an organization for which he now needs to consider succession plans, just as Jim Morton has had to think ahead to a successor to lead the New York Interfaith Center, which he established when he retired in 1997. Ted died while this book was in final preparation.

For those who are a decade or more younger than Ted, "the war" is the Vietnam war, which has left very different memories. Jane Fonda was just over thirty and an established film star when she met her second husband, Tom Hayden, who was already deeply involved in protesting the war. She had been living in France with her first husband, Roger Vadim, and returned in the late sixties to an America in which the activism of the civil rights movement was being displaced by the anti–Vietnam war movement, with the feminist movement developing alongside. "What happened, which is part of my DNA now, was the realization of the collective power of people working together," she told me. "I was a rugged individualist, I had no friends, women were rivals. I was not relational. It was my second act that coincided with the end of the sixties and into the seventies, when the women's movement needed women activists, and suddenly—it was like getting into a warm bath—'only together will we make a difference,' 'we want to make a difference, but we can't do it individually.' The other thing that is still with me is learning, mostly from the Vietnamese, about what strength is. That the bamboo is stronger than the oak. That the kind of strength that our culture thinks is important is ultimately not as important as compassion and flexibility and collectivity.

"The main people that I worked with during those years of my morning-to-night, twenty-four-hour, all-the-time activism, from about age thirty-two to fifty-two, when I married Ted [Turner], were men. It was led by men. I so admired my second husband, Tom Hayden. He had a depth of experience in the movement that I lacked, so I believed in his narrative and it became my narrative, yet I always knew that I would have to find my own narrative in time. It wasn't until my third act that I developed my own narrative, which is really a gender journey. It's a gender narrative. That part of the activism is different. Part of the sameness is the fact of optimism. I'm hopeful."

" 'I can make it better'?" I said, quoting back to Jane a phrase she uses repeatedly in her memoir.[2]

"Yeah. That's right. I can make it better, really can make it better. And I have a role to play in that.

"I'll tell you something that's different now. When I started off, I was ashamed of my differences from fellow activists. The movie *Barbarella* was playing, and I was a celebrity. I wasn't rich, but I certainly had more money than they did, and I could draw in money. And I wanted to become just like them so I could fit in and not feel that separation.

"Now I understand my role and I'm very comfortable with it. I'm not a visionary, I'm a cheerleader. I can help take the vision out to large numbers of people. The metaphor that I see is that I'm a repeater—you know, at the top of mountains they have those antennas that stick up that pick up the [radio] waves from down in the valley and carry them on? I see myself as a repeater. There have to be visionaries, and there have to be repeaters." It's a good metaphor, but it applies to only part of what Jane does. She also amplifies the message and the vision and transforms it by the decisiveness of her own engagement into a call to action and a reachable goal.

I had been pondering the ways in which Dick Goldsby and Ted Cross spoke about legacy, and before raising the question with Jane, I asked myself how I would use the term in thinking of her and found a series of different ways. Since I see my own legacy in my writing, I thought of her films and books. I thought of *Jane Fonda's Workout Book*,[3] which has made young women aware of how to care for their bodies, and I thought of her as a model for activism. Last of all, I wondered whether the conversations she and Tom Hayden had created among Vietnam veterans and servicemen had contributed to a new understanding of the psychological damage done by warfare even to those with no physical wounds—the mysterious maladies sometimes dismissed as cowardice and sometimes called in previous conflicts battle fatigue and shell shock, now understood in the wider context of post-traumatic stress disorder. I had a list, but Jane surprised me with a three-word answer: "My life story," she said.

"I thought of it as a book for women," she continued, "but men really responded to it. You know, there's the idea that you can't show vulnerability, you can't show weakness, you have to suppress emotion. And then this notion of 'good enough is good enough' is important, not in the same way as for women, but it's the same theme."

"The problem of trying to be perfect," I remarked. I wish [D. W.] Winnicott's concept of the 'good enough mother' were known by more young American women.[4] "You can't be the perfect mother," I remarked. "You know, I had that same experience with *Composing a Life*, that men responded to it, and some have complained to me about my writing about discontinuities and conflicting commitments as if these were only women's problems."

"What do you answer?" Jane asked.

"I answer that, as far as I'm concerned, women are human beings and these are human problems. I happen to have chosen female examples to look at, reversing the way that for centuries women have been reading books, ostensibly describing human beings, that were actually based only on men. Some men will not learn from a book in which the examples are women, and some men will. That's why I'm including men specifically in the book I'm working on now, to make it more accessible to more of the people that need it. That's really what it comes to."

Jane was struck by my bringing up the *Workout*. "I think I would have avoided mentioning it," she said, "because I've been so described as saying to women, 'You have be slim and glamorous and look like me.' I felt guilty about it, frankly, until I really thought about it more, and then it was kind of like, wait a damn minute, if I'm honest I have to go back to my experience as someone who thought she was extremely unattractive and unacceptable and suffered from an eating disorder. I had stopped the behavior, the acting out of my addiction, but the *Workout* for me was a way of taking control of my body. Liberation starts for a lot of us in our muscles. It took me, I would say, four years to get to the wait a minute stage. The purpose was to allow women who had no time and had young children to be able to own their bodies in their own homes. And I got letters like, 'I never wanted to go out,' 'I never could stand up to my boss, and now I can.' So I'm reluctant to claim the *Workout* as a legacy, but now that you have reminded me, yes, I think that is a legacy."

As Jane went on to consider the legacy question, she described how writing her memoir, *My Life So Far,* after twenty years or more of being "under the radar," had led great numbers of people to tell her how she had affected their lives. "Writing my book was a very liberating experience, and I went out on the road extensively when it came out. I spent almost a year traversing this country. I feel like all the different changes I've gone through as I've composed my life are fodder; they're the fertilizer for me to grow lessons from that will be helpful to other people. I learned in writing the memoir and traveling around to promote it that I can use my own experiences to make people who are reading them think about their own situation.

"I was struck by all these generations of women I met on three levels. There would be 'My favorite movie, *9 to 5,* oh, my God, it changed my life.' That kind of thing. Sometimes it was *Cat Ballou,* sometimes it was *Barefoot in the Park,* but different movies had intersected the lives of so many women. Then there were the women like, 'I marched with you in San Diego, do you remember?' 'I went to Chapel Hill when you spoke there in 1971.' And then there was the *Workout,* the women who said, 'I got through my pregnancy with your *Pregnancy, Birth, and Recovery* book,' or 'I recovered from mastectomy doing your . . . ,' and in a way it was the *Workout* stuff that was the most personal, you know, the way the music of Bonnie Raitt or James Taylor is like the wallpaper of your life for chunks of time that are embedded in you. That was kind of the way the *Workout* was."

"We came from a generation where women were not encouraged to be athletic," I said, "and along came midlife and bodies needed moving, so I think that's a very important legacy. It might not be everyone using the same videos, but the creation of a different body consciousness, which we were talking about earlier. I think you also helped make people realize they can have an effect by demonstrating, by activism. So much has been done to discourage citizen activism since that time in very subtle ways. Now, if you get fifty thousand people out demonstrating, it hardly makes the news, whereas it did in those days. I think that's still a legacy. It's there for people to think about. Maybe *legacy* is not the right word, but when I think about trying to get older adults more politically engaged, one of the things I think about is all the people who remember the sixties and seventies and left that behind, and I wonder whether that's something that can be reawakened."

Jane has a foundation that was endowed as a gift to her by Ted Turner, and she uses it to bring together her two birth children, one stepdaughter, and one informally adopted daughter who has become a member of the family, each deciding on the use of a share of the income. Jane's share goes to the Georgia Campaign for Adolescent Pregnancy Prevention and to a program she created called the Jane Fonda Center for adolescent reproductive health at the Emory School of Medicine.

"What I discovered," she told me, "was that the adults who were working with kids don't understand and don't like them. And so there was a need for the training of adults—social workers, juvenile court judges, nurses, teachers—with an understanding of adolescent development and how sexual abuse and racism affected them, training people to do relationship-based work, and developing curricula."

"You know," I interrupted, "what you're saying involves trying to get the people that work with adolescents to switch from seeing them as problems to seeing them as potential, and it's very close to the issue of people who work with the elderly and see only their deficits. They see them as vulnerable and as a problem, rather than seeing them as a source of strength for the society. It's that same switch—"

"From 'at risk' to 'at promise,' " Jane cut in. Realizing the connections between our interests had us both leaping into the exchange. A change in phrasing can make the difference in how people see each other, like Jane's use of the word *countenance*, making the connection to a face-to-face relationship, whereas I sometimes speak of recognition of the other. "That's what it means to me, you know, grokking the totality of a person,[5] countenancing their whole humanity. The role of parents or surrogate parents is to reflect back to the child their being-ness with eyes of love. Sometimes the eyes of the parents are covered with duct tape! That's what narcissism does to eyes! Then the child doesn't get that assurance of love.

"I've studied photographs that I found, after I wrote my memoir, of myself with my father, when I was probably two, and I see love in his face, and that says to me, Aha, very early on I was *countenanced* by my father. Not by my mother, but by my father, and that's partly where my resilience comes from, and then along the way mothers of my best friends countenanced me. They would do something that my parents never did, take me on their lap and talk to me about how I was supposed to behave, and, 'Are you hearing me, Lady?' 'Don't you think that that is the way it should be, Jane?'

"Some of the training that we do, that I love, is called *reflective supervision*. It teaches people who work with children the difference between 'you are a child-care provider' and the give-and-take relatedness that you can have with a young child, which is what teaches the child 'people are good and people pay attention to what I'm feeling and thinking.' You know? That's what we're trying to teach people who work with young people. It's hard with adolescents because they're prickly and they want to make you think that they don't care what you say and . . ."

"You felt that you initially didn't know that and you had to learn?" I asked.

"Oh, I had to learn it, yes. I had to learn everything. It's never too late, although it's a lot harder to heal those early wounds if you weren't there early on."

It occurred to me that Jane's awareness of what she had missed was what made her aware at this stage of her life of the need for teaching it. "The other side of it is that you know in your bones that that kind of regard, that kind of attention, is not something that can be taken for granted, it's not instinctive, it has to be learned," I said. "People who learn it from their own childhood may have no memory of having learned it, so the fact that you had to learn it at a later stage of your life means that you have the memory of the learning process, and that underlies your ability to build an institution that will do this. One of the things that has happened over the last half century is an empathetic rethinking of what human beings have to learn that tends to be taken for granted and *how* they learn it. It turns up in psychotherapy, and it turns up in athletic coaching and in physical therapy."

"Right," Jane responded. "This is the great historic contribution of the women's movement. I'll give an example. Freud as a very young psychoanalyst was listening to his young women patients, witnessing what was called hysteria, and as he built their trust they then revealed to him that they had been sexually abused by family members. He wrote a paper about it, and he was so shamed by his peers in academe that he withdrew his thesis and changed it into 'They are fantasizing.'⁶

"So a long time goes by to the early seventies and the beginning of feminism, with women going into various fields, including psychology, and they are taking on patients and participating in consciousness-raising groups. And in these consciousness-raising groups, they begin to say, 'You know, I don't know what I'm hearing, but I'm being told by many of my clients that they have experienced incest,' and then another woman in the group would say, 'I've had that experience,' and they began to realize that this wasn't one in a million, that this was very common. Why were they hearing this? They were hearing it because they were sitting face-to-face with their patients and responding empathically to their patients' pain and even crying with them, and they discovered of course not only the commonness of incest but that restoring relatedness to the therapeutic process is what heals." Jane told the familiar story with passion. "That changed everything. We now know that that limbic resonance between people is what saves lives and what allows people to heal. It really was the women's movement that brought that about."

"My sense, Jane, is that all the time that you spent with veterans and soldiers in the Vietnam era, sure you were involved in the resistance movement, in trying to stop the war, but you were also countenancing them and helping them to understand their pain and their own dissent. I would guess that contributed to the evolution of understanding of post-traumatic stress, not for framing the diagnosis but for helping veterans to be able to say why it was so awful and helping them to say it to each other."

"I'll never forget the first exposure I had to it, at Fort Ord," Jane told me, "with this young man who could not speak above a whisper and could not get the words out. I finally intuited that what he was trying to tell me was that he had killed a child, but he couldn't really get it out." When Jane told her father about it, he was angry, saying that a soldier shouldn't talk about such a thing, and she argued that he had to. "A lot of it came out of the FTA, the Free the Army Show. That's something the GIs came up with, but really they meant 'fuck the army' and there was a GI paper called *FTA* and our show was called *FTA*. We would meet with groups of GIs and listen, and yes, I think that talking therapy empowered a lot of the guys."

"That new understanding of trauma has illuminated so many other kinds of events that happened to people," I went on, "and yet we're still trying to persuade them of the damage that they're doing to civilians with their military adventures, to the children who see it, and to the soldiers themselves. How much of this society consists of people who are severely damaged either by abuse in childhood or by trauma as young adults?"

"People don't realize," Jane said.

"We abuse children in the same way in which we abuse the natural world," I went on. "We think we own it. I wasn't suggesting, you know, that you intuited or formulated the diagnosis of PTSD, but I think you contributed to the conversation that made it possible."

Like Dick Goldsby, Jane has been able to look at mistakes made in her youth, and perhaps the one she regrets most was allowing herself to be photographed in Hanoi beside an antiaircraft gun. "What happened to you has happened to many people. You got 'quoted out of context,' " I said. "A piece of your behavior got pulled out of its context and used."

"I regret that that photograph hurt some soldiers and their families, because they felt that an American who had benefited from a lot of things this country has to offer had turned against her country's troops, which of course was totally the opposite," Jane told me. "That causes me pain, and I'm really sorry about that. The right-wing politicians tried to make it look like I was a traitor. But I know what I am. I'm of the opinion that if you are true and clear and coming from a good place, it blows away in the ether."

"You know, we seem to have the idea that all criticism is hostile. We don't in this country have a clear understanding of loving criticism," I said.

"Our forefathers did—those deists!" Jane exclaimed.

"I think it's connected to a psychological issue about dealing with ambivalence toward parents that you love and you also hate a bit. You know, you can't not love them, even the children of abusive parents can't get rid of that love, but they do need to admit that something was wrong. When we criticize the policies of this country, especially in wartime, people say that makes you disloyal. It doesn't, any more than it's unloving for a parent to correct a child, and it's really important to keep making that case. Ambivalence is the human condition. There is not a parent on earth that hasn't occasionally hated their child. There's not a child that hasn't sometimes hated the parent, and that's just how it is."

"You know, it's one of the values of getting older," Jane said, "at least for our generation. I've lived long enough to have remembered and lived in Europe at a time when this country was revered for democracy and fairness and freedom and those things, and I particularly was exposed to it because my father was a kind of symbol of the things about America that people in other parts of the world held dear. To have experienced that and then watched our image deteriorate for the rest of the world was so painful."

Jane in her memoir criticizes herself as a parent, so I wondered how her experience of multiple kinds of parenthood had played into her effort to understand what it is to be a parent. "The thing about my book that seems to have surprised people the most is that I admit that I was not a good parent," she said. "That's not something you're supposed to do. But the fact is that I could not *not* 'fess up, because my daughter would have called me on it. So my goal was to communicate to my children, particularly to my firstborn, my daughter, that it had nothing to do with rejecting them. No matter what you try, until you've healed yourself, you end up repeating some of the same mistakes. And I repeated some of the things that . . . When I die she will read it differently. I'm urging people in my book that I'm writing about the third act to talk about these things while they're still alive.

"What has happened to me is . . . I can't just take off and go to Hanoi and do the things that I did. I can't—the way my activism manifested itself during my second act was physically really challenging, constant traveling and speaking. I can't do that now. What has shifted is that I feel more like a teacher."

As far as I can tell, Jane has been a teacher all of her adult life, but now her concept of what it means to be a teacher is shifting. Partly this is because she has become increasingly confident of her own values and of the validity of what she has to say. In order for her life story to become a legacy, she has to take ownership of it. But it also takes time to outgrow the narrow meaning of teacher as that person who stands in front of a classroom and to think about the way we teach through our actions and especially by modeling the process of learning as we teach. The future is built from what we are able to pass on, whether in words spoken or words on paper, actions taken or gestures made, but the modalities of teaching change in the course of the life cycle. In different ways, Cross, Ted, and Jane are putting what they have learned into the hands of a new generation they respect but cannot and should not control.

CHAPTER XI

Knowledge Old and New

WITH EACH PERSON that I have interviewed at length, I have begun in childhood, going even further back by learning about the background of parents. This book has been a study not of old age or even of late adulthood but rather of the ways in which the extended period of health and activity achieved by modern science fits into a lifetime, and of the potential contributions that period can make to human society. I have been exploring the idea that our new longevity is not equivalent to an extension of old age, years added on at the end, but rather a period inserted in the life course after the era associated with full adult participation and generativity but before the decline of old age, a period characterized by the accumulated experience of adulthood but endowed with health and energy, so that wisdom is combined with activity and often with activism for the common good. Continuing health makes it possible to make choices, and these choices reflect the ongoing ways in which individuals compose and re-compose their lives, intuitively seeking balance, fulfillment, grace.

Many writers have tried to capture what is distinctive about our species. *Homo sapiens* is also *Homo ludens* and *Homo faber.* Alfred Korzybski described our distinctive quality as "time binding," a characteristic that includes the ability to recall the past and to plan for the future, as well as the capacity to recognize and analyze sequences of cause and effect, a capacity that is amplified as knowledge is developed and passed on from generation to generation.[1] The invention of writing offered the possibility of time binding across millennia. Not only do human beings learn and teach but they do so across generations and across centuries.

The accumulation of scientific knowledge and technological possibility, however, has created a process of accelerated change in which the challenge of keeping up from day to day has actually undermined our capacity for long-term thinking and vision even as it has increased the future costs of bad decisions taken in the present. Korzybski titled a famous book, published in 1921, *Manhood of Humanity.*[2] I might have titled this one *The Second Adulthood of Humankind: adulthood* because females as well as males mature and continue to mature, often becoming less contrastively gendered with age; human*kind*—our kind—as a reminder that we are a species of mammal among other species, interdependent members of the planetary biosphere. Purposiveness, one aspect of time binding, can lead to disaster when narrowly focused and combined with high technology. Protection from the negative results of conscious purpose depends on a broader focus, an attention to side effects and collateral damage, and an awareness of the way effects circle back on causes, either for self-correction or for acceleration to disaster.[3]

As individuals, we live long lives compared to other mammals, and those lives are getting even longer, so that later adulthood is a time rich with memories even as it is shadowed by the fear of memory loss. Much happens in the course of any lifetime, and contemporary lifetimes are lived in the context of rapid social and cultural change. Yet wisdom is not simply an accumulation of information or experiences; it is the fruit of continuing reflection on encounters over time, a skill at drawing connections and finding similarities, looking for underlying patterns. It may be helpful to think of wisdom as a process rather than a possession, just as the strengths of several of the life stages—hope, love, care—reflect verbs as well as nouns. The bodily modalities of infancy that interested Erikson to begin with are verbs: taking in, holding on, moving, intruding. One of the weaknesses of English as a language of thought is our tendency to reify, to turn actions and abstractions into things. Perhaps all the basic strengths Erikson described should be rephrased as verbs.

One of Jane Fonda's first questions to me was about what changes and what does not: "You wrote, I think this was in *Composing a Life,* 'If your opinions and commitments appear to change from year to year or decade to decade, what are the more abstract underlying convictions that have held steady, that might never have become visible without the surface variation?'⁴ That really struck me, and I wonder, could you give some examples of how the abstract underlying convictions can be made more apparent because of surface variation?"

To answer this question, I used an example that my father often gave in discussing acquired and inherited characteristics:⁵ "A tightrope walker traditionally carries a thin bamboo pole, so very small variations in angle will restore his balance on the high wire—like the small adjustments in steering when you're riding a bike. Now, if you take that bamboo and freeze its position, so it ceases to be flexible, he will fall off the wire. That's why you can't inherit acquired characteristics. You have to have a range of possible adaptation, within which you are able to change, in order to stay alive when the environment changes or to correct for errors that might drive you off course. The variations preserve the underlying constancy.

"I've done workshops a couple of times for groups of Catholic nuns, and this is the kind of question they faced with all the reform that was started by Pope John XXIII. Here were all these women who had gone into convents with very specific ideas of what nuns did and what they wore. They had set routines, and the rules spelled it all out, so that they knew what they were committing themselves to, and all of a sudden that was being changed. The habits that nuns used to wear started out as modest, clean, unpretentious versions of what women wore when the orders were founded. And they got frozen, which didn't matter much for several centuries while change was gradual. But eventually, as styles of clothing changed, instead of conveying modesty, dedication, willingness to serve, the habits began to look grotesque and weird to people. Children were even frightened of nuns, or thought they didn't have feet, things like that. The rules didn't allow for other kinds of adaptation, so they snuffed out creativity and new learning.[6]

"The external symbols of the commitment the nuns had made changed in meaning because of the change in context, so it was time to ask, What is the message that's supposed to be conveyed by what we wear or how we live or whether we live in community or can live in separate apartments? How, in a new context, can we communicate a commitment that remains unchanged, instead of inadvertently communicating something completely different? Many nuns were upset and had a profound sense of loss. They didn't take the change as an invitation to reaffirm their basic commitment, because they mistook the externals for the commitment itself. This happened with liturgical reform also. Some people were really upset. The form of the service suddenly became different. Whoa! It was gone! It didn't mean the same thing! You have to stop and think to see that maybe changing the form was getting it closer to the meaning it always had.

"Those are two examples that I have in fairly developed forms. More personally," I went on, "my husband and I have lived and worked in different countries, and each time I have had to ask myself who I am and what I can do to use my experience and skill and express my continuing commitments in a new way in a new context. This is a kind of translation. After all, just to say 'good morning' or 'thank you' to someone, I may have to switch from familiar to unfamiliar words. It seems to me that if you don't have to deal with a change of context, you can skim along feeling that the specifics of a particular era, whether it's how you dress or the rituals you use or where you show up for work in the morning, are what life is about, without asking what the details of my day-to-day life refer back to. When the context changes, you need to rediscover what it's all about."

The tightrope walker analogy is a way of looking at evolutionary change, seeing that a change that seems adaptive in the short term might lead into a fatal cul-de-sac, as excessive size probably was for the dinosaurs. In the evolutionary context, the constancy that is preserved is survival. For human beings, we may want to consider individual survival as meaning something more than minimal brain activity in a vegetative state, looking instead for some surviving identity and connection to others. For human communities, the survival of value systems and ideas may seem more important than specific populations or customs. During the fifties, when we had air-raid drills at my school, crouching under our desks, and my father pointed out that this charade was an absurdity in a nuclear world, I asked him, Didn't he think it was important for Americans to survive and win the next war? He said all he "could really hope for was the survival of ten thousand relatively untraumatized human beings, regardless of nationality or race, who could start again." And yet the politicians were preparing for such a war as a way to defend the nation. Furthermore, the notion that nuclear weapons can be used for defense is one in which the technological means defeat the purpose.

What does it mean to survive? This is really the basic issue that faces everyone in growing older, the issue of how to affirm what is essential to one's identity in a context that includes both cultural changes and changes in one's own physical being. How do I grow older and remain myself—or rather, how in growing older do I become more truly myself, and how is that expressed in what I do or say or contribute?

I learned forty years ago to put my daughter to sleep on her tummy, but the changing context of knowledge now says that, to avoid crib death, infants should sleep on their backs—so my expression of love and care has been reinterpreted as a hazard.[7] Again and again, I find myself in situations where I know what "I" would typically do and find that, at seventy, I'd better do something different. My seven-year-old grandson wants to look over a fence to see a construction site, and the behavior that naturally expresses my relationship to him is to lift him up, but my back won't allow it. When I want to pass on something I have learned in life, I have to find ways of translating it to the experience of a different generation, just as I had to translate myself in adjusting to life in other countries. As I searched for a title for this book, however, I found myself rejecting titles which suggest that we can newly create ourselves in later life, yet this is a common rhetoric. One of the strengths of American culture is our belief that we can reinvent ourselves,[8] but one of the weaknesses is the willingness to discard earlier learning.

The challenge to creativity is to go forward drawing on what is useful and valuable in past experience without being constrained by it or continually looking backward. Civilization literally depends on what is passed on, but it depends equally on the capacity for every generation to modify and reinterpret what has been passed on. One of the questions to ask in Adulthood II is, What knowledge do I have that needs to be shared in some form before it is lost or overlaid by more recent, and perhaps dangerous, preoccupations? Yet just having knowledge that I regard as valuable does not mean that I will be able to pass it on, whether to a student or a friend or a grandchild. Paradoxically, it often can be passed on only if I am listening and learning at the same time, yet this contradicts our stereotype of the authority that might come with age. Becoming a mentor or a consultant or even a teacher involves not only affirming past learning but also embracing new.

As I think about the different people I interviewed, what strikes me is not so much what they know but their ways of engaging with the world, which have been developed and honed over time. I think of how Dick Goldsby has developed the patience needed as an educator, or how Hank Lawson has become an increasingly disciplined craftsman; of Ruth Massinga's practicality and Jim Morton's exuberant openness becoming ever more inclusive; of Dan Jepson's willingness to take care of others and Jane Fonda's growing capacity to combine public commitment with her inner truth. These are themselves forms of wisdom acquired and modeled in action, examples of knowing *how* rather than knowing *what*. They might be translatable into wise sayings, but because each of these individuals is active, at this stage of life they are *wise doings*, and the message they carry is more powerful than words. What I find in each of these lives is a pattern of learning, often through improvisation, often in spite of frustrations, that is ongoing.

When I interview people, I often have the sense that they are learning from the reawakening of their memories as they retrace the past. Memory is precious, but it is not always clear how to use it or what obligations one has to what has gone before. Looking back over a lifetime takes different forms. A body of professionals has evolved who help individuals through a partially formalized process of "life review," which has always in some sense been one of the preoccupations of old age, taking many forms and often focusing on one aspect of a life, rather than the whole. There are always surprises, as the remembering and retelling flow into the present and toward the future. Sometimes the answer to "What next?" is to reach back in time for something that has been neglected, perhaps for years. Some people return to a childhood home or seek out old friends long out of touch. Some people return to a skill that has been neglected, dusting off the grand piano or digging out an old set of watercolors.

Scholars often review their scholarly output and sort and catalog their papers as a way of looking back. A colleague, Robert Cohen, philosopher and historian of science, whom I see at Inge Hoffmann's seminar on life histories and case histories, is busy in retirement going through his professional papers and preparing them for archiving. Scholarship sometimes involves questioning old conclusions, but scholarship moves forward only when the earlier work is available.

My own papers are going, in installments, only very roughly sorted, into the Schlesinger Library, which is now part of Harvard University. I went back through all of my writings, from poetry to technical articles, in the preparation of the collection *Willing to Learn* and wrote an introduction to each item included there to explain the way the ideas were interconnected, one leading on to another.[9] It struck me at the time that nothing I had written about Arabic, which was the focus of my doctoral work and my first three years of teaching, had made it into the collection, one intended for general readers. So I wove it into a final essay about cultural diversity and becoming "nomads of the imagination."

As the world changes, we increasingly find ourselves onstage without a script, challenged to improvise; the skills of improvisation that actors learn turn out to be key skills for adaptation. My daughter once taught me a technique, used in training a group for theatrical improvisation, of piecing together a story one sentence at a time: simply begin each contribution with the words "Yes, and," affirming what the other has said before trying to extend or balance it.[10] After she taught me this technique, I realized that, as a teacher, I had gotten only halfway by habitually responding to student comments with a positive smile and nod, repeating what seemed valuable in the comment before going on to correct or amplify ("yes . . . , but . . ."). There was more to be gained for both of us from *and* than from *but*.

You might say that the *yes* expresses reception of what the other has proposed—a willingness to learn from the other—and the *and* an offer to convey something new in return. So in dealing with cultural differences, the appropriate path is to try to discover and acknowledge the good that is believed to be served by a particular behavior. Devout Muslims, male and female, believe that women and girls are protected by veiling and segregation, and under many circumstances this is true. Yes. And? But? *And* women and girls—responsibly protected by public order, equal laws, and education—can participate as equals and make unique contributions.

The historic religions are extraordinarily rich and diverse, which means that basic themes such as justice, truth, kindness, peace, and human unity, even versions of the "Golden Rule," recur in the scriptures of all the universalistic religions. As a result, when new ethical imperatives are recognized, it is frequently possible to find arguments and interpretations for them in traditional texts. For example, scriptures and myths from around the globe express wonder at the natural world, but the wonder and respect they evoke have often been little emphasized when there was wealth to be made from exploitation. Yet the ideas are still there, ready to be called forth by "Yes, and." It falls to those living today to frame the response to wonder that is appropriate to our perilous time.

Many Western feminists are rightly suspicious of all efforts to "protect" women as disempowering, but it's worth the effort to discover—

and reinforce—the underlying rationale. I have woman friends who are insulted if a man opens a door for them. I also have friends of both sexes who are insulted if someone sees their gray hair and offers them a seat on the subway. But we should never reject kindness, especially from someone who is remembering childhood lessons in courtesy. It is important to appeal to what people regard as the best in themselves.

Dialogues between communities are hindered by the fact that members describe their own faith in terms of ideal norms within the community while outsiders characterize them with negative examples of actual behavior in the past or present. Thus, Christians have mounted crusades and have sometimes owned slaves, Jews have sometimes been moneylenders, Muslims have sometimes become terrorists, and so on and on. Not only do such behaviors shape the response of others but we tend to be subtly influenced by our own behavior, wanting to feel justified. In each case, there are those who will rightly argue that the behavior was not representative. In no case does everyone who adheres to a belief system live up to the ideals of that system. Yet time and again we find examples of belief leading to altruistic behavior and to the institutionalization of altruism.

Passing on tradition is important, but there is more than one way to do it. One of the most striking aspects of the way we are beginning to spend our years of unanticipated longevity is the importance of ongoing learning and the willingness to learn, the readiness to set what has seemed important over a lifetime of experience and reflection into dialogue with new ideas and new scientific discoveries. Across the country, educational institutions are opening their doors to students in their sixties and seventies and beyond, sometimes seeking further degrees or skills needed in the contemporary marketplace and sometimes seeking the stimulus of exposure to other worlds of learning. The search for new learning complements the need to understand the most important continuities of each life, the strands that we might pick from the complex weave and say, This is who I am and what I stand for. I have argued that the longer lives in today's world mandate a process parallel to the consciousness-raising that women undertook in the sixties and seventies to free themselves from limiting stereotypes of who they were and what they wanted out of life—and above all, what they have to contribute to those around them.

"We have not yet really grasped what is happening demographically," I said to Jane, "because the discussion of demographic change has focused so much on costs and entitlements instead of on trying to understand what it means to have this additional healthy time, actually a new stage in the life cycle. The whole way people think about their lives is going to have to change. The question is, Can we contribute to the processes of change already under way so as to really enrich the entire community? My hope is that healthy longevity will mean not only longer lives but rather richer and deeper lives for people of all ages. We're becoming a different kind of human."

"We're still of course living with the paradigm that says that old people are a drag," Jane commented. "You know, that we're greedy geezers who are taking away what should be going to the young people."

"Sure. That's the American paradigm," I said. "But it hasn't been true of all cultures through history. I think greedy geezers has to do with rising health-care costs and entitlements, but that's just an overlay on the more basic but equally negative notion of older adults being obsolete, opinionated, inflexible, not understanding the needs of today. In fact, research shows that as people get older they become more open-minded, more tolerant of ambiguity, and less inclined to sharp black-white distinctions.[11] But the way to maintain that is ongoing learning, which is more and more coming into people's awareness in the culture. That's changing. But as with feminism, you have to internalize it and deal with your own stereotypes.

"Older adults have prejudices about each other. My godmother moved into assisted living in her eighties, and I asked her if she'd made friends, and she said to me, 'Oh, my dear, most of the people here are *so* deteriorated.' Well, many of them weren't any more deteriorated than she was, and she was very much herself. The point is, just as women have had to unlearn their stereotypes about other women as well as about themselves, so older adults have to unlearn the ageism that they learned thirty, forty, fifty years ago, because the condition of older people was literally different at that time. But that doesn't mean there isn't a lot in what they've learned in the course of a lifetime that's worth keeping. When I use an evocative term like *wisdom*, it has to include what I've been told, what I've experienced, what I've reflected upon, and also the world I live in now, looking and listening and continuing to learn. To be wise is to know that you have more to learn and to have spent a lifetime coming to terms with new knowledge. That, after all, is the place to start thinking about the needs of tomorrow."

The gathering at Upaya in 2007 where Jane and I were talking was in itself an exercise in the recovery of lost knowledge, for after the Long Island property was lost, the Lindisfarne community went through a series of metamorphoses. As the original group grew older, younger fellows and sometimes the children of fellows were brought into the circle. For a number of years, in the early twenty-first century, the fellows ceased to meet. Some of us are still exploring new territory, while a few are mourning the loss of projects that have stagnated or withered or been absorbed in a reduced form into the mainstream.

Still, I always find something to learn from these gatherings. Perhaps the most important element of Lindisfarne was the conversation across disciplinary and professional lines, conversation that has always been rare and that has weakened at universities in the same period. Conversation in which minds leap from subject to subject, suddenly becoming aware of parallels, moments of seeing things in new ways and moments of recognition, responding with "Yes, and . . . ," whether the juxtaposition is one of expertise or generation or culture, and even when the juxtaposition is one of different faiths.

It may be that the word *wisdom* refers not so much to what one knows but to a quality of listening, both internal and interpersonal. In other words, the willingness to learn and modify earlier learning is itself a component of wisdom, and the word refers to a process rather than a possession. What then would *active wisdom* mean? The ability and willingness to contribute to society by putting a lifetime pattern of experience and reflection to work—often, above all, by listening.

We do what we do and we learn what we learn and each of us has done some teaching. We would like to pass on what we have achieved, including the wisdom developed over years of experience. Few people die without leaving loose ends and uncompleted tasks that will wait for someone else to cope with them or take them up.

Yet as I look at my notes, the question that strikes me is this: What would have been left undone if the men and women I interviewed had lived only the years they might have expected a century ago, when average life expectancy was under fifty? They would all have been potentially bright and creative people, I feel sure, but some of them—most of the women—would have had their potentials limited and undeveloped. Poverty and ethnicity would have limited others, who benefited from being born later. Even more striking is the difference that ten or twenty years after age fifty has made in these lives, whether you look at achievement or wisdom or contentment. In many of these lives there is a visible watershed as they move into Adulthood II, but the transition that it represents often occurred later than the time at which their ancestors would have been dead or incapacitated.

Richard Goldsby and Barbara Osborne will make no more than a dent in understanding the immune system, but they will have contributed as scientists do, taking for granted that there will be more to learn, and they will have been part of developing the technology to produce needed supplies of human immunoglobulin as part of the battle against disease. When they met he was approaching forty, with two toxic and failed marriages behind him. Now in his seventies, he has had the happiness of his relationship with Barbara enriching every aspect of his life. He has had time to help his children establish themselves and has arrived at a warm and tolerant equanimity that seems to have been absent in his younger years.

Ted Cross sold his business in 1980, at sixty-eight, devoting himself to eliminating bias from the American system of higher education and protecting bird populations from habitat destruction. Neither of these problems is resolved, but he will have encouraged dozens of concrete steps in those directions and made the need visible to others. He founded his journal at sixty-eight.

Dan Jepson saw himself as "professionally dead" in 1973, but eventually found the contentment he had dreamed of in his life with Michael and the satisfaction he enjoys now in teaching music to autistic children. I imagine, although I cannot know, that without that his sense of frustration would have been acute and he might have died embittered.

If Jane Fonda had died at the height of her antiwar activism, when she visited Hanoi in 1972, she would not have shifted from protest to positive advocacy and philanthropy or discovered an inner peace and a nourishing faith. She could not have written about her life as she did in her 2005 memoir and I doubt that she could have played the part she played on Broadway in 2009 in the play *33 Variations,* an aging woman in a wheelchair discovering the meaning of her life.

So it goes. The early missteps remain, the tasks are uncompleted, perhaps necessarily so, yet each of these people and each of the others that I spoke to has grown and learned and deepened in the last decade. Some of us will leave behind scientific or artistic achievements, books written and organizations established, fortunes amassed or human suffering alleviated, but what we cannot fully pass on is what we have learned from experience and from reflecting on experience, because the living was necessary to the learning. All of us went in directions sufficiently different from our parents' so that our lives cannot be seen as their legacies, and our children will live their own very different lives. Instead of following in our footsteps, they may have learned our willingness to strike out on our own. If we try to tell them in words what we have learned from experience, they will learn something quite different through the passivity of listening. We will never be able to compute what was passed on simply by our presence.

We cannot pass on the Eriksonian strengths/virtues directly, but perhaps we can do so indirectly. We cannot instruct our children to trust, but we can try to be trustworthy and we can make a practice of showing trust in them; we can teach love by loving and will by consistency. We can even make them more beautiful by responding to their beauty. We can give them hope and courage for their lives by the way we respond to the diminishments of age and, at the last, by the manner of our dying.

Epilogue

WE END WITH ANOTHER STORY. When the Twin Towers fell, in 2001, I was sixty, not sixteen. I did not see how I might contribute to better understanding between the Islamic world and the West, but I was sharply aware that much of what divides us is ignorance and misunderstanding. I had been doing research and writing on other topics, and my knowledge of the Islamic world had become threadbare and out-of-date.

At the same time, thinking about the way people compose their lives had made me very much aware of the resources of memory and the way earlier learning can be recycled and informed by new understanding. As I followed the aftermath of 9/11, my years in Arabic linguistics and in Middle Eastern and Islamic studies were increasingly on my mind, with a nagging regret growing from the feeling that I have not sufficiently met the obligation to share the knowledge so expensively offered to me in my student years, knowledge badly needed in a society now preoccupied with fear and hostility toward the Middle East. That reflection made me aware that I had not maintained my knowledge but allowed it to grow obsolete.

Among the languages I have studied, Arabic was the one I fell in love with and regret losing. I first heard Arabic when I was sixteen and I crossed over from Israel, where I was staying, to Jordan, for in those days Christians were allowed at Christmastime to cross the border as pilgrims (and also, in the case of Christian Arab families, to visit kinfolk from whom they had been separated by war). Instead of visiting the Church of the Nativity, I visited refugee camps and carried that memory with me to the study of Arabic in college and to a continuing concern for peace in the Middle East. Sometimes when I hear Arabic spoken in the street, I fall in behind the speakers simply to luxuriate in the sound.

Above all, I loved Arabic poetry. In 2006 I spent an evening in Santa Fe at a home with a view of the Sangre de Cristo Mountains in the distance. As I sat with friends, we could see two distinct electrical storms wheeling across the desert and colliding with the mountains, and I found myself describing one of my favorite passages of Arabic poetry, written before the rise of Islam by Imru'u l-Qays.[1] There is even a word in Arabic for following the movement of a storm by observing the flashes of lightning.

As the poet tracked the storm from one familiar landmark to another, he piled on similes. The flicker of lightning reminded him of the flash of hands shuffling marked arrows in a traditional form of gambling, and then it reminded him of the distant oil lamp of a desert anchorite like those who still, at that time before Islam and the founding of the monastic orders, withdrew to solitary hermitages. The winds snapped the trunks of date palms on familiar oases and lifted the roofs of buildings. The twisted wrack of the storm wrapped around a rocky peak like raw wool around the whirl of a spindle. The storm dumped its baggage like a Yemenite merchant unpacking camel loads of colorful merchandise, and in the morning the larks sang as if they had drunk spiced wine.

Storms in Arabia can lead to sudden floods moving through the wadis, riverbeds that are dry most of the year; because the wadis are attractive places to camp, drowning has been a fairly common cause of human death in the desert, but what the poet spoke of was the muddy bodies of drowned animals, like the plucked up bulbs of wild onions.

I had translated the poem, and I had written about it as a linguist, but I had never seen a storm in the desert to really grasp what it meant to watch its wheeling movement. The memory of lines of poetry from years before was suddenly, wildly, alive in front of me.

So the Middle East began coming back, with the awareness that I had knowledge I needed to pass on. In the summer of 2007, at an international conference in Tallberg, Sweden, a Saudi princess spoke in defense of the status of women in the Islamic world, and I found myself introducing her and facilitating a conversation that had to be guided from attack and defense toward some degree of mutual understanding. At the same time, I was struggling to remember greetings and courtesy phrases of Arabic and seized by a heady excitement of rediscovery.

Major problems lie ahead as we confront the issues triggered by global climate change. On the one hand, we can expect heart-wrenching humanitarian crises, great numbers of people suddenly homeless or starving or reduced to refugee status. On the other hand, we can expect conflict and warfare when different communities look with envy at their neighbors and fear that their autonomy or access to resources will be reduced as arable land, fossil fuels, and potable water become scarcer. Some of these conflicts are already being expressed in terms of the differences between the Islamic world and the West, and understanding seems to be in short supply. Never before in history has it been so important to affirm that all human beings are kin and part of the interdependent life of the planet.

At the same time, it has become fashionable to suggest that all religious belief is pernicious. Part of this critique is a response to 9/11 and the particular form taken by anger in the Muslim world. Part of it is a response to the multiple mutually hostile fundamentalisms that flourish on different continents, which are themselves reactions to the threat of change. Still, the major religions of the world are not going to be replaced or disappear, for they have significant value in the lives of believers, and in spite of the horrors of the past, they sometimes have the potential to evoke cooperation and compassion. Judaism, Christianity, and Islam have many beliefs in common, starting from a belief in the Creator's entry in human affairs and concern for justice and peace, beginning with Abraham, evoking worship and wonder through a process of self-revelation. Knowledge of the range of human belief systems is an essential component of global literacy and not the property of specialists.

It felt like more than coincidence, then, for me to receive an invitation to go to Arabia in the summer of 2007. I had traveled in several Arab countries but never onto the Arabian Peninsula. The invitation came from Stephen Tolle, whom I had met once in Iran, who wrote:

> I represent the design team for the Society for Organizational Learning's (SoL) next global forum, which will be held in Muscat, Oman, from April 13–16, 2007. The theme of the forum is: "Bridging the Gulf: Learning across Organizations, Sectors, and Cultures"—our intent is to give people a direct experience of working across cultures, with a particular focus on cross-sectoral work, by sharing perspectives on building a better future. We are expecting about 400 participants from over 40 different countries (about 150 from the Gulf Region and the Middle East—including a contingent of Israelis), representing academic researchers, corporations, and NGOs. The session will offer a unique opportunity to explore common ground and possibilities for collaborative action.
>
> We would like to have you deliver one of the keynote addresses and host a plenary dialogue on cross-cultural learning for the forum. We think that your long experience in the Middle East and deep understanding of its cultures can offer valuable insight and help challenge the forum participants to question some of their strongly held assumptions.

The Gulf. The very phrase, of course, is a good example of the differences that divide us, for Arabia lies to the west of this patch of ocean and Iran to the east. Most American geographies speak of the Persian Gulf, which pleases Iran, Arabs call it the Arab Gulf, and some Middle

East hands carefully call it the Petroleum Gulf because of the massive oil reserves on both sides and beneath its waters. It was weeks before I grasped the fact that there would be participants from all around the world, because from the first moment I read the invitation, I was focused on the one third who would come from the Middle East, although in the end the arrangements for the Israeli contingent fell through. I told Tolle that I would come and suggested that I would also enjoy speaking elsewhere in the region, which led to engagements on university and college campuses in Oman, Bahrain, and Saudi Arabia.

In Oman I spoke at Sultan Qaboos University, in Saudi Arabia at Effat College for Women in Jeddah, and in Bahrain at the Royal University for Women. When speaking or traveling, I wore an abaya or loose tunics and head scarves as a gesture of respect. In each place I met with faculty and administration and sometimes with students in addition to the talks I gave. My main emphasis was on reciprocity in learning, where each side has something to teach and something to learn from the other.

The Society for Organizational Learning is focused on the application of systems theory to business and governance, and one of its key concepts is looking at any relationship as moving in two directions. Thus, instead of looking at government as exerting top-down control, systems theory reminds the observer of the ways in which the ruler depends upon and is affected by the ruled, and the dangers of attempting to govern without listening. Too often we think of teachers or physicians as acting upon students or patients—acting beneficently, to be sure, but unchanged by them. Even parents sometimes believe themselves to be guiding and forming their children without letting themselves be reshaped in the process. But if there is to be dialogue between civilizations, the learning must go in both directions, and each must acknowledge the need to learn from the other. This means encouraging curiosity and respectful mutual knowledge without proselytizing. In the area of belief, this is best done by focusing on the experience of believers rather than on theology and clerical expertise—after all, the clergy tend to be defined as teachers rather than as learners, and they may even stop at that definition.

The example I seized upon to open my talk was a set of ordinary greeting forms in Arabic. Often in English, when two people meet they greet each other symmetrically: "Good morning." "Good morning." In Arabic, it is customary to return a greeting with a further and different greeting, responding to one "hello" with "a hundred hellos," to "a morning of goodness" with "a morning of light." If someone offers me "peace" (or salvation), I may offer them "peace and the mercy of God and His blessing" in return. Thinking about these formal exchanges led me to wonder how often a professor or a priest or an industrial consultant approaches a student or parishioner or client with the assumption that he or she will be both teaching *and* learning something new.

This is even true in highly technical areas. New science and technology open new horizons of possibility and effective compassion but demand fresh ethical discernment in relation to tradition, a process that is often more complex than simple acceptance of the recommendations of technical specialists and engineers. To avoid reflexive rejections of change, it is important to embed the process of evaluation in programs to transfer technology and to be willing to learn what the other cares about. Where the same values co-occur in two traditions, they often do not have equal priority, leading to very different behavioral outcomes and judgments. For some, honesty is more important than kindness, while for others kindness is more important. In considering unfamiliar behavior, it is useful to ask what positive value that behavior is felt to serve and what alternatives might serve the same value. This is why passing on knowledge often depends on openness to new knowledge. Just as communities can learn from each other, so must older and younger generations.

In Oman I met a man who had represented his government in relief efforts in Southeast Asia after the tsunami of 2004. He was hospitable in the best Arab tradition, warm and welcoming to us as visitors to a culture he loved. But he was clearly aware of the suspicions Westerners have come to hold of Muslims since 9/11. Watching me carefully, he said, "I am a *jihadi*," using the word usually translated as "holy warrior." Fortunately, I remembered enough Arabic to know that *jihad* means not "holy war" but "effort" or "struggle," and it dawned on me that for him *jihadi* meant "activist—activist for peace and justice." This is the struggle we need to share, bringing reflection to action and vice versa, learning along the way. Yes. I, too, can continue that lifelong struggle.

References

Prologue

1. The Americans with Disabilities Act was anticipated in Section 504 of the 1973 Rehabilitation Act, which was the first disability civil rights law to be enacted in the United States and forbade discrimination and exclusion in federally funded programs.

I. Thinking About Longevity

1. I introduced the term Adulthood II in a keynote address to the American Society for Cybernetics annual meeting in 2005, to be available on DVD. See also Mary Catherine Bateson, "In Search of Active Wisdom: Libraries and Consciousness Raising for Adulthood II," in *Boomers and Beyond: Reconsidering the Role of Libraries,* ed. Pauline Rothstein and Diantha Schull (Chicago: ALA Editions, 2010), Chapter VI.

2. Mary Catherine Bateson, "The Future of Wisdom," April 4, 2006, http://ilfpost.org/?p=66. See also *Boomers and Beyond,* ed. Rothstein and Schull.

3. W. D. Hamilton, "The Genetical Evolution of Social Behavior: I and II," *Journal of Theoretical Biology* 7 (1964): 1–52.

4. The effect of the presence of grandparents on infant survival has been extensively studied both in contemporary field situations (India, Gambia) and historically through European parish registers (Germany, Poland). In general, the finding is that the presence of the maternal grandmother promotes survival, especially during the first year of life. A useful review of the research can be found in *Demographic Research* 20: 559–94, online at http://www.demographic-research.org/Volumes/Vol20/20=23.pdf (May 26, 2009).

5. Richard B. Lee, *The Dobe Ju/'hoansi,* 2nd edition (Fort Worth, Tex.: Harcourt Brace College, 1993).

6. Peggy Cappy, *Yoga for the Rest of Us: Essentials for Every Body.* DVD. WGBH/PBS, 2004.

7. http://www.rand.org/pubs/research_briefs/RB5018/index1.html (accessed January 26, 2010). The difference is about ten years.
8. Mary Catherine Bateson, "Getting Time on Your Side: Breakthrough Ideas for 2005," *Harvard Business Review* (February 2005), pp. 48–50.
9. Marc Freedman, *Prime Time: How Baby Boomers Will Revolutionize Retirement and Transform America* (New York: Public Affairs Press, 2001), and *Encore: Finding Work That Matters in the Second Half of Life* (New York: Public Affairs Press, 2007).
10. Mary Catherine Bateson, *Composing a Life* (New York: Atlantic Monthly Press, 1989).

II. Small and Beautiful
1. Erik H. Erikson, *Young Man Luther* (New York: W. W. Norton, 1958), pp. 100-104.
2. Nevil Shute, *Trustee from the Toolroom* (New York: William Morrow, 1960).

III. Liberation Time
1. Thomas Kuhn, *The Structure of Scientific Revolutions* (Chicago: University of Chicago Press, 1962).
2. Ibid.

IV. From Strength to Strength
1. Arnold Gesell, *An Atlas of Infant Behavior* (New Haven: Yale University Press, 1934).
2. Sigmund Freud, "Three Contributions to the Theory of Sex," in *The Basic Writings of Sigmund Freud,* ed. A. A. Brill (New York: Modern Library, 1938).
3. G. Stanley Hall, *Adolescence: Its Psychology and Its Relations to Physiology, Anthropology, Sociology, Sex, Crime, Religion, and Education* (New York: D. Appleton & Co., 1904).
4. Erik H. Erikson, *Childhood and Society,* 2nd edition (New York: W. W. Norton, 1963).
5. Erik H. Erikson and Joan M. Erikson, *The Life Cycle Completed* (New York: W. W. Norton, 1997).
6. Daniel J. Levinson, *The Seasons of a Man's Life* (New York: Alfred A. Knopf, 1979).
7. Gail Sheehy drew on all of these thinkers in her books *Passages: Predictable Crises of Adult Life* (New York: E. P. Dutton, 1976) and *New Passages: Mapping Your Life Across Time* (New York: Random House, 1995).

8. Erikson, *Childhood and Society*, figure 12, p. 273.
9. http://www.ilfpost.org/?p-275.
10. Brian L. Weiss, *Many Lives, Many Masters* (New York: Simon & Schuster, 1988).
11. Harris Poll 90, December 14, 2005, http://www.harrisinteractive.com/ harris_poll/index.asp?PID=618 (accessed January 2010).
12. Erikson, *Childhood and Society*, p. 268.
13. Mary Catherine Bateson, "The Earth, Our Kin," in *Crisis and the Renewal of Creation: Church and World in the Age of Ecology*, ed. Jeffrey Golliher and William Bryant Logan (New York: Continuum, 1996).
14. Stephanie Coontz, *The Way We Never Were: American Families and the Nostalgia Trap* (New York: Basic Books, 1992), p. 10.
15. Carolyn Heilbrun wrote about the new stage I call Adulthood II in *The Last Gift of Time: Life Beyond Sixty* (New York: Dial Press, 1997).
16. Oliver Wendell Holmes, "The Chambered Nautilus."

V. Acts and Chapters

1. Isaac Watts, in the hymn "Psalm 90," stanza 5.
2. Niles Eldredge and S. J. Gould, "Punctuated equilibria: an alternative to phyletic gradualism," in *Models in Paleobiology*, ed. T.J.M. Schopf (San Francisco: Freeman Cooper, 1972), pp. 82–115. Reprinted in N. Eldredge, *Time Frames* (Princeton: Princeton University Press, 1985).
3. Gregory Bateson, *Mind and Nature: A Necessary Unity* (New York: Bantam, 1980), pp. 100–107.
4. Mary Catherine Bateson, "Mother-Infant Exchanges: The Epigenesis of Conversational Interaction," in *Developmental Psycholinguistics and Communication Disorders*, ed. Doris Aaronson and R. W. Rieber, *Annals of the New York Academy of Sciences* 263 (1975): 101–13; *With a Daughter's Eye* (New York: William Morrow, 1984); *Composing a Life* (New York: Atlantic Monthly Press, 1989).
5. Erik H. Erikson, *Young Man Luther* (New York: W. W. Norton, 1958), *Gandhi's Truth* (New York: W. W. Norton, 1969); Erik H. Erikson, Joan M. Erikson, and Helen Q. Kivnick, *Vital Involvement in Old Age* (New York: W. W. Norton, 1986); Erik Erikson and Joan Erikson, *The Life Cycle Completed* (New York: W. W. Norton, 1997).
6. Bateson, *Composing a Life*, p. 3.
7. William Bridges, *Transitions: Making Sense of Life's Changes* (Reading, Mass.: Addison-Wesley, 1980).

8. To see how pervasive this phrasing has been, see *Women's Voices, Feminist Visions: Classic and Contemporary Readings*, ed. Susan Shaw and Janet Lee (Burr Ridge, Ill.: McGraw-Hill Higher Education, 2008).

9. *The Cloud of Unknowing* (New York: HarperCollins Spiritual Classics, 1981).

10. See, for instance, Steven Eric Krauss, "Research Paradigms and Meaning Making: A Primer," *Qualitative Report* 10 (December 4, 2005): 758–70, http://www.nova.edu/ssss/QR/QR10-4/Krauss.pdf.

11. Samuel Butler, "Life After Death," http://poetry_pearls.tripod.com/eEPoets/Butler.htm.

12. http://www.interculturalstudies.org.

VI. Focusing Multiplicity

1. René Dubos, *Beast or Angel?: Choices That Make Us Human* (New York: Charles Scribner's Sons, 1974).

2. René Dubos and James Parks Morton, "The Lichen Sermon," in *Crisis and the Renewal of Creation: Church and World in the Age of Ecology*, ed. Jeffrey Golliher and William Bryant Logan (New York: Continuum, 1996), pp. 11–21.

VII. Pleasure and Responsibility

1. Alex Comfort, *The Joy of Sex* (New York: Crown, 1972).

2. Konrad Lorenz, *Autobiography*, Nobel Lectures 1973, http://nobelprize.org/nobel_prizes/medicine/laureates/1973/lorenz-autobio.html (accessed January 2010). The theory of "innate teaching mechanisms" is developed in *Evolution and the Modification of Behavior* (Cambridge, Mass.: Harvard University Press, 1961).

3. Sigmund Freud, "Three Contributions to the Theory of Sex," in *The Basic Writings of Sigmund Freud*, ed. A. A. Brill (New York: Modern Library, 1938).

4. Erik H. Erikson, *Childhood and Society* (New York: W. W. Norton, 1950).

5. Nena O'Neill and George O'Neill, *The Open Marriage: A New Lifestyle for Couples* (New York: M. Evans, 1972).

VIII. A Time for Wholeness

1. D. J. Kennedy, "Thomas Aquinas, Saint," *Catholic Encyclopedia*, http://www.newadvent.org/cathen/14663b.htm (accessed January 2010).

2. Jane Fonda, *My Life So Far* (New York: Random House, 2005), p. 104.

3. Mary Catherine Bateson, *Composing a Life* (New York: Atlantic Monthly Press, 1989), Chapter X.

4. Elaine Pagels, *The Gnostic Gospels* (New York: Vintage Books, 1979) and Karen L. King, *The Gospel of Mary of Magdala: Jesus and the First Woman Apostle* (Santa Rosa, CA: Polebridge Press, 2003).
5. Alfred North Whitehead, *Religion in the Making* (New York: World Publishing/Meridian Books, 1960), p. 16.

IX. What We Pass On

1. *Thinking AIDS* (Reading, Mass.: Addison-Wesley, 1988).
2. Richard Goldsby, *Race and Races* (New York: Macmillan, 1971).
3. Mary Catherine Bateson, *Composing a Life* (New York: Atlantic Monthly Press, 1989).
4. Erik H. Erikson, *Childhood and Society* (New York: W. W. Norton, 1950), pp. 268–69. Erikson is quoting Edmond Rostand, *"Mille petits dégoûts de soi, dont le total/Ne fait pas un remords, mais une gêne obscure,"* Cyrano de Bergerac, act V, v. 5.

X. Shaping the Future

1. Richard Dawkins, *The Selfish Gene* (New York: Oxford University Press, 1999).
2. Jane Fonda, *My Life So Far* (New York: Random House, 2005).
3. Jane Fonda, *Jane Fonda's Workout Book* (New York: Simon and Schuster, 1981). The video appeared in 1982 and was followed by some twenty other videos between then and 1995, many of which have been reissued as DVDs and in various collections.
4. Donald Winnicott, *Mother and Child: A Primer of First Relationships* (New York: Basic Books, 1957).
5. *grok:* to understand profoundly through intuition or empathy. Coined by Robert Heinlein in *Stranger in a Strange Land,* http://www.thefreedictionary.com/grokking.
6. Since the debate about Freud's revised interpretation, triggered by Jeffrey Masson (*The Assault on Truth: Freud's Suppression of the Seduction Theory.* New York: Farrar, Straus & Giroux, 1984), it has become clear that although some of the cases of very young children reported by Freud might have been based on fantasy or suggestion, substantial numbers of girls and boys do suffer sexual abuse by trusted adults, especially family members.

XI. Knowledge Old and New

1. Alfred Korzybski, *Science and Sanity: An Introduction to Non-Aristotelian Systems and General Semantics,* 5th edition (Chicago: Institute of General Semantics, 1994).
2. Alfred Korzybski, *Manhood of Humanity: The Science and Art of Human Engineering* [1921], 2nd edition (Chicago: Institute of General Semantics, 1950).
3. Mary Catherine Bateson, *Our Own Metaphor: A Personal Account of a Conference on Conscious Purpose and Human Adaptation* (New York: Alfred A. Knopf, 1972).
4. Mary Catherine Bateson, *Composing a Life* (New York: Atlantic Monthly Press, 1989), p. 15.
5. Gregory Bateson, "Ecology and Flexibility in Urban Civilization," in *Steps to an Ecology of Mind* (San Francisco: Chandler, 1972), p. 506.
6. Mary Catherine Bateson, "The Construction of Continuity," in *Executive and Organizational Continuity: Managing the Paradoxes of Stability and Change,* ed. Suresh Srivastva and Ronald E. Fry (San Francisco: Jossey-Bass, 1992), pp. 27–39.
7. L. P. Lipsitt, "Behavioral Aspects of Crib Death: The Rise and Fall of Alternative Hypotheses," *Current Directions in Psychological Science,* July 31, 2003.
8. Robert Jay Lifton, *The Protean Self: Human Resilience in an Age of Fragmentation* (Chicago: University of Chicago Press, 1999).
9. Mary Catherine Bateson, *Willing to Learn: Passages of Personal Discovery* (Hanover, N.H.: Steerforth Press, 2004).
10. http://www.improvforeveryone.com/2010/02/improv-games-yes-and/.
11. Gene D. Cohen, *The Mature Mind: The Positive Power of the Aging Brain* (New York: Basic Books, 2005).

Epilogue

1. For background on the poet and translations of his poem, see http://www.bbc.co.uk/dna/h2g2/A3994176. A literal translation, made for purposes of linguistic analysis, may be found in Mary Catherine Bateson, *Structural Continuity in Poetry: A Linguistic Study of Five Early Arabic Odes* (Paris: Ecole des Hautes Etudes, 1970).

Mary Catherine Bateson received her undergraduate degree from Radcliffe College (BA 1960) and her Ph.D. from Harvard (1963). She has taught at Harvard, Northeastern, Amherst, and Spelman College, as well as overseas in the Philippines and Iran. From 1987 to 2002 she was Clarence J. Robinson Professor of Anthropology and English at George Mason University, spending half her time writing in New Hampshire and becoming Professor Emerita in 2002. Since the fall of 2006 she has been a Visiting Scholar at the Center on Aging and Work/Workplace Flexibility at Boston College and a special consultant to the Lifelong Access Libraries Initiative of the Libraries for the Future. Until recently she has been President of the Institute of Intercultural Studies in New York City. She divides her time between Cambridge, Massachusetts, and Hancock, New Hampshire, and has a married daughter and two grandsons. She is the author of *Composing a Life; With a Daughter's Eye: A Memoir of Margaret Mead and Gregory Bateson; Peripheral Visions: Learning Along the Way; Full Circles, Overlapping Lives: Culture and Generation in Transition;* and *Willing to Learn: Passages of Personal Discovery.*

A NOTE ON THE TYPE

This book was set in Minion, a typeface produced by the Adobe Corporation specifically for the Macintosh personal computer, and released in 1990. Designed by Robert Slimbach, Minion combines the classic characteristics of old-style faces with the full complement of weights required for modern typesetting.

Composed by Creative Graphics, Allentown, Pennsylvania

Printed and bound by RR Donnelley, Harrisonburg, Virginia

Designed by Maggie Hinders